EMPOWERING

A Process to Activate Y...

Chock full of relevant information, insights that insp... ...s and processes that accomplish their intentions, this book delivers! Whether you are seeking help connecting with your divine inner spirit or looking to add new tools to your medicine bag, *Empowering the Spirit is* an invaluable addition to your spiritual library.

Nicki Scully, Author of *Alchemical Healing: A Guide to Spiritual, Physical and Transformational Medicine, and Planetary Healing: Spirit Medicine for Global Transformation*

Empowering the Spirit is "right on time" for a world in creative chaos in need of great change. When "yesterday's soul purpose has devolved into today's ego agenda" it is time to step back from our busy lives and activate our spirit from within to help midwife us through the transformation process calling us forward. *Empowering the Spirit* lives up to its name as a guiding light in a changing world.

Linda Star Wolf, Author of *Shamanic Breathwork, Visionary Shamanism and Spirit of the Wolf*

Empowering the Spirit is a book of inspiration . . . a vision of what our life can become as we invite Spirit to infuse every breath of our human experience here on Earth. Yet it is also a book that provides techniques and processes to assist us in navigating through the nitty-gritty of daily life . . . the physical, emotional and mental challenges that provide the grist for our growth and our evolution in consciousness. The wisdom that overlights this book comes not only from Judith's many years of experience as a transpersonal psychotherapist and teacher, but also from her personal journey which has empowered the Spirit within and opened access to the higher realms of consciousness.

John Horneker, Author *of Quantum Transformation: Guide to Becoming a Galactic Human*

Judith Corvin Blackburn gives us a great gift in her book *Empowering the Spirit: A Process to Activate Your Soul Potential.* Beyond her many years of clinical practice as a transpersonal psychotherapist and teacher she brings her higher guidance to bear in the pages of this book. The result for us, her readers, is inspiration, insight, tools and exercises that lead us to a deeper understanding about personal and spiritual power. She helps us to see how we came in with a spiritual contract, or "pre-birth agreements" that allow us to fulfill our soul's purpose. New to this edition is an exploration of our multi-dimensional nature and the most important piece of the great shift we are currently in: How to clear our individual energy field of emotional blockages and dysfunctional beliefs in order to positively impact the world around us as we co-create the New Earth. Thank you Judith for honoring your sacred contract and writing this book.

Thea Summer Deer, Author of *Wisdom of the Plant Devas: Herbal Medicine for a New Earth*

Judith Corvin-Blackburn is a gifted teacher, writer and spiritual leader. Her book, *Empowering the Spirit: A Process to Activate Your Soul Potential* is full of wisdom, enlightening ideas and practical applications for daily living. It is a wonderful roadmap for the experience of a soul-centered life.

Ruby Falconer, Co-author of *Shamanic Egyptian Astrology: Your Planetary Relationship to the Gods.*

Empowering The Spirit - living and teaching about what Judith refers to as a *spirit directed life* has been so very helpful and inspiring for me and my students at Soul Studies Institute. I highly recommend this work of art!

Wendyne Limber: Author of *Intimacy Without Responsibility: The Conscious Evolution of Love*

Do you wonder how to access the wisdom of our Divine Source and how to utilize this guidance in our everyday experiences? By following the processes shared in *Empowering the Spirit*, readers will absorb the loving presence and laser-precise guidance of gifted intuitive/ teacher/counselor/ facilitator and author Judith Corvin-Blackburn. Judith lives the life she visualizes and shares what she has learned in an easily absorbed and extremely useful format so that the reader can create the life Judith knows is possible for all of us, lives that together create new communities of peace and mutual support. A must-read for anyone seeking to understand, as well as to thrive in these swiftly changing times.

Yvonne Scott, Author of *SIMPLY GARDEN SMALL! End hunger and restore health with creative food-growing strategies from around the world.*

EMPOWERING THE SPIRIT

A PROCESS TO ACTIVATE YOUR SOUL POTENTIAL

Judith Corvin-Blackburn

EMPOWERING THE SPIRIT
A Process to Activate Your Soul Potential
JUDITH CORVIN-BLACKBURN

Published by
Healing Concept Publishing
Whittier, North Carolina
Revised 4th Edition
www.empoweringthespirit.com

Copyright © 2005; Copyright © 2006; Copyright ©2007; Copyright ©2013;
Electronic Edition Copyright ©2012
by Judith Corvin-Blackburn
All rights reserved.

ISBN: 0615699111
ISBN-13: 9780615699110

ACKNOWLEDGMENTS

Friends, family, clients, students – To name all the people who have been instrumental in the inspiration and creation of this book would be a book in itself.

Thank you to my early readers: Susan Hardesty, Wendy Allen, and most especially Janice DiGirolamo for her insightful and insistent feed-back without which this book might never have made it into the world.

Thank you to my dear friend Yvonne Scott, for all her help and support to make the Kindle edition and now this newest print edition, a reality.

A very special thank you to my daughter Rhiannon for the use of her beautiful water lily photo on the cover, for saving the day with her talented re-design of my first Kindle cover and for her keen eye and advice for this book's interior design. Thank you to my son Jonathan, for his ongoing technical support and to my daughter Lizzie for her inspiration.

My deep appreciation for Linda Star Wolf for her consistent support of my writing and teaching, and to Pat Cummings for her author photo and the irrepressible spirit she brings to her art of photographing.

Thank you to Eric Hendrix for his editing suggestions, as well as help and patience with my "back page," and to Norma Hendrix and Bonnie Rubenstein for their feedback on my cover design.

And always my unending gratitude to my husband, Dennis, whose love, support, insight and humor never ceases to amaze me.

dedicated to PLANET EARTH
with love

TABLE OF CONTENTS

INTRODUCTION	xiii
"IMAGINE" Exercise	xvi
CHAPTER 1: THE PREMISE	1
Assessing Spirit's Power in our Lives	2
Ego-Driven vs. Spirit-Directed Living	3
Moving From Our Hearts	9
Self-Observation	12
CHAPTER 2: OUR COLLECTIVE ISSUES AROUND POWER	21
The Relationship between Power and Empowerment	22
Roadblocks to Empowerment	24
CHAPTER 3: RECLAIMING BALANCE	33
1st Chakra	35
2nd Chakra	40
3rd Chakra	43
4th Chakra	49
5th Chakra	53
6th Chakra	60
7th Chakra	63
The Upper Chakras	66
Embracing Our Power	67

CHAPTER 4: GETTING FREE FROM THE COLLECTIVE TRANCE   69

   Collective Limiting Beliefs   71
   Collective Beliefs of the Emerging System   87
   Uncovering and Transforming Limiting Personal Beliefs   88
      Life Path Story   96

CHAPTER 5: CLAIMING OUR BIRTH & BIRTHING OUR VISION   101

   The Dark Night of the Soul   103
   Why We Chose Our Birth   103
   Opening to Purpose   116
   Identifying Pre-birth Contracts   124

CHAPTER 6: REINCARNATION & OUR MULTIDIMENSIONAL SOUL   127

   The Clearing   130
   Observing Our Resistance   132
   Techniques for Healing Our Multidimensional Selves   142
   Welcoming our Magnificence   146

PART TWO   153

CHAPTER 7: CREATING EVOLVED RELATIONSHIPS   155

   Codependency and the Separation Myth   158
   Loving Partnerships   159
   Parent/Child Relationships   171
   Sibling Relationships   185
   Friendships   188
   Work Relationships   192
   Soul Groups   195

CHAPTER 8: FAMILIES FOR THE NEW PARADIGM   199

    The Evolution of the Family through Reclamation of Feminine Power   201
    The Dynamics of Conscious Family   203
    Envisioning the Family of the Future   216

CHAPTER 9: SPIRITUAL COMMUNITY   221

    The Collective Resonance   225
    Taking Charge of our Vibrational Field   228
    Creating Community   232
    We Are the World   234

You may say I'm a dreamer, but I'm not the only one.
Perhaps someday you'll join us, and the world will live AS ONE.
John Lennon

INTRODUCTION

I have been birthing this book for so long, I have lost count of the years. It has soothed and inspired me; scared and frustrated me. But it has never stopped demanding that I complete it. On one level, it is a compilation of all I have learned about the human experience and the process of emotional and spiritual development, both from my 35 years as a transpersonal psychotherapist and teacher, and from my personal journey to live a conscious, Spirit-directed life. On another level, it is infused with Higher Guidance, with Divine inspiration which sneaks up on the page and startles me, and which resonates so clearly in my soul as truth, that I ultimately cannot question its wisdom.

This book, for me, is a sacred contract. Part of me longs to let it go, to move into a comfortable retirement full of family, friends and travel where I pursue my own spiritual development and help the world in quiet ways. But I know in my heart that times are too dire. The old world is dying and those who know how to midwife the new are being called to speak out as loudly as we are able.

We have the capacity to be wondrous beings, powerful beyond imagination. We have the power to heal ourselves and activate healing in others. We have the power to heal our Earth, to cure our diseases, to right our social wrongs. As we open our hearts and express our highest spiritual potential, we collectively create the conditions that will propagate this new world. To carry this out, we need to surrender to our intuitive guidance, living our lives aligned with this guidance, thus enabling our Spirit to lead the way.

The more our Spirit leads, the more fully we become ourselves, embodying the vibrational frequency of our souls. As we do this, each of us becomes free to make our contribution. Yet, like me, you are likely to find inner resistance to stepping fully into this power and the role it will bring you. This book sets out to help you identify and break through this resistance, while directing you toward creating a spiritually awakened life and ultimately, a spiritually awakened world.

The process I present in this book is to help you empower your own Spirit to direct your life rather than be led by the desires and fears of your ego. It is full of techniques that have worked for me as well as for numerous students and clients. Living in this manner has provided me with innumerable joys and I believe it will do the same for you. These techniques will teach you ways to continually face your ego's fears and then act from Spirit anyway. They will also teach you how to take full responsibility for the creation of anything that is occurring in your life while continuing to be loving and supportive of yourself. As you understand fully that you are energy and that you are continually interacting with everyone and everything in your environment on an energy level, and as you take full ownership of this energy, you will make what I believe to be the evolutionary leap.

Throughout the pages of this book are a multitude of exercises, examples and suggestions to help you personalize a strategy to put your Spirit more fully in charge. Chapter One outlines the book's premise and helps you assess how active you are allowing Spirit to be in your life. You will learn to identify the blockages that keep you from being led by your heart and to define them more clearly in order to break through them. You will also learn ways to help you observe yourself more consistently.

In Chapter Two, we explore our collective issues around power, as well as our roadblocks to empowerment. A lengthy self-assessment will give you a stronger understanding of your particular challenges as well as suggestions for mastering these challenges.

Chapter Three explains how essential it is to be equally well-developed on the physical, emotional, mental and spiritual levels in order to step into our full spiritual power. We look at each chakra from this perspective, both to determine what needs our attention and to create healing in the areas which call. In Chapter Four, we look deeply at the collective and individual beliefs that interfere in our progress. Suggestions and exercises are then offered for transforming these beliefs. I present a new cultural belief system that needs to be operational in order for us to shift into the new paradigm. Exercises for helping you step into full empowerment and to create the next chapter of your life are presented as well.

To fully empower our Spirits and become who we have come here to be, we need to understand why our soul chose the circumstances of our birth and our childhoods, resolve any unfinished emotional pain, and ultimately embrace all our experiences from the perspective of how they have helped and can continue to help us carry out our pre-birth agreements. This allows us to clearly define and carry out our purpose on the numerous levels. Chapter Five provides you with insights and tools needed to do this.

The next step in our journey is to understand ourselves in terms of our multidimensional nature. Chapter Six provides you with perspective and methods to heal your soul's issues from other lifetimes and welcome all aspects of your being, so you can experience the joy of wholeness and step into this evolutionary imperative.

In the second part of this book, we look at how to expand what we have learned as individuals into healthy, spiritually based relationships, families and communities. Spirit knows that we are interconnected on all levels. While clearing our individual energy fields has a positive impact on our world, the more skilled we become at expressing and combining our co-creative energies, the more wonderful a world we will create. Throughout the book is always the message that every time you clear the emotional blockages and dysfunctional beliefs that interfere with you following your Spirit, not only do you enrich your own life and the lives of those dear to you, but you help us all. We need you.

IMAGINE

I wonder if you can imagine you are living on planet Earth which is now teeming with loving, spiritually awakened people.

See yourself in this environment and feel yourself in a state of total and utter relaxation. There is no tension or tightness in your body, only a loose gentle flowing feeling accompanied by a sense of strength.

Imagine a wondrous feeling of warmth around your heart and feel this loving energy radiating throughout your body and then out to all who come into your presence.

Feel all the energy centers in your body fully operative, spinning with ease and continuously rejuvenating you down to the tiniest cell.

Imagine your voice like a finely tuned chime – resonant, warm and clear – always speaking your truth.

Realize the deep awareness you have of all the other beings who are vibrating at this same frequency, who are part of this magnificent symphony of energy that is wrapping itself around the globe. Know when you are in this consciousness, you consistently feel connected to the Earth, to Spirit, to all Beings of Light, to all life on the planet. Breathe into this imagery: Breathe it into the deepest parts of yourself. Breathe it into your fears and doubts, your areas of shame and guilt. For as you breathe this imagery, you begin to create this for us all.

Imagine that we have reclaimed our Mother Earth, ridding her soil water and air of the harmful pollutants of the industrial age. Our Earth has become lush and green once again, the violent storms are over, and the blue sky and brilliant sun give way to gentle rains as needed, and then reappear to revitalize our world.

Imagine loving families and communities: People bonded together from their hearts, no longer projecting their pain and hurt onto others, but healing whatever arises inside them so that their interactions with all others are based on love. Children thrive, animals thrive, gardens thrive.

Imagine resources distributed so the physical needs and comforts of all beings on our planet are met. Each person is aware of their unique contribution and carries out their work joyfully. We appreciate all contributions equally: the artists, the healers; the organizers, the teachers, the gardeners and farmers, the builders and all who have the talent to provide for our physical needs.

We have created a world based on love, trust, faith and abundance, and it is a very nice planet, indeed

I: THE PREMISE

Collectively we stand on a precipice, on the edge of an evolutionary leap, poised and ready to jump into the Unknown. This leap is about becoming "Spirit-directed," rather than ego-directed. The old way has taught us to live by the dictates of our ego: to operate out of a survival paradigm, which keeps us seeking love, acceptance, material security and approval from others. The new way asks us to empower ourselves so that we can align our lives with our spiritual nature. It asks that we trust our intuitive guidance, open our hearts, and make a commitment to being mindful. It asks that we free ourselves from societal expectations and from the opinion of others.

As we learn this, our morality comes from within because in our hearts we understand what is right and what is not. It becomes easier for us to attune to Divine Will and to make conscious choices in our lives from this perspective. We learn how to love ourselves more deeply, how to validate ourselves more strongly, how to release old emotional wounds, and to trust that whenever we make life choices based on the call of our Spirit, what we need will be provided.

The great emphasis of the past few decades on personal growth and inner healing has been an essential forerunner in the process we are being asked to undertake. It is a prerequisite. In order to relegate our ego to the service of our Spirit, we need to have a healthy and empowered sense of self. If we are still functioning out of emotional wounding, feeling victimized or disempowered in our lives, going into spiritual mode will likely be an escape route, not an authentic passage. The more empowered we feel, the more we take responsibility for the quality of our lives. The more responsibility we take, the more our Spirit can operate and help us to make choices that will activate and ultimately fulfill our individual and collective spiritual destiny.

The process for becoming Spirit-directed as presented in this book, takes us through both inner and outer terrains. It begins by identifying how active we allow Spirit to be in our life and suggests practices to increase its influence while easing the influence of our egos. It helps us identify and put closure on any residual wounding that has not yet been released by our inner work. Removing emotional blockages and transforming limited belief systems allows our vibrational field to pulsate at a higher frequency than ever before. This strengthens our connection to our spiritual and creative abilities, because we have cleared the blocks that create dense energy. We become more able to consciously connect to our energy body and to honor the now freed-up intuitive flow within us.

Large numbers of us on the planet are going through this process simultaneously. It is collectively changing our view of ourselves, allowing us to embrace the concept that we are made up of light, rather than the dense matter of clay; that we are really light beings. It is also bringing to our awareness that we are multi-dimensional, and that to further this journey, we must accept all the multi-dimensional parts of ourselves: the Divine, the ingenious, the petty and the cruel. Once this is in order, we can focus on creating spirit-directed relationships, families and communities. If you feel ready for this process, read on. This book provides you with numerous exercises, examples and images to help on your way. I suggest you keep a journal handy.

ASSESSING SPIRIT'S POWER IN OUR LIVES

The Relationship between Ego and Spirit

When we are Spirit-directed, we use our ego as a tool. Because Spirit lives in the present, it needs the ego to help it interface with the 3-dimensional reality of our world. Our Spirit presents us with our higher vision: why we are here, why people and events come into our lives, what skills or resources we have contracted to use in this lifetime. Our egos help us to navigate in the material world. It is through proper use of the ego that we can most effectively actualize the desires of our Spirit.

Being Spirit-directed does not mean we become Pure Spirit. On Earth, we intentionally have our personalities; that is part of the earthly experience. We need our personality, which includes our ego. It adds to our unique energetic blueprint. When we can consistently use our ego to support our Spirit, rather than to keep us stuck in a lower vibration of fear and addictive desires, we have made the leap and are now Co-creating with the Divine.

There is a wonderful story about the Buddha that for me shines light on this. Every night Buddha would say that Mara, loosely translated as temptation, would come to visit him, and every night he would have tea with Mara. On one hand, he was saying that temptation never disappears even if you are the Buddha, but to me this is a wonderful metaphor for how our Spirit can relate to our ego. Our ego is not going to go away. It will continually visit us. So sit it down for tea. This will do two things: first, since your Spirit is the host, It will be in charge of the interaction. Your

Spirit can be sweet and gentle with your ego, but not allow it to sit at the head of the table. And second, the "tea experience" will have a calming effect on the ego, settling it down so it is more open to helping your Spirit carry out its Divine plan.

Since ego does not go away when we become Spirit-directed, it needs to take on a new job description. It becomes employed by our Spirit to help us create guidelines and to help us develop strategies on ways to best negotiate Spiritual guidance in our present life. When we have developed a healthy ego, a healthy sense of self, we are able to work within our personality structure to optimize this Guidance.

For example, my Spirit is directing me to work on this book. I love to write. I love to inspire people to feel more empowered and to connect more deeply with their own Spirit. Nevertheless, each writing day I face the self-doubts of my ego, the fear which likes to suggest I am not up to this task. Because I am Spirit-directed, I can observe my ego, and find strategies so that I will not lose my Spirit-direction. I may do this by using my ego to create time frames ("write for an hour no matter what judgments may arise, then take a break, do something fun, and come back for another hour.) I may do this by employing my ego to note all the reasons I do not have to be attached to an end product. ("My life is fine either way.") I can notice how I focus on negative assumptions about my abilities, and use my ego to substitute these old negative beliefs with self-encouragement so that I become my own cheering squad, energizing my Spirit and helping me make the right choices to manifest what Spirit is asking of me.

Objective self-observation is the primary tool for assessing how much Spirit is leading in your life. Once you can objectively observe the areas where Spirit is in charge, and the areas that are still being run by ego, you can set the intention to make the necessary changes. Throughout this book, I will be helping you identify and understand the fears and their origins that keep you stuck in ego. You will learn to recognize and overcome programmed responses that keep you from listening to your intuition. And you will be able to uncover the subtle beliefs that inhibit you from stepping into your full co-creative power and how they are still operating in your psyche, which in turn gives you the ability to shift them.

Ego-Driven vs. Spirit-Guided Living

We often hear the term 'Go with the flow.' This term implies surrendering to the guidance of our intuition and the guidance of our Spirit. It implies ease. It suggests that we can just lie on our backs and float down the stream of our lives enjoying the view, trusting we will arrive at our desired destination. Except, what about the rocks in our way, or the rains and wind that churn up the water so we want to grab on to something for dear life, or the heat and cold that make us so uncomfortable we want to get out of the stream and take cover? Our Spirit, if we can let it, will respond to these obstacles by being mindful and responsive, thus keeping us out of harm's way. Our ego, on the other hand, responds to these obstacles with fear and doubt, often pushing us to get out of the stream and stay stuck in old familiar patterns. "Go with the flow," suggests that if we just relax everything will be fine; everything will be just as it is meant to be. But the ego does not trust; it does not believe this. It assumes we have to make things happen or else nothing will occur. It believes that going with the flow makes us passive and therefore vulnerable, and that vulnerability is a sure invitation to get hurt. We have been trained to fight the flow, to push upstream, and thus unconsciously to create more obstacles.

So consciously wanting our Spirit to lead the way, and assuming this will bring us great harmony in our lives is not enough, we also have to activate courage as well as our inner resources to free ourselves from the strong resistance of our ego. Understanding how we allow our ego to undermine us in our quest is the first step. The next step is learning to realize when our ego is in charge. Below I have listed some qualities for you to watch for, as they are signals that your ego is over-riding your Spirit. As you read through, ask yourself what is still active in your life.

Qualities of Being Ego-Directed

- A sense of being driven
- Tension, stress
- Worry and concern about the future
- Fear-based decision-making
- Shutting down feelings: going numb
- Living in the past: past hurts, past successes, past relationships
- Feeling superior or inferior to others
- Focusing on other's reactions to you; feeling a need for others approval & acceptance
- Exhilaration about accomplishments
- Deflation about "failures" or shortcomings
- Judging yourself and/or others
- Being attached to achieving a goal
- Feeling overwhelmed
- Trying to logic everything out

As you go over the list, notice if there are questions which come up for you. For example, you might hear a part of yourself defend the experience of being driven. "How else do people get things done?" Confusing motivation with drive is common in our society. And sometimes the distinction can only be made by paying attention to how each quality feels in your body. When we are driven, we generally feel a sense of urgency. That urgency, in and of itself, is a quality of the ego. For Spirit, there is never urgency. All things happen in their right time.

The ego operates out of the belief that without some stress we will do nothing. It does not understand that we can be moved to action effortlessly. Tension and stress tax our systems. They tend to be propelled by fear. When we feel this, it is a sign that our ego is in control and that the conditions this creates are making it difficult for us to attune to our Spirit.

When we are aligned with Spirit, being motivated to action is in the natural flow. Spirit will be encouraging us, cheering us on. Whatever we do will feel good, inspiring, and energizing. It will not have the stomach-wrenching intensity of drive, or the adrenaline rush of excitement that comes when we are in achievement mode. It will have the quality of a choreographed dance: We make one synchronized step after the other, effortlessly and in a state of grace.

The concept of feeling better than or less than another human being always comes from our ego. Whenever we feel smug or lacking, our ego is running the show. This is different from understanding that we may be farther along in the process of self-development than others, or that others are farther along than we are. We are all teachers and students in the spiritual realm: we are all in different grades, but we, as souls, are never more valuable or less valuable than another.

This holds true for judgments as well. Notice how you feel when you are judgmental about yourself or another person. There is a tightening in your body. Your heart energy cannot flow freely. While we have the right to distinguish between behavior that supports a loving way of life, and behavior that supports a negative, destructive way of life, to hold another or ourselves in judgment takes energy away from our Spirit. We all have a right to our choices. Some choices that may appear negative may bring extremely important information that will ultimately propel us along. This is easy to see when we are operating from Spirit. It is almost impossible to see, when our egos are in control.

Our culture views goal-setting as essential to living a successful life, and there is nothing wrong with setting goals when they can be seen as guidelines. Goals, properly set, give us direction. All of you reading this book, for instance, have a goal to become more Spirited-directed. When our Spirit is in charge, we will be enjoying the process of moving toward this goal, but we will not feel emotionally attached to it; therefore we will not be looking at this in terms of success or failure. Being Spirit-directed also gives us the flow or flexibility to allow the goal to change when needed. If our egos are running things, the goal is what counts, and our feelings of self-worth become dependent on whether or not we achieve our goals. In this way, being goal-orientated operates counter to our Spirit.

When the ego is directing you, not only do you tend to feel overwhelmed, you are not able to honor your feelings. The ego operates most effectively when we are numb. It can tolerate impatience and frustration, because that tends to fuel its high stressed, or in some cases, depressed energy; but to be in a genuine flow of feelings, to allow ourselves to consciously ride the wave of joy, or grief, or even anger and fear, gets in the ego's way. So when we are ego-directed, we will generally feel shut down or frustrated. It is also likely we will feel victimized. The ego clings to victim beliefs like "my life is always so hard." Until we are able to identify how this is operating in our life and free up our flow of feelings, Spirit cannot fully be in charge.

When we understand how our emotions work, and we begin to get a sense of what I call "Unconscious Intention" (more on this in Chapter 4), we realize that logic in itself will not help our self-development. With logic, we assume that because we know a thing to be accurate or we know what we want, we will automatically behave in ways that support this. We are complex entities who often act counter to logic. The more we are able to access heretofore unconscious beliefs that run counter to our conscious intention, the more successful we will be at clearing the way for our Spirit to lead. When unconscious beliefs and motives are being activated in this way, we want to keep them from having power in our life. If we are tuned into our emotions, they will signal us when there are beliefs that need to be brought into our conscious awareness in order to be transformed.

Take a moment to assess how frequently and in what capacity ego is currently directing your life. Pose the question, "What percentage of my life is currently run by my ego?" Note the very first number which pops into your head. It is very important that you do this with spontaneity. If you think about this too much, you will not get accurate information. The percentage that pops in spontaneously will give you a sense of how reliant you are on your ego. You might want to refine the question, by asking for a percentage in different areas of your life, areas such as relationships, work, parenting, and friendships. Be aware that ego does not give up its control easily and that a high percentage response does not mean you have not made progress. Simply understanding the distinction of being ego-driven vs. Spirit-directed is an important step, as is the ability to honestly assess where we are.

Listed below are the kinds of qualities that are operative when we are allowing Spirit to direct our lives. These qualities exist when we quiet our ego, tune into our hearts and align our personal will with Divine Will. Quieting our ego in this manner may begin as a fleeting experience for you, but it will continue to build in frequency as you consciously choose activities that will nurture this: activities such as meditation, yoga, prayer, intention-setting, visualization, breathwork, journal-writing, as well as any energy work that helps you clear and attune your chakras. Using these techniques is vital to developing the optimum relationship between our Spirit and our ego.

Qualities of Being Spirit-Directed

- **A feeling of calm and well-being**
- **Non-attachment to outcome**
- **A sense of higher purpose or mission**

- Focus on growth; on the journey rather than the destination
- Open-hearted treatment of self and others
- A quiet mind
- Ongoing ability to observe one's thoughts and emotions without attachment to judgment
- Ability to observe others and the world without judgment without attachment to judgment
- Feeling in sync with life
- Freedom from being influenced by the reactions of others
- Feelings of being connected to the greater whole – to all of humanity and all other life forms
- Sense of limitlessness and unlimited potential
- Trust that all will work out for our highest good
- Faith in oneself and in Divine Order
- A loving and joyful heart

When we are Spirit-directed, we do not have to see the rocks in the stream ahead of time. We know we can use anything that is in our path for our development and that our development is ultimately to serve all life. Flowing is easy if we know we can handle the obstacles. Certainly, we do not want to crash head-first into the rocks, rather we want to be able to trust our intuition to signal us as we approach a rock. Then we can pause and take time to understand the message that this rock is bringing us. When the waters are unsettled we have the ability to center and trust that the ride, no matter how bumpy, can support the needs of our Spirit and that it will give us an opportunity to fine-tune our "navigational" skills. This brings a deep and abiding feeling of well-being.

Ask yourself now "What percent of my life is currently guided by Spirit?" Again, note the first figure that pops into your head. Divide this into categories as before: "What percent is spirit leading me in my relationships? In my work?" And so on.

This is not precise science, and the details are not important. If the sum of percentages from ego vs. spirit does not add up to 100%, it does not matter. The purpose of these "percentage" questions is to let your intuition give you an overall sense of where you are in this process. This will help you set more realistic intention for using this book.

Another clue about how active ego or Spirit is during your day is to notice your relationship with time. Whenever we are focused on events from the past or concerned about our future, our ego is in the driver's seat. Spirit wants us to learn from our past and to create images of our future, but when this comes from our egos it will have a different qualitative feeling. There will be an emotional charge that is usually a negative one. Remember the ego holds fear, and believes that this is a good thing because it will help us survive. It is very one-dimensional and quite ignorant of the emotional and spiritual part of us. It cannot bring us a joyful life, but hopes that if we are busy enough, we will not notice. When we are emotionally connected to Spirit, our heart is open, we feel a sense of well-being or joy, but there is no emotional charge – rather there is a sense of peace that permeates our entire being. If we learn to notice when we are focused on the past or future, we will then be able to use various techniques to bring us back into the present such as taking a deep centering breath and focusing our total attention on the act of breathing. The more we practice this, the more adept we will become.

BEGIN WITH AN INTENTION

As you go through this book, keep focused on its purpose which is to activate a process within you: the process to empower yourself to jump off that precipice; to empower your Spirit to lead your way. You will learn to consciously embrace and participate in this evolutionary leap. Personalize this by creating a statement or an image which contains your deepest wish or wishes for empowering your Spirit. If it feels right for you, include your wish for empowering the healing of our planet as well.

Take a moment, breathe deeply, and focus your attention inwardly. Now ask: "***What change would I most like to see in my life from reading this book?***" Let images or words float gently into your awareness.

For some of you, the answer will be quite specific like going back to school; leaving a relationship; changing jobs. For others of you, the answer will be more general: "Trusting myself more; speaking my truth more often; being more authentic with others." Write this intention down. Our mind is very powerful, and we want to give it as many ways to support our desired changes as possible. Writing down an intention energizes it. Another way to energize your intention is to state it in the present tense implying that it is already happening: "I have a new Spirit-supporting job." "I speak my truth with ease."

As we evolve individually, we evolve collectively. We understand that we are all interconnected, and our well-being impacts our communities, our countries, and our planet. So adding a "collective" purpose for your intention energizes change in a larger arena. Using our examples from above, it would be something like "I have a new Spirit-supporting job where I am serving the best interests of humanity." or "I speak my truth with ease, and model this for others."

As you read through this book, keep your intention in mind. You might want to say it out loud each time you begin to read. The more you are able to focus on your intention, the more you are activating your Spirit to help you create it.

MOVING FROM OUR HEARTS

While Divine guidance and spiritual information enter our bodies through our upper chakras, it is the heart which offers us the clearest spiritual direction. Learning to recognize our heart energy, to listen to its wisdom and to follow its yearnings, is part of the way we empower our Spirit to lead us in our lives. Doing your emotional healing is essential. Without this level of healing, you are less able to reconnect with your heart and to read its signals accurately. Conversely, deep emotional healing automatically connects us to our heart, and helps us to open and honor this energy center. We are then capable of focusing our awareness here, and can feel Divine love within us and around us. We need this kinesthetic connection. It shows us what to trust as we continue to shift into this new way of being.

Blockages

Those of us who are too afraid, who are actively (albeit unconsciously) blocking this process, are being propelled into undue suffering: disease, depression, anxiety, addiction, emptiness. This is not the punishment of God or the Higher Beings; it is our natural response to damming up our energy: We create blockages. The more intensely we resist the wisdom of our hearts, the bigger the blockage. The bigger the blockage, the more it affects our lives.

Blockages are created by our egos. In our culture, and over most of our planet, we have so disconnected from faith and inner spiritual direction that we hold a collective belief that our egos must protect us, rather than allowing God-energy to do its work. This puts an enormous amount of pressure on the ego and causes us to develop unhealthy defensive strategies to help us feel "safe." Be aware that spiritual direction is not the same as religious direction. Our globe is filled with different religions that dictate rules to live by. While all religions have Spirit at their root, too often the rules of the religion are ego-driven. "Follow our rules and you will be a good person; you will be saved... don't follow our rules and you will be bad, and in danger." Whenever beliefs of any kind create more separation and fear, this feeds our ego, not our Spirit.

Another pervasive form of ego involvement that interferes with Spirit is the phenomenon of denial. Denial keeps us from looking honestly at ourselves and our environment. My favorite personal example of denial was when I woke up one morning, 6 months and very obviously pregnant with my third child, and I said to myself "maybe the test was wrong." For a split second, I totally believed this was possible. I was going through fear, from my ego, that I would not have the energy to parent another child, that I would not be able to balance the inner call to fulfill my work on the planet, and the needs of this new baby, and it was this anxiety that created the momentary denial. What struck me most from that experience was that for that moment, I was actually able to believe the absurd.

It is this denial in its extreme form that allows mothers to be in close proximity to their children being beaten or molested and to "believe" it is not happening. It is this denial that allows us, when consistently confronted with the destructive behavior of addicted spouses, children, parents, or friends, to minimize its significance and deem it not a problem.

Denial is the primary method we use to ignore our hearts, and thus it keeps us from empowering our Spirit. Because our ego-driven denial is a manifestation of our fears, the more scared we are, the more we cling to it. It is an indication of where we are unable to activate our faith and to surrender to Spirit. A commitment to courage and to brutal self-honesty is called for if we are to break through this. Most of you who read this book will already have made major inroads here. Still there are likely to be areas where you are not following your heart, and these will be permeated with denial and its corresponding fear.

So start by asking yourself *"What am I still pretending?"* Using your journals, ask yourself this question over and over again, and each time you ask, write down whatever comes into your head. The rules are: No censoring. No worrying if it makes sense. No judging. No wondering about the accuracy of what comes in. Let yourself do this for 20 - 30 minutes of uninterrupted time repeating the question over and over, and each time writing the first thought that pops up, no matter how silly, extraneous, or false it may seem. After you finish, look over your writing for themes and surprises. Accessing this previously unconscious information gives you important clues about the blockages currently in your path.

After we identify where denial is active in our lives, we can look at the fears that drive the denial. I encourage you to return to your journal in order to dig deeper in uncovering these fears. Go through the list on what you are still pretending, and next to each item write down what fears may be driving this. As an example, if you wrote that you were pretending a relationship was meeting your needs, you might be afraid of losing some financial security and/or of being alone. Much of this book will be presenting techniques to help you move through these fears, so the earlier you can identify them, the more effective use you can make of the chapters to come.

The Risk Factor

Part of breaking through fear is about activating courage. We need to be able to take the risk of following our heart and ultimately to risk life as we know it, in order to follow our Spirit. This takes will, and the ability to stand behind our choices and to cheer ourselves on. Anytime we move beyond our comfort zone and things turn out well, we create an inner resource that we can use for future change. It will begin to grow exponentially. Conversely, anytime we refuse to take a risk that is initiated by our heart and by our intuition, and opt for security instead, we disempower ourselves. This tends to activate a downward cycle.

Think back to a time when you acted from your heart, despite your fears. Can you go back to a decision where your head was advising one thing, but you followed your feelings instead. Or a time where significant people in your life were advising you against a move, but your heart won out. I am not talking about decisions based on denial or momentary impulse. I am talking about decisions where, even though you go against commonly held wisdom, you know it is the right thing for you. Always, in these instances, things work out because you are following the call of your Spirit. So find a time in your life when this happened. You might want to write it down. If you are unable to access such a decision, it is time to get the show on the road. Notice if there is currently a change or decision you are feeling drawn by your heart to make.

There are several times in my life where I have followed my heart. Had I listened to my parents or even my friends, I would likely have made an alternate decision that would have created blockage for me. Many of these decisions looked impulsive to the outside world, but my spirit was strong and I was willing to take responsibility for my choices. It is with deep gratitude that I look back on these because the "easier" path would have been to follow conventional wisdom. Had I done that I would have greatly impeded my journey and put myself through needless suffering. I have spoken of many of these decisions in my book: ***JOURNEY TO WHOLENESS: A Guide to Inner Healing***, so I will not go into them here.

Instead, let me give you a simple example from my husband's life. My husband came from a lower middle class background. His family had a strong belief that you work to support yourself and your family, not for personal fulfillment. When he and I first got together, he had been working "alternative" jobs for many years. He had managed our local food co-op, baked bread and served lunches in an alternative restaurant, and taken odd jobs, as needed, usually involving physical labor. He had four years of college, but had not finished his degree. After we got together, he went back and finished his undergraduate degree, but continued to work in alternative employment, usually for friends. These were "laid-back" jobs with just enough compensation that combined with my part time income got us by.

After my second child was born, I worked part time at a non-profit counseling collective while my husband stayed home with her. But the economic demands of our family, which at the time included my two children and my husband's daughter from his first marriage, grew too great. An opportunity opened at the local post office for him to be a mail handler. The pay was good, the benefits were great, and we thought we would be on "easy street". For seven years, my husband sorted mail, mostly on the midnight shift. It helped us a lot economically. We were able to buy a house and have some modest savings. He was also going to school, one class at a time, to earn a Master's degree in labor relations, an interest that developed while being a union steward at the post office. He would joke daily as he went off to work that he was going to "the steaming pits of hell." By this time, we had four children between us. When my son reached an age where we were comfortable putting him in childcare, my practice became relatively prosperous. It was at this point that I said to my husband, "Why not just quit your job, finish your degree and do the work you love?"

He pondered this for bit. He knew in his heart he wanted to work for a service-oriented labor union. He knew that his master's degree and experience might give him an easy entrance. He also knew that he had a secure job. I was self-employed. He was also 45 years old, and there was a lot being written about how tight the job market was over 40. Had he asked his parents or any members of his family what they thought, they would have told him he was crazy. My family would probably have said the same thing. Our friends would have been more supportive, but might have hesitated agreeing with such a risky decision. Nonetheless, he allowed his heart to lead. We came up with a plan that allowed us about 6 months to pay off some bills, and then he resigned and enrolled in school full-time. This was in August. By mid-April of the next year, his Masters close to completion, my husband applied for and was offered a paid internship at the very labor union he had hoped to work for. Within three weeks of his employment, a staff representative abruptly quit. As one of the council directors was asking a manager if he knew anyone who might be good for the job, my husband walked by. The week before, my husband had been assigned to work with this manager on a job out-of-town, giving them a chance to get to know each other. Within an hour, my husband was called into the director's office and offered this job which involved a free car, a significant raise, a salary and benefits that surpassed the post office, and the work his heart had led him to.

I give you this example to encourage all of you. I have experienced this phenomenon repeatedly in my life. If we listen to our Spirit and follow our hearts, if we are willing to defy conventional wisdom, break free of tribal consciousness, if we are willing to take the risks our Spirit is leading us to take, it always works in our best interest. It is the leap of faith that Spirit demands of us, and this is the key to creating the lives we want in partnership with the Universe. If you have not yet had the experience of doing this, you may want to include the ability to take appropriate risks as something you will gain from reading this book.

SELF-OBSERVATION

Being aware of the call of our Spirit is the first step in becoming Spirit-directed. We all get called, but many of us are in the habit of ignoring this. Developing a skilled method of self-observation allows us to pay attention to what is really happening for us. We might choose not to act on it, that is always an option, but we will no longer be able to claim ignorance.

The more we are able to observe ourselves and our interactions objectively, without judging ourselves or others, the more we will notice when we are being Spirit-directed and when we are letting our ego lead. I always tell clients to become researchers of themselves and their lives. Researchers do their best to remain objective. I suggest to clients that they watch themselves with that level of detachment in order to collect important information that relates to whatever area of growth they are pursuing.

The four main areas of self-observation to focus on are: Body sensations, emotional charge, thoughts that go through your mind, and environmental experiences or feedback. Each of these provides important signals.

Observing Your Physical Body

We all differ in terms of how aware we are of our bodies. Some people feel very disconnected from their bodies, while others attune naturally to body signals. Our bodies are by nature, finely-tuned mechanisms. They give us the ability to experience many types of sensations, all of which have messages for us. Learning how to use the breath to quiet the mind, will allow you to notice the sensations of your body and therefore give you more access to the signals it provides.

Take a deep centering breath and notice where you hold tension. Is your stomach tightening? If so, that is probably fear. Does your stomach hurt? This could be fear or guilt. Is your chest or throat tight? Usually that indicates sadness. Are your shoulders hurting? This could indicate anger or feeling burdened. Does your heart area feel relaxed and open? This is when love and joy can flow freely. Are you feeling a deep sense of calm? Then you are aligned with your Spirit.

Create an intention just to notice, remembering to put judgment aside. If judgment comes, which is natural, just observe it and send it on its way. It may take a lot of practice to begin to interpret what you are noticing, and to do this with objectivity. Be gentle with yourself. Just breathe and notice, and give yourself credit for being willing to do this. If you stay committed to this practice, the rest will begin to unfold.

Observing Your Emotional Body

To observe the emotional body, notice your moods as well as any internal feeling of activation or agitation. It is easiest to notice that we are experiencing an emotional charge when we are angry or scared. As you observe this, do your best to label it, saying for example, "My anger is activated now" or "I'm observing anger getting triggered for me." Realize as you label this objectively, you quiet down any tendency to judge your emotions. At the same time, you are detaching enough from the emotion so as to minimize it having control over you. It is important to let yourself feel this emotion, to go into the experience of it as energy that is coursing through you, to honor it, to notice if it is asking you to do a deeper level of healing or to deal with something in your current life. Make a commitment to follow what is being asked, and then allow it to move on its way. You can use the same technique with fear. With fear, it is also helpful to say reassuring and comforting things to ourselves, focusing on our ability to act with courage and to stay safe.

Sadness is generally felt as heaviness. It is similar to depression, but without the sense of guilt, worthlessness, and all pervasive hopelessness. With sadness, nothing feels like much fun. But simultaneously, if you are able to observe the sadness objectively and therefore without judgment, you will find that it is not particularly painful especially if you are able to cry freely as a way to release it. (Crying out of sadness feels good; crying out of anger does not.) Once we release it, we open ourselves to more joy.

Excitement is more complex. Many times we are feeling joyful when we are excited. But excitement is often a sign that our ego is getting stroked, or anticipating getting stroked. This is where paying attention will help you sort things out. Where joyfulness brings a deep sense of fulfillment and calm, excitement tends to throw us off center. On the other hand, when children get excited, they jump and dance and carry on. This is not ego. It is a spontaneous expression of joy. Their Spirit is celebrating. So if you have retained that childlike quality, your excitement may be coming from your Spirit. The more skilled you get at self-observation, the more you will get an accurate interpretation of what is truly going on with you.

One of the hardest concepts for people to grasp is that we are capable of feeling contradictory emotions simultaneously. We have the ability to feel joy even as we are feeling sad, and to hold both of those feelings in our awareness. We can feel anger and still feel our hearts brimming with love, and hold both of those feelings at the same time. This happens more easily once our emotions are flowing freely and therefore aligned with our Spirit. When we have reached this level of emotional expertise, we can consciously focus on the love energy in our hearts while noticing our anger is activated at the same time. One's ability to observe this, however, generally comes after a great deal of emotional healing and a lot of practice watching the self.

If noticing your emotional responses are difficult for you that is an indication that there is a need for more emotional healing. A good therapist can help you explore why it is difficult for you to tune into your feelings. It is likely that you carry old messages that it is not okay to feel, and you will need to begin with transforming these.

Watching Your Thoughts

When we are 100% aligned with Spirit, we have no thoughts. We are totally connected to Stillness. This, however, is a very rare experience for humans, even for humans who spend much of their time in prayer and meditation. Typically the mind races about, filled with all sorts of interesting stuff. If you have not yet practiced observing the workings of your mind, I highly recommend you do this now. Remember to keep your sense of humor. When you can observe the many layers of thoughts that run through your mind, you will notice how silly and often bizarre many of them are.

To begin this process, focus on your breath, taking deep, relaxing inhales and exhales, and putting all your attention on your breathing. Do this for several minutes until you settle down enough to step back from your thoughts. Now notice what starts popping in. It is likely you will start to run through your plans for the day. Then, typically, judgments will come. You may be putting yourself down or judging others. Just watch and see what happens. Fearful thoughts like to jump in as well. The more we can see this, the less we will become attached to our fears and therefore the less emotional charge and intense body sensations we will have to experience. We will explore our thoughts and belief system in more detail in Chapter 4. For now, do your best to just notice what thoughts are coming through your mind.

Messages from the Environment

As we truly realize that everything is interconnected, that we are all part of a giant web of Consciousness, we realize that every interpersonal interaction and every experience that comes to us from our environment is really a reflection of ourselves. Being able to watch our interactions and experiences consciously is the first step to extracting the important messages, often cloaked in symbols, which our environment brings to us. We have powerful electro-magnetic fields. These fields draw to us the exact lessons our Spirit is wishing us to learn. How intense and dramatic these will be generally depends on our ability to accept subtle messages and work with them. If we can pick up on subtle signals, then we will not need crises to learn our lessons. Working with these signals allows us to grow more aware of when we are in flow, which helps us surrender to the wisdom of our Spirit. This surrender then draws to us some awesome blessings, inspiring us to continue this process of growth.

If you are having any external difficulty, whether it is a relationship or some life situation, do your best not to get stuck in the struggle. Instead, ask what is the message this experience is bringing to you. Even if you are not getting a clear answer, you have put the process in motion. Again, the more you practice this, the more skilled you will become at tuning into the symbolic message of the situation. This will help you create the necessary shift that can make your lessons and your life considerably easier.

As we practice this level of observation, we learn that while everything is bringing us lessons, nothing is to be taken personally. The purpose of the lessons and blessings are to bring us into closer alignment with our Spirit. It is only our ego that feels wounded or inflated when we have interactions or experiences that we judge to be good or bad.

As you begin to practice these four levels of self-observation, notice when your Spirit is being fed and when you are feeling deflated. The more aligned we are with our Spirit, the more we feel good in our life, in ourselves, in our interactions and activities. Remember, our life does not have to be problem-free for us to feel good. Rather, our obstacles and problems are viewed as challenges and opportunities for more soul development. When we have empowered our Spirits, this perspective becomes as natural as breathing.

Current Life Observation

Think about the areas in your life where you most honor your Spirit, where you most follow your heart. Notice the sense of empowerment you feel in these areas. Then think about the areas of your life you where you least honor your Spirit. Write them down, and jot anything that comes to mind about why these areas are difficult to hand over to your Spirit.

Healing Exercise: Observing Your Day

Think about your typical day. What makes you feel happy? Do you find yourself waking in gratitude for the wonderful life you have, or do you often feel disenchanted, dissatisfied? Spend an entire day observing yourself, or if you prefer, go through a day in your mind and make your observations. Remember to be the researcher: curious and without judgment. Whatever you become aware of whether positive or negative, keep an attitude of "isn't that interesting."

Here are some questions you might want to focus on as you observe yourself going through your day.

- *How do I generally feel when I wake up in the morning and what am I saying to myself?*

If you regularly wake up feeling good and energized, this is a sign that you are living your life in harmony, and that you are not being bogged down by old emotional issues or fearful, limiting beliefs.

- *Do I do a morning ritual, or some sort of morning "practice?"*

For instance do you start your day off with a prayer, with some Yoga, do you do a stretch or two, say affirmations, sing a song? If so, does this ritual center you and give you a positive outlook? Clearly if this is the case, you are getting a strong indication that important parts of your life are in order. Conversely, if it is difficult for you to keep to some sort of morning practice (and be aware that even a 5 minute practice can make a huge difference), try some self-observation to figure out what you are doing to sabotage this. Remember to suspend judgment.

- *Upon awakening, how do I greet and interact with the other people in my home?*

If you have a family with young children, notice how it feels to get them started on their day. If you have a partner, does it feel good to wake up next to him or her? Do you feel a sense of harmony in the daily life of your household? If not, can you think of simple changes to help create this?

- *How do I feel heading off to work?*

Is there anticipation? Is there dread? Do you feel this is an obligation you must fulfill? Are there people in your work environment with whom you feel a loving connection? Are there people at work who sap your energy or push your buttons?

If you do not work outside your home, ask:

- *How do I feel once I'm ready for the main part of my day?*

Are you feeling motivated and excited? Are you bored? Are you feeling connected to some passion be it gardening or reading or working on a project? Are you feeling directionless? Lonely?

- *Once I get to work, how does that feel?*

Is it better than anticipated? Do you feel energized or do you feel forced to do work that seems disconnected from any real meaning or joy? What are you learning from your work? Are you expanding your intellectual understanding of things? Are you expanding your emotional awareness by observing your work relationships and noticing where they are functional and/or dysfunctional? What are the spiritual/soul lessons for you, the deeper symbolic meaning as seen from your soul's perspective? For example, having a critical supervisor gives you the opportunity to break free from painful emotional patterns put in place by a critical parent. If you see yourself taking on more than your share of responsibility, this may be the Universe's way of saying to you, it's time to learn to stand up for yourself, and only do your part.

- *Are there people who trigger me emotionally? And if so, what is the message here for my growth?*

Our working environments tend to be ripe with dramas and traumas, which if dealt with from a higher perspective and a sense of personal power can increase our consciousness and serve as opportunities to break free of soul-restricting patterns. Look carefully and consciously. Sometimes the most difficult situation is the one we will look back on with the most gratitude because it can be used to propel us forward. So scan your work environment carefully. It may well be the things you hate that will be turn up to be serendipitous.

- *How do I feel when I am heading home?*

When you are finished with work, do you head home anticipating loving, pleasant contact with your family, or a solitary peaceful retreat? Or do you have a sense of discomfort or stress about what you may have to deal with when you come into your home? Difficult relationships in our homes occur for several reasons, but remember whatever is not working in the relationship mirrors our own internal conflict. For example, if you observe you are being treated disrespectfully, you have the option of finding and working with a part of you that views yourself in a disrespectful manner. Once you have done this work, you will no longer tolerate being treated this way, even if that means severing the relationship.

- *How do I feel walking into my home?*

If you have children who live with you but are separated from you throughout the day, how does it feel to reconnect with them at the day's end? Are you looking forward to seeing them? Do you get a sense of warmth and open-heartedness when you or they come home? Or do you feel overburdened or overwhelmed with responsibility? Do you feel resentful that your time is not your own, or that you spend all your energy caring for them to your own detriment? Or perhaps you might feel a combination of love and warmth coupled with feeling overwhelmed and resentful. Do you have a difficult relationship with one or more of your children?

When we can observe our children and our relationship with them objectively, we notice that, in addition to being blessings, they are also lessons. The challenges they present us symbolize areas where we need to do some growth. So do your best to observe these areas carefully, being loving and gentle to yourself, but also allowing the reality, the honesty of the situation, to shine forth. Trust that there are always solutions; always ways for things to get better, and make an inner commitment you will seek these ways for yourself.

If you live alone, how does it feel to come into an empty house? Is it peaceful and pleasant? Do you feel lonely? Does your houses provide you with a sense of well-being or are there painful feelings attached to it? Do you see an orderly environment, or do things seem disjointed and chaotic? Again, without judgment, just notice. What you experience walking into your home provides you with important data.

- *Are my evenings spent in ways that feel good to me?*

If you have been active all day, evenings need to be a time to relax, to "kick back" in order to rejuvenate. If your evenings are structured and hectic, make a note of this. If they seem to drag on interminably, make a note of this as well.

- *How do you feel as you go to bed?*

As you get ready to go to bed, do you feel peaceful and ready for sleep? Is this the first moment of quiet you have allowed yourself all day? Are you anxious that you may not sleep or that your sleep will be disturbed? Again, pay attention.

- *How do I spend my time on days when I'm not working?*

Notice how you spend your time when you are not at work, using the same perspective as suggested above. All activity can bring us lessons. All contacts can elucidate important aspects of us. If non-working days have little activity and outside contacts, then pay attention to what you do with your time, to your thoughts and to the signals of your emotional and physical body.

After doing this exercise in each area of your life, you should notice a marked increase in your ability for self-observation. Eventually, you will find you are able to watch your thoughts, your feelings and motivations with ease, and ultimately use that information to empower your Spirit to more fully lead your life.

2: OUR COLLECTIVE ISSUES ABOUT POWER

Empowerment is both our divine gift and divine connection. Within all of us is a wealth of unlimited possibility which flowers only in the fertile environment created by our becoming empowered. It is then that we are self-referenced enough to listen to and act on the call of our Spirit. While the path to empowerment is exquisitely simple once we allow Spirit to co-create in our lives, our learned resistance to allowing this is strong. This is because our present cultural paradigm holds numerous fear-based beliefs that must be identified and exorcized before we are empowered enough to fully release our life to the direction of our Spirit. The paradox is we need to feel in charge of ourselves and our lives enough to surrender this job to Spirit, and to ultimately be able to discern what Spirit is really asking of us.

To come to a place where we are taking charge of our life demands that we go through the process of understanding and transforming our emotional wounding and our self-defeating beliefs, while making sure that all parts of ourselves are participating in this process. Good psychotherapy typically guides people through this. But be aware that the healing process has many levels. It is rather like school. In the early grades we learn the basics: how to read, write, and compute. In the early psychotherapeutic part of this process, we learn how to make insightful connections, how to increase our self-esteem, how to relate to others more effectively. Some people stop here. It is a place where life can go reasonably smoothly as long as we do not look or feel too deeply.

Those of us committed to furthering our "education" may quickly go on to higher grades. Others may hit an intense life lesson that compels them to re-enter the process. At this next level, we become skilled at recognizing and trusting our feelings. We are not just intellectually free of the old wounds; we clear our emotional body as well. We also learn that the self/Self is many layered, is in fact multi-dimensional, and we increase our ability to identify and transform the parts of ourselves that are not aligned with our Spirit's empowerment. These are the disenfranchised parts that hold our fears and limiting beliefs.

The next several chapters will offer insights and exercises to support this new growth in you. In this chapter, you will have an opportunity to deepen your awareness of your issues around power and empowerment. This will provide you with clarity about where there needs to be more growth in order for you to fully empower your Spirit. We begin by looking at different models of power. Next we look at how we are collectively taught to block empowerment. I will ask you to do a self-assessment designed to access all the beliefs and feelings you carry around power which have blocked or are currently blocking your way, and suggest ways for you to break through these.

THE RELATIONSHIP BETWEEN POWER AND EMPOWERMENT

If we were to ask a random group of people to define the word power, many would perceive it as the ability to force one's will upon others or to dominate and control a situation. Clearly this has been the predominant view of power in our culture. This view of power is about the ego's need to control in order to feel safe. Empowerment, on the other hand, is about a sense of inner power. It brings with it the awareness that security does not come from controlling one's external world, but by being in harmony with one's heart and inner wisdom. This is why being empowered is such an essential step in becoming Spirit-directed.

When the patriarchal paradigm began to develop over 6000 years ago, it could only gain a stronghold by suppressing the right hemisphere of the brain, the side which corresponds to the Feminine principle. "Feminine" qualities such as intuition, spiritual connection, and emotional sensitivity started to be invalidated. This was a time in history where agriculture had developed to the point that surplus could be created. This created a shift away from tribal units working for the collective good, and introduced the concept of private property. The left brain, which corresponds to the Masculine principle and which includes logical thinking and calculation abilities, needed to develop in order to find more sophisticated ways to keep track of goods, property and distribution. The left brain categorizes and separates. These qualities supported the emerging patriarchal structure. Because the right brain is holistic and its perception is immediate and inclusive, it became viewed in the collective unconscious as dangerous to "progress".

As the Masculine principle ascended, people shifted toward a belief in one male god, kings began to rule wielding great power over the masses, and women and children lost status and rights, ultimately being viewed as property of husbands and fathers. The psychic division from this paradigm shift created a separation and thus a deep soul wound within each individual as the division and hierarchical relationship between the male and female parts of the psyche occurred.

Looking at power from the above perspective, we can see that left-brained or male power is the ability to be focused and forceful. It is an external power. When it is working cooperatively with the right brain, the feminine hemisphere, it uses force only with compassion and only for protection. It can be fierce, but appropriately so. It does not derive pleasure or ego satisfaction from displaying itself. Since the advent of Patriarchy, where male power was disconnected from the feminine, it has come to be defined as a way to dominate others. In disconnecting from the feminine, it has gone haywire. It has separated from emotions, intuition and Spirit. It now has no anchor, no sense of Self. Force is used for its own sake, to cover up and distract from the pain of the psychic rift that resulted from this disconnection.

Hitler's regime was a manifestation of this disconnected male power at its extreme. People cannot participate in atrocities if they are spiritually connected, and spiritual connection comes to us through the right hemisphere of our brains. The Nazi regime was the expression and mass culmination of centuries, even millenniums, of the self-abuse caused by this psychic rift. If people were connected to their internal wholeness, they would not have been able to be controlled, and certainly could not have been so cruel to their fellow humans. When we are connected to feelings and to Spirit, to right hemisphere or the feminine consciousness, we have no desire to harm others for we know internally that we are all One. Only when we are disconnected can we develop the ability to use dominance and force. This disconnection creates our capacity to be ruthless and to create child-rearing practices that train children, especially males, to bury and even lose their capacity for empathy or compassion.

Female power or right-brained power is the ability to be anchored to love, Spirit and intuition. It is an internal power. When it is connected to the masculine, it is able to bring forth vision and transformation. When it is disconnected, it has no means of external protection, no means to set boundaries which can result in chaos, martyrdom, victimization and madness.

Feminine power had to be submerged, distrusted and invalidated for patriarchy, a paradigm of dominance rather than equality, to gain ascendance. Men and women were taught to disconnect from their internal opposite, so that men began to lose access to their inner feminine, and women began to lose access to their inner male. Females were devalued and taught they were powerless and needed to rely on their fathers and husbands. Women, as a group, held no societal or economic power and bought into the cultural myths that their inner wisdom, their inner power was silly or dangerous and something to stay away from.

By invalidating the feminine, males who might be tempted to access their own feminine power were also ridiculed. One of the greatest insults to boys or men was to say they were somehow like girls or women. All that was feminine came to be associated with weakness. All that was masculine became associated with strength, which in turn became defined as external power. Since it was considered feminine to feel, we have for centuries conditioned men not to feel. Since it was considered feminine to honor the intuitive, men for centuries have been conditioned to believe that intuition is fantasy.

With the advent of the women's movement in the late 1960's, women began to shift belief systems that had been alive for eons. Two overtly contradictory and equally important things began to happen. First, women joined together in consciousness-raising groups. While we did not talk of our inner male or inner female, or even about empowerment, we did talk about no longer allowing male dominance to separate us from each other. We began to appreciate and honor the feminine, and collectively formed a commitment not to be overpowered by the male hierarchy. We shared our wounds, released our rage, and reclaimed a deep sense of ourselves.

Simultaneously we began to insist that we be accepted into heretofore male arenas and we developed our "male" side in order to survive in the world of men. We learned to be forceful, assertive, independent, and even power-hungry. We decided anger felt better than tears, and that strength as modeled by males, was what counted in terms of economic and societal success. Some of us sacrificed our inner life in this process, but many of us soon began to realize that not only were we capable of competing with men on their own turf, but we had something of extreme importance to add to the equation. We rediscovered the nature of feminine power, and were able through our internal integration, to bring forth a vision that could heal our culture in all arenas. We happened upon empowerment.

As we became more aware of this, we began to educate the men around us. Some men reacted with fear and anger, but others, aware things were not right in the world or in their life, saw that a new perspective was needed and appreciated the women in their lives as friends, lovers, colleagues, and teachers.

This awareness is deeply transforming our society. We are now beginning to understand and develop true power, the integration of the male and female aspects; the yin and the yang. We are reclaiming wholeness. It is this energy that empowers our Spirits and it is the claiming of this power that will propel us into a positive future.

Roadblocks to Empowerment

There are a multitude of factors which encourage us to block empowerment. Our patriarchal religious traditions warn against personal power. They teach us to distrust our inner goodness and they claim we are easily seduced by evil and therefore must abdicate to strict "god-made" rules. The concept of original sin as told in the story of Adam and Eve is an obvious example. In addition to the old religious stories, the written history of our earth contains horrifying misuses of power. One of our collective fears is that we will obtain power and use it to harm others. This reinforces that belief that we cannot trust ourselves, that deep down inside we are sinful. Fearing we are inherently bad, we learn to distrust our inner awareness. We are then easily convinced that we must look outside ourselves for a moral system to follow. This begins the process of giving away our inner power.

In reality we all have our "shadow" parts: parts that can hate, avenge or seek to dominate. We also have great ability to shine the light of our awareness on these parts, to send them love, and to not allow them any expression that would harm others or ourselves. We are not born with the desire to harm anything; the shadow develops as we are hurt, invalidated, repressed and oppressed.

Another belief that keeps us from becoming empowered is the belief that we are undeserving. It is the internal question: "who am I to have such awesome gifts?" This creates a norm of setting impossible standards, which drives the belief that we are not good enough and therefore feeds our view that we are not worthy.

Fear of self-delusion is another block: "I can't be so smart, wonderful, and powerful, I must be hallucinating." "If I really were so exceptional someone would have recognized this and let me know." But of course because we have become distrustful of our own awareness, we often ignore or misinterpret that inner knowledge which is telling us we have a contribution to make, and that we can be part of creating a loving, healthy world for ourselves and our planet.

Another looming but often unconscious fear is that everyone will envy and therefore hate us if we admit to and act from our power. We fear that we will be alone, abandoned and/or generally under attack. A part of us may be saying, "Great, bring on my inner power... let me be who I am meant to be," while another inner voice of fear and maybe experience says, "Oh, yeah, and then we will be shunned or burned at the stake." Fear of isolation, as well as persecution, is a significant force interfering with our empowerment. The great irony here, is that the more empowered we are, the more we are connected to our inner path, which in turn connects us to all that is. Once we experience that connection, we realize that we are never alone.

Refusing to own our inner power can also come from a 'rescue' fantasy: the childhood dream that someone will come rescue us from all our pain by healing us with their love. If we take full responsibility for our lives and our reality, we fear we might lose out on this. "If I fully take care of myself, who will care for me?" In a culture that has long defined love as co-dependency, it becomes hard for us to believe that love can exist free of neediness.

Some of these beliefs and fears about being in full power are with us at birth, whether from other lifetimes or cellular memory. These may be core soul issues. Since there have been innumerable times in history where people were greatly persecuted for shining their light, and we are in a time in our history where there is opportunity and collective need to clear out these issues, there are many souls presently born on our planet who wish to resolve and transform these beliefs and fears. This clearing is vital for us to move into our full power.

ACCESSING OUR OWN FEARS ABOUT POWER:

Below I have identified several issues that commonly serve to keep us from claiming our full power. The more conscious we are of our fears and how they hold us back, the more ability we will have to transform them.

The following is a simple assessment tool that provides insight into how you may be blocking power in your own life. Go through these statements and notice what fits for you. Call on your inner wisdom or Higher Guidance to help you be more objective. The following statements are divided into different categories to help you be more specific.

Fear of Misusing Power:

Most of us have had experiences where we have "power-tripped" or manipulated others for our own ends. Some people do this strategically, consciously; others tend to be more subtle and/or unconscious. Since most of us do not like to see this quality in ourselves, we tend to rationalize our actions and have difficulty noticing when we misuse power. If you are having trouble identifying times when you used power inappropriately, go back into childhood, as we often give ourselves more permission to see that time in our life more honestly. Misusing our power often happens in close relationships, whether through manipulating our parents or siblings or engaging in "game-playing" with friends and romantic relationships. We also can end up misusing power if we believe that we know what is best for others.

Which of the following statements fits for you? As you identify these, write them down and sit with them for a moment to fully grasp the message.

1. *I feel uncomfortable whenever I find myself in a position of authority.*
2. *I often think other people are making poor life decisions for themselves.*
3. *If I give others advice, I worry they may follow it and it will not work out for them.*
4. *If I give others advice and they do not follow it, I judge them negatively.*
5. *I attract people into my life who manipulate me into doing things their way.*
6. *When people ask my opinion or I have an opportunity to express my opinion, I am hesitant to give it unless I know everyone will agree with me.*
7. *Every time I come close to getting a promotion or improving my work situation, something messes it up.*
8. *I have a difficult time seeing myself as an authority, even on subjects I know well.*
9. *It is easy for me to speak in an authoritative way for a while, but if this continues for any length of time, I leave the situation or create enemies that force me to leave the situation.*

As implied in the above statements, those who believe they have misused or might misuse power often avoid situations where they have positions of influence. Conversely, some people with this fear find themselves taking on authority, but end up creating personal dramas where they end up feeling victimized by the experience.

Feelings of Unworthiness:

Believing we are unworthy is more prevalent in our society than the golden arches of McDonald's. It is truly everywhere. As with other inner beliefs, some of us will know this consciously and other's will not. If you go around feeling that others are better than you or you cannot measure up in some way, then your beliefs of unworthiness lie near the surface. If you go around feeling you are better than others, you are the only one who knows how to do things well, etc., those beliefs of unworthiness are buried under messages that you must excel, be perfect, or be generally superior to others. You may also vacillate between these two extremes.

Sadly, our society conditions us to create impossible expectations of how we should be. This starts in childhood, often with the following scenario: Our parents were not happy or emotionally fulfilled. They expected their children to fill the void in them and unconsciously withheld love and/or acceptance until we did. So we came to believe this was our job. Some of us did this by taking on great physical responsibility such as taking care of the house and younger siblings; others of us did this by taking on deep emotional responsibility, trying to bolster our parents so they would feel successful. Some of us were abused and blamed ourselves hoping this would help our parents change. Others of us sacrificed our own sense of self to go out into the world in ways that pleased our parents, rather than ways that reflected who we were. And we all failed because we were trying to do something that only our parents could genuinely do for themselves. Since we were just children, we internalized this failure as our fault and concluded that we were not good enough.

Go through the following statements and notice what fits for you. Again, take your time, and let the phrases move deeply into your consciousness, jotting down the blocks.

1. *No matter how much I am doing, I always feel I should be doing more.*
2. *No matter how well I am doing, I always feel I should be doing better.*
3. *When people give me compliments, I am not sure they really mean it.*
4. *I have a difficult time hearing others say good things about me.*
5. *I often feel guilty.*
6. *I see other people as more competent and successful than I am.*
7. *When things go well in my life, I assume something bad will have to happen.*
8. *I often feel angry at people around me for not being more competent.*
9. *When I try to picture living a fulfilled, joyous life, it seems unimaginable.*
10. *I typically do more or give more than 50% in my relationships.*
11. *I typically expect others to do more than I do in relationships to prove their love.*

Breaking through core beliefs of unworthiness is not an easy task. Once you recognize their source, however, you are on your way. There is always some source in our childhood experiences. This does not mean we have not brought these feelings in with us from experiences we have had in other lifetimes, but working through the experiences in this lifetime is usually enough to vanquish this belief.

To fully empower our Spirits we must learn both to transform these beliefs and keep them from being in charge of any part of our lives. Our Spirit is not unworthy. Our Spirit does not hold these beliefs. The more power we give our Spirits, the more we are able to release the beliefs of our ego.

Lack of Trust in Our Inner Knowing:

One of the most destructive aspects of our societal conditioning is how we are trained to disconnect from our internal or spiritual wisdom. In religious families this often happens by being taught we must believe only what our particular religion tells us is true. In non-religious families, we are generally urged to conform to the larger beliefs of our culture. If, as children, we see energy fields around people and somehow have the ability to speak of this, we more than likely would be told this was our imagination. The same holds true for seeing, hearing or sensing angels or other-dimensional beings, and for psychic impressions and intuitive understandings. We are taught to trust only our outer senses which have limited perceptual ability because of this conditioning.

Our sensory perceptions can be limited simply by not having language to describe phenomena our culture does not believe exist. Thus our ability to perceive what is truly real becomes severely restricted. If we are told we are imagining things as young children when we experience subtle phenomena or intuitive impressions, we take this as truth. If we have no words to describe what we are seeing and sensing, and no validation from other sources, we soon learn to ignore these phenomena and assume they do not exist or perhaps worse, think there is something wrong with us for experiencing them.

As children, we are also taught to distrust our feelings when we are told our feelings are inaccurate or silly, or that our perception of what is happening to the people around us is wrong. Classic phrases like "I'll give you something to cry about." "It's silly, (or wrong) to feel that way." "You don't really mean that." "Mom & Dad were not angry at each other." "Daddy wasn't drunk." etc. contribute to this.

All of this type of conditioning disconnects us from our Essence and limits our ability to know and understand who we truly are. Were we not limited in this way, we would likely know from childhood what our uniqueness was; what gifts we were to develop in this lifetime. We would have some general, if not specific, understanding of why we have come to Earth.

This is not to discount the fact there are those of us who do intuit their purpose early on, and carry it out no matter what the conditioning. Generally these people have parents or some adult in their environment who believes in them and validates them. People with this experience are currently the exception, not the rule. Their Spirit is so clear and powerful that all else is unimportant. For most of us, however, our Spirit began a process of shrinking in importance at birth until, by adulthood many of us barely know how to get in touch with it.

Go through the following statements, and notice what fits for you.

1. *I often feel unsure of myself.*
2. *Before I make an important decision, I have to talk it over with several people and make sure they think I'm doing the right thing.*
3. *I chose to study things in school that others suggest for me: my parents, other relatives, teachers, spouses or peers.*
4. *I felt going to school for what most interested me was impractical and thus a waste of time and money.*
5. *When I get a feeling about a person or situation, I often talk myself out of trusting this feeling.*
6. *Part of me knows I have certain gifts, but unless other people tell me I have them, I fear I might be imagining them.*
7. *Whenever I do not listen to my parents or authority figures who are important to me, things do not work out.*
8. *I surround myself with people who think my ideas and/or beliefs are ridiculous.*
9. *I surround myself with people who always agree with my ideas and/or beliefs.*
10. *I would rather do what is known than experiment with something new & unusual.*
11. *I feel it is really important to behave in ways others think are normal.*
12. *I am not comfortable sharing any ideas or beliefs I have, unless I know that the person that I am sharing them with thinks or feels the same way.*
13. *When I think about not conforming, not fitting in, I get scared.*
14. *I often find myself questioning my true motives or intentions.*

Learning to trust our inner stirrings, our inner goodness, and our emotional and psychic impressions is essential if we are to fulfill our life purpose. We need to muster the courage to step outside of conventional wisdom. Many of us have been so intimidated or humiliated when we have shared these 'stirrings' or impressions, we carry enormous fear: Fear we are crazy, fear no one will like us, etc. Every time we give in to that fear, we move away from being authentic. Every time we confront our fear and go with what we feel inside of us to be true, we empower ourselves to move closer to becoming the powerful beings we are meant to be.

Activating courage and relearning to trust ourselves is not an easy or simple process, so go easy on yourself. It usually takes a long time for us to finish reclaiming who we are. But at the same time, be proactive. Until you step out of your comfort zone, you will not be able to develop the strength to keep moving forward. You can take baby steps, but you must take some steps or you will not be able to empower your Spirit.

"Original Sin"

To accept the concept of original sin on a psychological level is to believe that we are inherently bad, and therefore should not trust ourselves. The degree to which we accept this will correspond to the degree of personal power we relinquish. Early conditioning has enormous force in our psyches. If that conditioning was supported by the powerful presence of a religious community, this force intensifies. We must break out of this conditioning to successfully come into our inner power and connect with our spiritual essence.

Notice what fits for you in the following statements:

1. *I was taught to believe there is only one way to Salvation.*
2. *I was taught that people are sinful by nature, and if they do not conform to "God's teachings," they will be damned to eternal hell.*
3. *I sometimes fear that I am not following God's will because I have strayed so far from the religious teachings of my childhood.*
4. *Whenever I trust my own perceptions rather than those of an outside authority, I feel scared and/or uncomfortable.*
5. *I still feel angry and resentful about my early religious training.*
6. *I constantly question and doubt myself and my motives.*
7. *I worry that I am leading myself astray.*
8. *I feel some of my past or present behavior is sinful and I have not forgiven myself.*

If you answered "yes" to any of these questions, it is likely that your early conditioning about original sin is having some negative influence in your life. In future chapters, I will give specific exercises and suggestions to help you shift any core belief systems which block your way.

Waiting for Our Fairy Godmother:

Most of us did not receive the emotional nurturing we needed in childhood. This is partially due to our societal belief that we must repress emotions in order to survive. Many of us were abused as well. When we suffer abuse and/or emotional deprivation as children, we often create a fantasy that involves someone coming to our rescue. When no one does, we may feel cheated or undeserving. When we become adults, many of us still have an inner child that clings to this fantasy. This is a fantasy that dies hard.

This fantasy, combined with a generally unconscious belief that no one rescued you because you were undeserving, creates a strong inner resistance to embracing your full power. This is an issue that tends to affect women more often and more intensely than men. For men, this may be reversed. As a man, you will likely believe that you can only become worthy if you rescue the 'fair maiden.' This is a complex issue which I will discuss more in depth as you read on.

For now, go over the list below, and see what fits for you. Remember to take your time and let the phrases seep in.

1. *I remember as a child hoping God or someone would come and fix my family, or take me out of my family.*
2. *I expect my spouse or romantic partner to take care of me in ways that my parents did not.*
3. *When I have to take care of myself and my own problems, I feel resentful and unloved.*
4. *I am tired of always having to take care of myself.*
5. *I am tired of always having to take care of everything in my life.*
6. *I feel cheated when I look at the lives of other people. I find myself wondering why they get to have things I don't have.*
7. *If I can do everything for myself, I won't need anyone else and therefore I will never find true love.*
8. *If no one ever rescues me, I will always believe that I may not deserve to be treated well or have good things in my life; therefore, the only way for me to believe I am truly good and deserving is to have someone rescue me.*
9. *I need other people's love in order to feel full and loving of myself.*

As I mentioned above, this is a complex and usually unconscious dynamic which is tied up in our societal definitions of love as well as in our childhood wounding. Because it is directly related to issues of self-worth, much work may need to be done here in order to get free of it.

Fears from Other Lifetimes:

Just as we need to bring into conscious awareness and understand our childhood experiences and how they have impacted our relationship to power, so too we need to uncover any relevant experiences our soul may be carrying that are currently influencing this. For some of us, it is impossible to come into full power if we are not aware of our pre-birth belief system and the experiences and fears which may have driven these beliefs.

Looking at psychological and emotional issues held from other lifetimes can be tricky territory. I sometimes find people have a persistent desire to work with other lifetimes because working with this one feels too painful and immediate and other lifetimes seem much more romantic; thus working with other lifetimes could potentially become a way to avoid what is most needed to heal. Conversely, important soul experiences will remain hidden and therefore outside of our ability to heal them if we do not access them. My personal experience suggests other lifetime work may be essential if we are to understand and heal all the blocks to empowerment.

If you have worked a great deal on your emotional and psychological healing, have no sense of any repressed memories in this lifetime, and are still having difficulty fully empowering your spirit, it is time to look at other lifetimes. I will go into this in depth in Chapter 6.

THE POWER TO TRANSFORM

The transformation to become Spirit-directed is powered by the strength of our intention. Understanding what real empowerment is and the subtle or not-so-subtle ways we block this, gives us the conscious awareness needed to activate this intention. Our ego responds to our fears and wants then to strengthen its hold on us. So walk with the awareness you have gained from this chapter and simply notice how you may be affected by this. When we learn how to observe this process without attaching to our fears, we have learned how to stay conscious and to therefore clear the path for our intention to manifest.

Notice when you are feeling empowered and Spirit-directed. You will notice when you are there because you will have a clear inner experience of peace and well-being. When you are in this state, it is a good idea to encourage and praise yourself. I see this as a positive way to engage the ego, for our egos respond to our approval. This is a very different dynamic than looking outside ourselves for validation. This is the way we invite our ego to tea, enjoy its company and enlist its cooperation.

3: RECLAIMING BALANCE

In order to allow our Spirit to be in charge of our lives and still function effectively in the world, we need to find the equilibrium between our Divine nature and our earthly existence. The foundation of a Spirit-directed life is balance. This means our physical, emotional, mental and spiritual aspects need to be developed evenly. If these aspects are not all well developed, we can get stuck in the dualistic nature of the earth plane: unable to honor our Spirit and/or unable to "pay the rent." We also need to balance our intellect with our heart which allows us to access Higher Consciousness, and have loving, healthy, compassionate relationships. Our Spirits can use all of these aspects to guide us into our Sacred Purpose, but it is up to us to ready each part for this use.

This chapter will provide you with a deeper understanding of each aspect's part in empowered functioning. You will learn methods to identify areas of imbalance, and ways to gain more balance. I will take you through the chakra system and show you how to use it to diagnose and heal your imbalances.

FOUNDATION ISSUES

It is the norm in our culture for people to develop one or two of their core aspects, while the other aspects languish. Since we need healthy development in all four areas for full empowerment, the greater the unevenness of our development, the more difficult it is for us to feel powerful and connected.

Imbalances can manifest in a multitude of ways. As an example, many in our culture develop primarily on the physical or material plane. Athletics are stressed, as is material success. We all know people who have excelled in these areas yet have little or no sense of self, no ability to sustain loving emotional relationships, and little awareness of the meaning of their life.

Often I see new clients who have done much spiritual work, yet have no emotional foundation. They may have a great deal of psychological insight, but the emotional body has remained unhealed. Unhealed emotions typically carry with them inaccurate beliefs that affect a person's self-esteem and feelings of safety in the world. An unhealed emotional body would also suggest that the mental body is out of alignment, and that this person is carrying deep unconscious beliefs which surround their emotional wounds. These beliefs can magnetize a great deal of suffering in their lives.

Underdevelopment on the physical level can manifest in several ways. There are those who carry unconscious fears about survival and belonging. These fears continually impede their material well-being. The stress this creates distracts them from new growth, often keeping them in a state of anxiety. Others will sacrifice their emotional and spiritual well-being for financial security. There are those who have developed spiritually and have done some mental and emotional healing, but maintain a negative relationship with their bodies and thus create frequent or even terminal illnesses.

The first step in this process of reclaiming balance is to realize where we have developed unevenly, and to understand there are old belief systems, old feelings of guilt, shame and unworthiness, old resentments and/or old fears that have created this unevenness. Collective beliefs also impact us and can activate fear which, in turn, will exacerbate any existing imbalances. While any part of the energy field affects all other parts, it is still possible to separate, analyze, and rebalance ourselves chakra by chakra, with various chakras corresponding to the physical, emotional, mental, and spiritual levels of our development. This allows us to go through our healing in a systematic way.

What do you know already about your development? Are you a person who needs to figure everything out but is not very comfortable feeling your way through things? That would be an example of being more developed on the mental than the emotional level. Do you have wonderful ideas and deep caring relationships, but never are quite able to put these ideas into action, into creation? This might suggest you are well developed mentally and emotionally, but have work to do on the physical. Are you able to easily manifest prosperity but not loving relationships? That would be an example of having some mastery over the physical, but needing more growth in the emotional realm. Understand as well, that being underdeveloped in any one area can negatively impact the other three areas.

Think about your imbalances as you read through the chakra material. Chakras 1 & 2 correspond to our development in the physical world. Chakras 3 & 4 correspond to our emotional development. Chakra 5 and chakra 6 have more to do with the mental plane, although chakra 6 is a bridge to the spiritual. Chakras 7 & 8 connect us to the spiritual plane.

1st CHAKRA:

This is the energy center found at the base of our spine. As Anodea Judith says in her book *Wheels of Life*, "…this is the foundation of our whole system, the first building block upon which all the other chakras must rest." (p.62) This chakra is also our energy connection to all of life on the earth and the seat of tribal consciousness. We are an energetic ecological system: My well-being is your well-being. Our well-being is all part of the well-being of our planet. When we heal base chakra issues, we know that no matter what, we are secure and that we have access to everything we need to support our well-being on Earth.

Spiritual traditions tend to discount the importance of this earth chakra. To deny its beauty and importance is to dishonor our Mother Earth, for it is she who sustains this amazing physical form of ours in which consciousness can develop in extraordinary ways. Not only is this the seat where Kundalini energy can rise up our spine, it is the place where we become fully connected to the earth by putting in our energetic roots. When we are without this connection, we can literally find ourselves falling on our face time and time again, as we try to function in the world.

In balancing our base chakra, we need to learn to meet the demands of our physical survival with ease so that our health and our body's daily needs can be taken care of reflexively. This frees us to focus on our higher energies. It also allows us to experience the deep enjoyment of being on the earth. We become free to fully experience the sensual pleasures that being in the human body offer us. Leaving behind conditioning which diminishes or even demonizes the value of this, is an important part of healing this chakra.

There are many experiences which can create base chakra damage. If you were physically or sexually abused as a child, and/or lived in physical chaos and insecurity, you may have developed several beliefs which inhibit your ability to enjoy being in your body. Also, when our bodies are abused by adults in our environment, we feel as if we no longer have ownership of this most personal possession. The younger we are when the abuse begins, the more vulnerable we are to this. We may turn against our bodies, believing somehow it is the body which has caused us this pain. We may feel unworthy because we are in this particular body. Often in sexual abuse, the abuser convinces the child that they "asked for" the abuse. Thus in a child's mind, it is the body which causes the problem. Also, children often survive abuse by dissociating from their bodies. They may develop the ability to mentally go to other dimensions, often spiritual dimensions to compensate for what is being done to them physically.

As adults, this split may become accentuated. One may be highly intuitive and conscious, but experience ongoing "physical world" problems. The symptoms experienced may vary, but often include one or more of the following: ongoing financial struggles, frequent physical moves, ongoing physical illness, difficulty in caring for the physical environment by living in disarray, difficulty caring for the body such as poor grooming, eating disorders, addictions to food, alcohol or other drugs which deplete the body's health, deep ambivalence about remaining in the body which may include a history of suicide attempts, and/or an abundance of suicidal thoughts, frequent crises or frequently having the "rug pulled out from under you." These are all base chakra maladies.

If you suffered from childhood abuse which has alienated you from your body, deep emotional work is called for in order to fully shift the base chakra imbalance. If you have already done this emotional healing, the exercises suggested for this chakra can help immensely.

What has been called "poverty consciousness" is another base chakra issue. This is the belief you will never have enough. It can stem from a childhood of poverty, but can exist even when there have been no shortages of needed things. When one is in poverty consciousness, much energy is devoted to fearing there will not be enough to survive. People may have millions of dollars and still fear they will not have enough. This is about the lack of being able to trust that one will be secure on the Earth. Healing this imbalance puts us back on solid ground.

Unlike symptoms that are the result of abuse, poverty consciousness is generally not deeply-seated. Often it stems from a belief system based on scarcity. Our society continuously reinforces these types of beliefs, so detaching from the old is called for here. Go outside. Reconnect with Mother Earth. Notice you can drop a seed into the ground, give it a little water and let nature do its work to bring it to fruition. Be mindful of the magnificence of this planet, of all the beauty and sustenance the earth holds for us. Trees bear fruit. Oceans and lakes spawn fish. There is abundance everywhere in nature. So it is with our material well-being. We live in an abundant world. While there are many who believe they must horde this abundance, they truly cannot interfere with our attracting what we need. So look for the abundance rather than the scarcity and notice how you feel.

The health of our base chakra also determines how we connect with our family, our ancestry and with humanity as a whole. The more developed we are here, the more we experience the truth that we are connected to all of Life. Think about this for a moment. Whether you are in the midst of a huge city or by yourself in a desolate area, you are energetically connected to all of humanity, to all living things, and to all of creation. This is the birthright we are given when we come into human form. It is only our belief system, individually and collectively, which keeps us from this awareness. When we fully reclaim our power, we know at every level of our being we are not alone. Physical distance becomes irrelevant.

Our energy system is an electro-magnetic field. Reflect on this. Electricity generates power into the world. And magnets draw things to us. We have the capacity to program our energy field to draw to us what we need. Your base chakra, if functioning correctly, can be programmed to magnetize whatever is needed to be comfortable on the earth. This is important if we are to continue our spiritual empowerment because then we allow ourselves to relax about our physical well-being, freeing us to put our energy into more spiritually creative pursuits. I equate this to the well-organized person who never wastes time searching for things or redoing things, and who efficiently carries out mundane tasks. This person then has easy access to the time and energy needed to experience other things. If we are disorganized, we are always in a state of turmoil and inefficiency. So it is with our physical well-being. If it is running smoothly, if our health is good, if we are easily prosperous, if our environment is free from clutter, our energy is freed up for the more important work of our Spirit.

Many times when people tune into Spirit ambivalence rises up – on one hand there's a feeling of love and awe for this wondrous part of us, on the other, there is fear about where Spirit might lead us if we surrender. Certainly this is a state most of us are in whether we are conscious of this or not. Since, the way to our evolutionary future is to take the leap into the unknown, dealing with this ambivalence is preparation for this leap.

To be on the Path, to be fully Spirit-directed, means to sacrifice our old definitions of security. It is our egos that provide us with the illusion of external stability. Typically we look to our ego to create goals and expectations for ourselves. That helps us feel safe. But it is that type of safety we are called upon to give up. Will it be scary? Of course. But only to your ego.

Visualization: Releasing External Security

Close your eyes for a moment and see if you can be so quiet you can hear your Spirit speak to you. Take several deep breaths to quiet your mind. Ask Spirit what It wishes to tell you right now. What feelings, images or words come for you? Do your best to censor nothing, and release any concerns about where the words you may hear are coming from. Just pay attention to what they are. Pay attention too, to the feeling of attuning to Spirit. How do you feel about this experience? Are you aware of ambivalence?

Can you imagine being able to handle the experience of having every external thing you count on suddenly stripped away? Can you imagine that all of your earthly possessions are gone? All the people who love, nourish and anchor you in your life suddenly disappear? What would happen to you? How would you handle this?

See yourself in this state for a moment... outside somewhere, all alone in a strange location, no possessions or resources, nothing external to rely on. What is the first thing you would see yourself doing? Would you scream? Cry? Immediately search for food and shelter? Pray? If you were guaranteed some minimal sustenance, do you feel you could survive like this?

Think about World War II. Many people were literally yanked out of comfortable affluent lives, all their worldly goods taken from them, they were separated from their loved ones, thrown into cattle cars and transported to strange and hostile surroundings where they were asked to endure the unendurable. We are all familiar with the horrors of this, but what we are less familiar with, and what is relevant to the questions I am asking of you, is the resilience of the human spirit.

An inspiring example of this comes from Viktor Frankel's personal account in his book, ***Man's Search for Meaning***. Frankel was imprisoned in a concentration camp as a teenager. He came from a comfortable Jewish family in Austria. While in the camp, where he was living under unbearable conditions, he observed that the people who were able to survive and keep their humanity intact were those who had a deep sense of what he called inner meaning. I would call it connection to Spirit. It allowed them to be kind to those around them, not turn into terrorized animals, and to keep a belief there was a purpose to all experience no matter how horrible.

I read his book just after graduating from college. The first half is his description of life in the camps. I was able to tolerate reading about this because of his marvelous sense of compassion and objectivity; he was able to view these experiences from a higher perspective. Not only did he survive, but he went on to utilize this potentially soul-shattering experience to strengthen his sense of self, his faith and his consciousness.

Inspiring as well is Saint Francis of Assisi. Saint Francis came from affluence and could have had an easy life. Instead he chose to enlist as a soldier and was immediately captured and thrown into an isolated dungeon. It was here he experienced the ecstasy of Spirit. He was able to go into a deep state of surrender and would later consider his year of "imprisonment" as a deeply fulfilling experience.

Saint Francis, as well as people who survived the concentration camps spiritually intact, provide us with an allegory of what true empowerment can be. Any human being who can go through such horrors and keep their connection to the Divine, models to us the deepest level of the potential power we have as a species. All vestiges of physical security can be stripped away and we still have the ability to trust and to connect to our Divine nature.

Return to the scenario I presented you earlier. You are there in a strange isolated place, no possessions, no loved ones... nothing of your old life... only you and the earth and the sky. Breathe into this vision for a moment. Can you feel the fear coming up? Use your imagination to make this as real as possible. If you can get a sense of fear, you will be able to do a more honest self-assessment. This is an essential first step to creating the inner balance we need. When you can imagine the fear, go to the next step which is to think about what you can do to calm yourself. Take some time with this. Then visualize doing it.

When I did this, I saw myself in a barren place. I was quite scared until I centered my breath and closed my eyes and asked for Divine protection and guidance for myself and my loved ones. Once I had calmed down, I was able to assess what was available for me to survive; what food sources might be found, what shelter I could create or find, etc.

The next thought which came had to do with using my ability to manifest what I needed. Most readers will be familiar with the laws of manifestation to one degree or another. When utilizing this law at its highest level, one can instantly create any material reality one chooses. As Paramahansa Yogananda explains in his book *The Autobiography of a Yogi,* this is possible by using our mind to increase the vibrational frequency of the molecules in our energy field so they are moving at the speed of light. As all physical manifestation is made of light, this allows us to bypass the physical laws of the third dimension. I have not evolved to the point where I am able to consciously shift my field or the energy field of objects around me to create immediate manifestation, but I know my thoughts are magnetic and powerful and that they get focused during prayer or mediation. So I saw my next step was to go inward and focus on what I most needed, trusting the Universe would provide this for me in some way. I understood that it may come to me in ways I could not prescribe, but if I stayed openhearted and aware, I knew I would have what I needed for my soul's development, and this allowed me to keep a sense of inner peace.

Imaging this type of scenario helps us know who we really are because we become free of the anchors of our consensus reality. By consensus reality, I mean the commonly held beliefs of our culture that give us a limited view of reality; they are useful beliefs for surviving within the culture, but dysfunctional in terms of mental, emotional and spiritual development because they negate large portions of what existence really holds. These beliefs negate the creative power of our mind and our capacity to become fully conscious. They tend to negate the power of our hearts and our capacity for love, even when our physical survival seems threatened. They negate the awareness that our bodies have an energy field which can magnetize what we need. These beliefs also minimize our capacity to open to Divine wisdom and guidance. Seeing ourselves breaking through these beliefs in our imagination creates a new inner resource for empowerment.

Chakra Healing Exercise

Go back to the visualization described above where all your earthly possessions and people have been stripped away. Imagine long roots growing from your base chakra and going deep into Mother Earth. Imagine her smiling at you, and speaking to you. Feel her energy flowing up through those roots and into your base chakra. See those roots filled with her warmth and nurturing. Then realize all humans have energetic roots that form a root system and connect everyone on the planet. Are you able to breathe into this and experience it as real? How does it change your experience? How do things look? How do you feel? What do you find yourself saying to yourself? Can you imagine feeling connected with the energy field of your loved ones even if they are thousands of miles away?

Now focus on what you need and desire for your material well-being. What is necessary for your physical survival and your day-to-day comfort? We can have abundance in our life without being excessive or greedy. Create an image of this for yourself. If you do not get visual images, allow words to form. Experience the feeling of this well-being. Then put these images, words and/or feelings into your base chakra. Picture them there and draw Mother Earth's energy up through your roots, filling your chakra with her power. Visualize your chakra as a magnet pulling to you the images you have placed there.

Use this visualization in your daily life. Notice what you need to support your material well-being right now. Put those images in your base chakra. Let the Earth's energy flow up through your roots, and feel the magnetic energy of this center draw in those images for you. Do this visualization every day for a while. With clear intention and focus, you can magnetize whatever you want to create.

If you can feel the magnetism of this chakra, you will attract what you are imaging. If you are unable to feel the magnetism, you can still draw this to you. Some people are able to feel the magnetic pull, while others may have a more developed visual or auditory sense.

If you are not attracting what you are imaging, then there are likely old issues to heal. Remember our unconscious intentions are very powerful. We need to bring these intentions into consciousness. I discuss this more in chapter 4. Once you have you have uncovered these unconscious intentions, you can identify and work to shift these self-defeating, fear-based beliefs.

2ND CHAKRA

The sacral or sex chakra is found at the sacral vertebra. It corresponds to the lower abdomen, womb and genitals. It is in this chakra that we begin to separate from the "tribe" and to form our individuality. It is here we can feel life force energy as our own and understand our ability to cocreate with the Universe. Our bodies have now become our point of reference and from here we begin to relate to "the other" outside of ourselves.

This center holds the deep and powerful energy of pleasure and sensation; of creation and procreation. This is the center of passion, that vital force which allows us to relish in the beauty of life in the body, and calls us forward to carry out our incarnational purpose. As we learn to honor this chakra, we learn to honor our physical body. As we honor the integrity and energy of our physical body, we realize our need for the "Other," that which is outside ourselves, to create a sense of completion. This is represented by a physical partner and/or a partnership with the Divine or with Divine inspiration.

Similar to the first chakra, the 2nd chakra has been devalued in our culture. We have been encouraged to bypass these lower chakras, to disconnect from our body and to view the body as unclean or unholy. How incredibly sad and what an insult this is to Mother Earth. Sexuality in its highest expression, runs Spirit through us. It is a way to connect us with the Divine.

Our societal images of sexuality debase us all. When you have gender inequality, you cannot have sexual balance or sexual health. Our 5000 year experience with patriarchy threw the energy of the second chakra into deep disharmony. How can you have a sexually healthy society when females are viewed as property, married off as girls by their fathers for economic gain, and thus often sexually abused by their husbands? Healthy sexuality is impossible when women were "owned" by their husbands, and when sexual intercourse became seen as a "wifely duty." As men and women were disconnected from being equals, so the Divine could no longer be an equal partner in heterosexual relationships.

Imbalances in this chakra cause all sort of problems; from sexual addictions to being sexually numb. It can lead to child sexual abuse as well as sexual assault. Physiological problems whether with impotence, infertility or other reproductive dysfunction also originate in this chakra. Remember, this is the energy center which propels the creation of human life. This is the energy that is essential for creative expression. It is no accident that most artists, poets, musicians and literary figures have generally challenged the sexual repression of their society.

Repression of the energy of the second chakra often comes from our fear of pleasure, which stems from our labeling pleasurable experiences as unholy or bad. This is the height of irony. Our Mother Earth offers us all sorts of natural pleasures: the warmth of the sun on our skin, wonderful and varied tastes and fragrances from the wealth of her gardens. Oceans and lakes allow us to bathe, float, and surrender. There is visual beauty everywhere in nature; it is simply the nature of things. It is the nature of the Divine in form. It provides us all sorts of blissful experiences. Our physical bodies are filled with pleasure centers: our lips, tongue, breasts, genitalia are the most intense of these, but everywhere on our skin, loving touch brings pleasure.

When we repress our natural sensuality and sexuality, it becomes distorted and demands our attention in unhealthy ways. It is like the experience of depriving ourselves of certain foods and finding that we can become obsessed by them. So it is with sexuality. Repress it and it will come inappropriately. In order to keep it successfully repressed, one has to deaden the body, which in turn, makes the energy field denser.

The other side of this imbalance is to utilize pleasurable sensation to momentarily fill an inner void. We become stuck in the extreme of second chakra energy, not knowing how else to feel good. Usually this is coupled with imbalances in the solar plexus and heart. This imbalance is part of what drives pornography, sexual exploitation, abuse, assault and addiction. It is simply the other side of the coin of repression.

Healing second chakra imbalances can be complicated as they are typically paired with emotional imbalances (3rd and 4th chakras.) Our sexuality is the most personal part of ourselves. It is the entrance to our private selves. Violation, shame or blockage in this center reverberates throughout our soul and deeply affects our energy field.

Anodea Judith in her book, *Eastern Body/Western Mind,* explains how the second chakra is connected with our ability for empathy and socialization. When we have no access to second chakra power, we are not able to sort between our own feelings and those of others. We may either interpret all the emotions we sense as our own, thereby leaving us unable to see another's feelings as separate from ours, or we lose ourselves by continuously giving our power to others in relationship; letting others' voices have more say than our own. In the first case, there is a narcissistic dynamic where no one else's feelings count. In the latter case, only other people's feelings count. It is impossible to be in our full power and to have healthy intimate relationships until this is shifted.

Chakra Healing Exercise

There are two contact points for this chakra; the first is an inch or two above your pubic area in line with your navel. See if you can locate this by putting a finger there, closing your eyes and noticing if you can feel any energy swirling or a sense of warmth. If you are sensitive to this, you will be able to locate this chakra with some ease, if not, just let yourself guess. Once you have established an approximate place in the front of your body, imagine a straight line originating outside your body going through this point, and straight through to your back. The place where this line would come out is the point of the second chakra on your spine.

Imagine a swirling cone at each of these points. One cone is drawing energy from outside of yourself to you; the other is pushing energy out into the world. Where the energy meets in the center is where it is transformed: so we draw in the "other", pull it to the center point of this chakra, transform it with our unique vibration and send it back out into the world in creative form.

If you have a loving sexual partner, visualize drawing in the purest of their energy through one of these points (use your intuition–for some of you the energy will enter through the back point, and for others through the front.) If you do not have an appropriate partner, then make one up. Let this energy flow to the midpoint between the front and back. For women, this will be in the center of the womb. Let this energy swirl for a moment or two, capturing your unique individuality in this most personal of centers. Feel the warmth. Then notice it swirling out the opposite point. When you swirl it out, you may wish to visualize an idea you want to put into form or a project you wish to bring to completion. See that form or project attached to the energy as it swirls from the midpoint out into the world. Ideally, you will be feeling a sense of warmth, sensual pleasure and creative force.

If you have been sexually traumatized in this lifetime and have not yet healed this, instead of or in addition to the above exercise, do the following. Visualize a loving spiritual presence, an angel, a guide, Jesus, Divine Mother, the Goddess or any spiritual archetype that you resonate with. Let your imagination make one up for you. It can be a composite of loving, accepting people you have known, or even characters in books or in the media. Imagine this loving being sending you a beam of light filled with love. Draw this beam in through this chakra and feel yourself cleansed and purified.

I would suggest you practice both the base chakra and second chakra exercises for a while. If you have located blockages in both these chakras, do them one at a time, waiting to work on the second chakra until you have finished with the base chakra. If you feel you do not have much blockage in either of these centers, you may do them at the same time, starting at the base.

3RD CHAKRA:

The center of this chakra is found in our solar plexus and is connected with the navel. This chakra is the center of our personal will and seat of our personal power. A strong sense of self which supports healthy self-esteem and self-confidence is the key for this chakra to be fully functional.

While the second chakra puts creativity into form, it is the third chakra which initiates action. At optimum functioning, this energy center is in perfect alignment to the outer world. If there is a task to do, a project to promote, a mountain to climb, a mission to complete, people who have healed their 3rd chakra issues will face these challenges with ease. They will meet the world confidently, but not arrogantly. Their self-esteem will be strong and authentic, connected to their Spirit. They will be able to utilize the 1st chakra's stability, and the 2nd charka's passion and creativity, alchemizing their energies with their will, to bring forth magnificent personal power.

It is from this chakra that we beam our individual expression into the world. If we have been disconnected from our individuality, have never successfully connected to our unique identity, we have no way to carry this out. Because the 3rd chakra is one of our two emotional centers, emotional trauma from childhood can cause deep imbalance here. This type of trauma tramples our sense of self. When we lack the ability to appreciate our self, we become disconnected from our will, which in turn, creates feelings of powerlessness. Our emotionally dysfunctional culture makes it enormously difficult for children to grow up with a strong sense of who they really are. Finding our identity is the primary task of adolescence, and it is the rare family that knows how to support this process in their children. This is even more difficult when our educational and social institutions largely inhibit this. This lack of self and its ensuing feelings of powerlessness cause people to respond by dominating others or by being stuck in a victim role, or both.

Every time we misuse our will to dominate others, we re-injure our own energy field. In order to dominate and control others, we have to shut off our ability to honor and love (2nd & 4th chakras).

We become even more disconnected from ourselves. While, we may feel our egos puffing us up if we carry the illusion these acts make us powerful, to those of us who understand that we are all interconnected, it becomes clear that any time we do harm to another, we are energetically hurting ourselves.

Each time we misuse our power to victimize ourselves, we re-injure our energy field as well. This also shuts off our ability to honor and love, but in a very different way. Unlike those who dominate, people in the victim role withhold their soul's energy from the world. They consciously identify with their powerlessness which further injures the 3rd chakra. From this place of powerlessness, they either project blame outward, or assume unconsciously that they are bad, defective or unworthy and so deserve this ongoing victimization.

The psychological patterns of these 3rd chakra issues are complex. Fear of power or fear of misusing power operates at a deep, unconscious level. Our souls often come in with these patterns from experiences in other incarnations. The emotional patterns which are more easily accessed come out in traditional therapy, as people seek help in overcoming their childhood wounds. The soul's wounds tend to stay in hiding until the more obvious imbalances become identified. The emotional outcomes of these wounds are guilt, shame or a combination of the two.

People, who have shame-based patterning, hold a belief that they are defective. Many try to defend against this feeling by adopting a perfectionist attitude which leaves them terrified to accept criticism. This is because criticism triggers the awareness they are imperfect, which translates in their psyche as proof of their defectiveness. Because it is impossible, as humans, to not have imperfections, people with this pattern tend to project blame onto others for any failings they feel in themselves, because looking at their flaws feels dangerous. They are also extremely vulnerable to addictions. There is another hidden dynamic here: a person who is shame-based often assumes all others are defective as well, which operates as a rationalization for whatever hurt or harm they may perpetuate.

It is also common for people who hold this level of shame to become the perpetual victim. This is a difficult cycle to break. If they take any responsibility for creating their victimization, they could believe this to confirm their defectiveness instead. This keeps them trapped in a dysfunctional cycle, and thus consistently disconnected from tapping into their genuine personal power. Once the shame is released and the wounds from the situations which have produced the shame are healed, then this dynamic can be shifted.

People, who are guilt-based, have formed their personality around the criterion that it is important to be a good person. Simultaneously they carry the belief that they are not good enough. They are generally not able to overtly dominate others, for this goes against their criteria of "good." They find immobilizing their own will preferable to overpowering another's. Of course, this will do harm on subtle levels as typically the resentment which builds from dishonoring themselves will be projected onto those they are "sacrificing" for.

Because they feel they can never measure up, people who are guilt-based are often high achievers or over-achievers. But their area of achievement rarely has to do with their true purpose. Rather they sacrifice their true Self and may spend enormous time and energy acting in ways to gain others' approval, their parents' or society's or both. Because they feel that no matter what they achieve or how much they do, they are never quite good enough and can never do enough, they are extremely vulnerable to depression.

People who are guilt-based typically display a different quality of victimization than people who are shame-based. Their outer life may not be as affected: they are unlikely to keep losing jobs or homes, or being victims of assault, robbery, and tragedy in general. Instead, they suffer from emotional victimization and often become the classic martyr.

These are the patterns which need to be healed before we can tap into the deeper beliefs and fears from other lifetime experiences where we may have either misused our power or been persecuted for this power. Once we have healed the guilt/shame patterns, we will no longer feel victimized or have a need to project blame onto or dominate others. It is then we become ready for the deeper understanding and healing which will fully align the power of our 3rd chakra.

Our task is to reclaim our individuality and identity. Carolyn Myss in *Anatomy of the Spirit*, talks about the core lesson of healing this chakra being "Honor Oneself." In order to fully honor ourselves we must have a sense of our individual identity. Sadly, our society often drops a steel door to block this important passage.

It is common knowledge that identity is supposed to form as we go through adolescence. Yet notice the ways we make it difficult for teenagers to explore and appreciate their uniqueness. While the darkest days of "zero tolerance" seem to be over, we still have schools and the culture in general operating off of the belief that we need to control our teenagers rather than guide them. Culturally, we seem to feel the need to keep teens from any experimentation and questioning of authority, which are two significant means by which adolescents begin to get a sense of who they are. We also seem unable, both in our families and in our culture, to validate why this would make teens so angry, depressed and anxious. Instead we choose harsh unreasonable penalties or prescription drugs to keep them under control. How ironic, for if we collectively honored and empowered the adolescent spirit, simultaneously providing them guidance and validation, this teenage energy which we all have, would empower and impassion the rest of us in our own transformation. Instead we cut ourselves off from this wonderful resource and conspire consciously or otherwise, to impede this process.

There is no mystery here. We are a society of people who are not encouraged to seek, to question, to find our uniqueness. The late 60's and early 70's gave us a momentary break. Those of us who were young and part of this movement believed we could change the world, and this empowered many of us to break loose, explore and "find ourselves" despite general societal and parental disapproval. By the late 70's it was over. Soon the media began to label this movement "the 'me' generation" implying that quests of this nature were simply based on selfish hedonism. I see this as an attempt to shame people and disconnect them from that sense of self. By the 90's, policies to repress our youth became more intense than ever. We claimed these were to save teens from the ravages of drugs, alcohol, unsafe sex and truancy, but we simply kindled their rage, broke their spirit, and/or taught them more skillful ways to lie.

These inappropriate and fear-based "solutions" exist because of our collective 3rd chakra wounding. It is during late adolescence that our power begins to surge. While, of course, we lack wisdom and perspective at this age, we make up for it with our incredible passion and energy. This is what JFK began to tap into when he formed the Peace Corps. Our sexuality is also awakening with great force at this time. Instead of preaching abstinence and repression, we need to say "Wonderful! Honor yourself! Honor others. Be responsible and enjoy. Love one another. Care about our world. Begin to listen to your inner voice."

Can you imagine a class for high school seniors on inner voice? Or a class based on social and community activism? How about a class on honoring the self and others, and understanding sexuality as an energetic force and an energy connection? Instead we force our youth into a curriculum based on outdated world views and tedious and often meaningless facts and theories. Then we wonder why they are still so attracted to drugs, alcohol and casual sex.

As we heal the third chakra, we find our deeper identity. This identity is connected to our purpose on the planet. If enough of us activate this, positive collective change is inevitable. Perhaps this is why we find such powerful resistance to this, both inwardly and outwardly. We have been taught to fear change of any kind, despite the obvious fact that we will not survive without it.

When we are finally able to activate third chakra energy, we become unstoppable. It is the proverbial fire in the belly. And this bright burning flame then allows us to purge and purify the old beliefs and social constructs which hold us back. If we are in energetic balance, always acting from an open heart, our Spirits have a momentum so strong that the old doubts and fears become irrelevant. As we claim our true power and individuality, we will be able to carry out what we have come to Earth to do.

Suggestions for Healing

Traditional family dynamics in our society invalidate children both emotionally and spiritually. It is a rare family where parents are open and mature about their feelings, and know how to honor their children's emotions. Instead, we typically tell a child their feelings are weak, silly or simply wrong, thus disconnecting them from their emotional core. We invalidate children spiritually by not seeing and appreciating their essence: the essential part of them which is separate from, and sometimes at odds with societal expectation. One of the primary symptoms arising from this legacy is an inability to trust ourselves, our instincts, our intuitions and inspirations. This, in turn, supports a belief system where feelings of powerlessness and disconnection from self are the inevitable outcome.

While many of you have left much of this behind, it is still unusual to find people who are not struggling with these feelings in at least one area. To identify where this may still be active in your life, you might wish to ask yourself the following questions. Stay aware that areas which are not fully transformed hold conscious or unconscious beliefs that promote feelings of powerlessness. After each question, stop, take out your journals, and spend a few moments making your list.

- *What areas of my life are still not to my liking?*
- *Where do I still deal with self-esteem issues?*
- *Where do I hold back my authority?*
- *When and in what areas, do I invalidate my perceptions?*
- *Am I expressing and acting from my full potential in my work? In my relationships? In my friendships? With my family of origin? With my children? With my community?*

Now you might want to prioritize which areas you still need to work on. Be aware, if you are a person who tends to compensate for inner feelings of powerlessness by dominating or controlling others, or through over-controlling various areas of your life, you may have more difficulty getting in touch with your powerlessness. This comes from holding an inner belief that any sign of weakness will bring hurt or other types of ego wounding to you, and that a show of bluster or self-confidence will substitute for genuine self-esteem. If this description fits you, I recommend you first journal on all possible beliefs you may have and messages you have gotten about feeling weak or vulnerable. Once you have done this you can begin to write transformation statements for them. For example, if you were made to believe that any sign of weakness was an invitation for others to take advantage of you, a transformation statement would be "I can keep myself safe while I own my feelings of weakness and vulnerability." And then imagine what would be a safe environment for you to do this.

For those of you who are more easily aware of your feelings of powerlessness, take a moment to focus on the areas where this is still operating in your life. Then try to identify the fear that gets evoked and drives your sense of powerlessness. If you are not conscious of this fear, notice if there is tightness in the solar plexus area. Sometimes it may feel difficult to breathe deeply. Tightness in the solar plexus involves the diaphragm. This tightness keeps us from fully utilizing the power of *prana* or life force energy. We know that breath pulls in life force energy, so when this area loosens, the life force is freed up. Then we can become fully energized simply through breathing.

It is important to identify fear in order to break through it. If you have worked long and hard to feel empowered in your life, you may tend to resist acknowledging fear. Yet it is through our ability to acknowledge our areas of fear, and then access our courage to deal with them, that we become fully empowered.

Carolyn Myss in *Anatomy of the Spirit*, speaks of the how the chakra system corresponds to the tree of life in the Kabbalah. The third chakra corresponds to two branches on the tree, one for endurance, and the other for dignity. Endurance is our ability to face fear and challenge and continuously activate our courage. Dignity comes from honoring and esteeming the self, and living in integrity. We need to develop these important qualities to re-balance this chakra.

The third chakra is also a place where we tend to draw in emotional energy from others. An intuitive sensitive person, who is sometimes referred to as "psychic sponge," typically stores the pain they soak in from others in this chakra. Most, if not all of us who are sensitive to subtle energy, are sensitive to other people's feelings. If we have not learned to be conscious and to activate an energetic filter to protect ourselves, we are carrying around pain which does not belong to us. This pain creates blockages in this chakra, and therefore interferes in our fully igniting our power. Holding another's pain makes us part of the problem, rather than the solution. If you have never been to an energy healer who can cleanse this area, I strongly advise this. If this is not comfortable or available to you yet, then go to the ocean, or soak in a salt-water bath, and envision the water washing away all of the pain you have been carrying for others: for your parents, your partner, your children, your friends, your clients; maybe even for the world.

Chakra Healing Exercise:

Rub your hands together until you begin to notice warmth emanating from them. Then place your hands over your solar plexus area. Breathe in and out for a few minutes and just notice this area warming and relaxing. Take your time. Notice how comforting the warmth is.

Now visualize a sun shining from deep inside this part of you. See it radiate to your hands, and hold this image. Bask in this.

Next visualize this sun growing bigger and bigger until it covers the entire solar plexus area from the navel to its center which is few inches below your heart. Feel it radiate light and warmth out your back as well.

Ask the sun to shed light on anything blocking the optimal functioning of this chakra and write it down. Close your eyes again and visualize this sun melting away this block. Breathe into this image for several minutes.

Notice that in the center of this sun is a pilot light. As you focus on this, let the image of the sun recede and the bright strong flame of the pilot light come to the foreground. This pilot light activates or ignites the qualities of the healed third chakra: a sense of self, a sense of empowerment, a strong sense of dignity and integrity, and the courage to move your vision forward into the world.

Now allow an image to form of what you wish to activate in the world. Let it heat up and expand from the flame. Then envision this going out into the world, emanating from the center of your authority where there is no room for doubt or fear or guilt, only the pure burning vision of clarity and purpose. As with the other exercises, repeating this daily for a while will bring you optimum results.

4TH CHAKRA

This is our heart chakra and it is located around the area of our physical heart. A fully open heart chakra spans the whole width of the chest. This chakra is the mid-point between the upper and lower chakras in the body, symbolizing the balance of Heaven and Earth, Spirit and Matter, Divine Love and Earthly Love.

In this energy center we find our kindness, our compassion and ultimately our humanity. The heart is the place of relationship and relatedness. It is also the place of self-love. When we honor ourselves at the 3rd chakra, we gain self-respect. We know our personal rights and personal boundaries, but it is the love generated from the heart chakra which fills us with compassion, tolerance, acceptance and sweetness for ourselves and others. Our hearts are also full of wisdom; the more we learn to "think" with our hearts, the more aligned we are with our spiritual path. Dissolving our heart blockages and opening our hearts completely is the key to stepping into our full evolutionary power. Heart energy, while exquisitely tender, is powerful enough to shift the world.

When this center is fully operative, there is a perfect balance between the love we can receive and the love we are able to give to others. The opening and spinning of this center is an incredible source of pleasure, well-being and joy. Like the 3rd chakra, the heart chakra deals with our emotional energy, and since our society is filled with people who have been emotionally wounded, it is the norm in our culture to shut this center down.

Anodea Judith, in ***Wheels of Life***, says "The task of chakra four is to integrate and balance the realms of mind and body. In so doing, it brings a radiant sense of wholeness to the entire organism and a realization that we are an exquisite inter-penetration of both spirit and matter." (p. 212) Thus, it is in this center that we are able to process the light of the Higher Realms with the substance of the lower realms. And through this integration, we gain the ability to have wonderfully balanced relationships with others. The core of our well-being and the well-being of the planet depends on our ability to heal the wounds of the heart. This is a central challenge of the evolutionary leap: Our hearts must open for us to survive.

The most challenging and the most important place to begin when healing this chakra, is to do an honest assessment of how much we are able to love ourselves. The amount of self-love we can activate is a measure of the degree we are able to truly love others. When I deny myself this love, I feel a profound inner lack which in turn creates deep and often unconscious feelings of resentment.

We learn to deny ourselves love as children usually from the experiences we have in our families. The vast majority of us had parents with issues around self-love. Because of this, they were not free to exchange with us the unconditional love we all deserve and need for our optimum development. While I believe that all but the smallest minority of parents truly love their children, parents who have not healed their own hearts, cannot promote full self-love in their children.

Look inward now for your own limitations on self-love. Close your eyes for a moment and ask your inner wisdom to give you a percentage to represent the amount of self-love you have activated. Then pay close attention to what you say to yourself, to any feelings of guilt or shame which may come up in you, to times when you feel scared of fully loving someone else, and to times when you feel scared of fully receiving love from someone else. Pay attention as well to your intimate relationships. How equal is the exchange of love in them? How close do you allow yourself to get to others? This all connects to your ability to love yourself fully. Also be aware that when we have fully healed our hearts, we become invulnerable to other peoples' opinions of us. So notice when you are able to follow your heart no matter what versus when you are concerned about gaining approval from others.

There was a wonderful little book published in the 1960's called **The Lazy Man's Guide to Spiritual Enlightenment**, by Thaddeus Golas. Golas points out that it is easy to feel love for ourselves when we are doing everything "right," but true self-love is our ability to love ourselves when we have done everything wrong, when we are at our very worst. So pay attention to how you feel about yourself when you are having mean thoughts, or you have just yelled at your child, or you have been unreasonable in an argument. Pay attention to what you are saying to yourself after you have made a mistake or done a poor job at something. When you find your unconscious reflex in situations like those above, is to be comforting and nurturing to yourself while still being able to take responsibility for any negativity you might have put onto others, then you have begun to master real self-love. When you notice your unconscious reflex is not to love yourself in these situations, love yourself for noticing.

Self-love is also connected to how open we are to allowing Spirit to direct our lives. If we suffer from a lack of self-love, we will have a limited ability to receive love directed toward us from others. We will unconsciously block or discount this love. This includes Divine Love. We must feel worthy to deeply accept the incredible unconditional love of the Divine. And that is often not an easy task.

Inner child work is very helpful here, since it is the child in us who has internalized feelings of being unlovable and unworthy. Sending our love to this child and creating imaginary "Spirit Parents" to also send love and nurturing to this child, is a very healing exercise. I cover this in depth in my book ***JOURNEY TO WHOLENESS****: A Guide to Inner Healing,* so I will not go into the specifics here. However, if you are not aware of how to send love to the parts of yourself who feel unlovable and/or unworthy, it is essential you develop this resource in order to fully heal your heart.

When the heart is healed, no harm will be done to the self or to others. When we feel full of love, we can only wish others the same pleasure. When I notice my heart chakra is open and spinning, I consciously send love and healing energy to everyone I see or meet. As we make the evolutionary leap, we begin to understand that to do this literally changes the energetic field of all. Imagine all of us feeling full of love, bursting with love, overflowing with love, and directing that same quality of love outward to all who are around us. Certainly this is my idea of paradise.

The energetic twin of a lack of self-love is the tendency to withhold love. One does not exist without the other. They also create each other. If I have little love to give myself, I have even less to give another. If I feel myself unable to love another, it intensifies my feelings of being unworthy of love.

You may believe you are able to love others more than yourself. You may be a person who is very giving and caring. And yet, if you do not have your heart filled with self-love, what is it that you are really giving another? And where does the feeling originate from? The foundation of co-dependent relationships comes from a belief that our value is only from doing for others. This belief causes us to continually pour out energy to those around us from an inner state of unworthiness rather than from an inner state of love, joy and fulfillment.

If you are a person who tends to over-give, ask yourself the following questions: ***If I give less, would I feel guilty? Would I fear others would no longer want to be with me, or find me of value? Would I feel as if I am not following through with my obligations?*** Often we are giving out of fear, guilt or duty. This distorts love and energetically keeps you and those you give to out-of-balance. If you can recognize this in yourself, do your best to give yourself love for this awareness. Work with your inner child and set your intention to transform this pattern.

Conversely, you may notice that in your fear of feeling unloved, you ask your loved-ones to continuously prove their love, to sacrifice for you, to give in to your demands however unreasonable, hoping futilely that this will help you feel loved. Since this can never be successful, it is not unusual for people who have this pattern, to become emotionally, verbally and even physically abusive as the unhealed third chakra projects blame outward, and the unhealed fourth chakra makes it impossible for love to be received.

We are so out of balance as a society that it is rare for people to be fully able to give or receive love. It is not until we reclaim ourselves, and re-balance our hearts that this begins to change. So often, people have no concept of what healthy love is: they simply have not been exposed to it. Instead they try to conform to the cultural mythology by behaving in ways they believe people who love should act.

Look within yourself to observe and to identify any imbalance you have here. Look also at what makes you feel safe to give and receive love, and at what creates feelings of fear and insecurity which may close you down.

To reach full empowerment, we must have open, balanced hearts. This is the central difference between the old model of power and the new. The old way teaches that reaching our external goals is what brings success. Success is defined by what is manifested in the material and mental planes; our emotions and Spirit do not count. The new way asks the heart to be healed and defines success by our ability to be loving, cooperative and true to ourselves.

Chakra Healing Exercise:

Imagine you are sitting by the gentlest of streams. The water is crystal clear. The day is perfect. The sky is a brilliant blue; the sun is bright, warm and soothing. You are sitting on lush, green, sweet-smelling grass that is soft and even. Birds are chirping. The air is fresh and the breeze is pleasant on your cheeks. You dangle your fingers into the stream and allow the cool water to wash over them. As you do this, imagine all the old wounds, all the guilt, fear, obligation, all unloving feelings and all feelings of insecurity washing away.

Now rub your hands together until you feel their warmth and lay them gently on your heart. Breathe deeply, inhaling through your nose and exhaling slowly through your mouth. Let your all of your wounding, all of your hurt feelings, flow out with the breath.

Bring your focus to your heart center and imagine that you are drawing the breath in and pushing it out through this chakra. Feel your heart protected by your hands. Notice how safe you feel. Your heart can now open in total protection. Keep breathing this way until you can feel the warmth of this center. If there is any constriction here, if your heart is having difficulty relaxing or difficulty releasing feelings, say something sweet to it. Let it know how much you appreciate it.

Say the following: "Oh, heart, I am deeply grateful for you who keeps my body alive, who keeps the life force of my blood circulating, and who holds the ability to deeply connect me to all others and to the Divine. I send you my deepest thanks and ask you to relax, to open, and to allow me to experience you in full bloom."

Wait patiently, breathing slowly, in and out, and visualize a beautiful lotus gently opening its petals in the middle of your heart. Next see a brilliant beam of golden light emanating from your deepest core and on the exhale beam this light out through the heart chakra. On the inhale, imagine there are magnificent celestial beings beaming this brilliant golden light back to you, and draw it in through your heart. Keep this process going, allowing the warmth to grow. Allow the feelings of well-being to spread throughout your body. Then smile and express your gratitude to the Divine as you bathe in the glow of this love.

5TH CHAKRA

This center is located in the upper throat area, and holds the energy of sound, communication and self-expression. This chakra is also connected to resonance and the expression of Divine Will. The lessons of this chakra are to speak Universal Truth as well as the subjective truth of your own heart. It is at this place in our energy system that we enter the mental realms.

All matter originates from energy. All energy is a vibratory field which creates a resonance. It is this resonance which connects us both to the Divine and each other. Balancing the throat chakra, which deals with the resonance of our voice and the vibration of sound, is essential.

It is the norm in our culture to not speak the truth. Often we do not even realize what our truth is. Children, who speak of perceptions that differ from the mainstream and/or from their parents, are redirected, gently or otherwise, to give up these perceptions. Parents usually do this out of their own fears, or out of the collective belief that good parents socialize their children to align with the beliefs of their culture, rather than to stay in harmony with their Spirit. Fitting in with society is viewed as far more important than validating a child's awareness. Sadly, few parents are conscious of Universal truths and their importance to our well-being.

Because of this, blockages in this chakra are extremely commonplace. If they are not put into place in young childhood, they certainly are by adolescence. Studies have shown that young adolescent girls give up voicing their opinions in order to feel more accepted by their peers and teachers. And while adolescent boys have more societal permission to speak out, by the time they reach puberty, they are already disconnected from inner wisdom. This is because emotional and spiritual perceptions have been seen as feminine. In our homophobic society, young adolescent males are easily shamed into abdicating their inner wisdom to fit into society's skewed view of masculinity. Since it is this deeper wisdom which connects us with Divine Will and puts us into a state of harmony, our culture has made it very difficult for males to have access to this.

Mass culture tries to get to higher truth through religion. The norm here is to teach children to repeat pat beliefs without questioning them. While these beliefs have vestiges of Divine truth, they have been so misinterpreted and institutionalized over the centuries or millennia, they no longer vibrate at the higher frequencies necessary to align us to Divine Will.

This is not to say that no one has ever found their way to higher truth through religion. There are certainly individuals who are able to get to the essence of these teachings and perhaps instinctively understand their deeper meaning. But those individuals constitute a minority. In general, religion has contributed to people being disconnected from their inner wisdom and therefore from the Divine. Imagine what happened to the collective throat chakras of Western Civilization when "heretics," often women healers and midwives, were burned at the stake in the name of religion.

As we are shifting out of the old paradigm, we have begun to collectively reclaim our voice. We are choosing to live by our faith, not by external doctrine; to listen to our inner wisdom, not the dogma of the society. The more we allow ourselves to speak our truth, and connect through intuition to higher wisdom, the closer we become to establishing harmony on Earth.

Aligning with higher truth comes simultaneously from within and without. As we heal our lower chakras, we have the security of knowing we can survive, and the passion and power to move forward. As we heal the heart, loving intention surrounds our actions. Intuitively we know that being connected to Divine truth allows all parts of ourselves to resonate in harmony. We must heal our throat chakras to create this resonance. As Anodea Judith says: "...Our ability to function as a unified whole depends upon the coherent resonance of the many subtle vibrations within us. *The task of the fifth chakra is to enhance this...*" (**Eastern Body/Western Mind**, p. 305.)

As we come into the full realization of how this energy affects our entire vibrational field, we come into an awareness of the importance of what the Buddhists call "right speech." Right speech creates energetic harmony. "Wrong" speech creates discordance which separates us from parts of our soul and therefore from the Divine.

So what is "right speech"? What does it mean to truly speak from our hearts? One thing it means is we must be connected to our feelings because our feelings give our bodies signals to determine if we are speaking our truth or simply relying on intellect. Our society, in its reliance on the left-brain, has considered feelings as irrelevant and unscientific. Truth is defined by "empirical data," that which could be seen and measured.

The implication here is saddening. We consciously have left the heart out because we do not trust it. What we call empirical evidence has been severely limited by our inability to fully perceive what is. How do you measure that which you have been taught not to perceive? How do you define truth when you have been cut off from inner knowing?

This leads us back to the heart, back to the importance of emotional awareness. We are in the process of reclaiming the ability to truly speak from the heart. The more healed our heart chakra, the more this can happen.

Another important aspect of right speech is to release judgment. Our minds have been trained to dissect, to analyze and to compare. Thus judgment becomes second nature. Internal judgments cause one level of disharmony. Speaking judgments out loud intensifies this. It creates a negative reverberation between those you judge and yourself, even if you have not communicated the judgment directly.

Notice this for yourself. Pay attention to when judgments arise. Notice how you feel when you are experiencing an inner judgment. Judging ourselves or others, creates a tightening, a tension in us. Once you are able to observe yourself going into judgment, label it as such, and ask to be released from it. There will be a loosening, a relaxing. Since judgment will continue to cross your mind, realize this is an ongoing process.

Become aware of what happens to you energetically when you speak the judgment out loud. When you notice yourself doing this, take a moment and scan your energy field. Some of you may have the skill to do this visually, but all that's needed is to notice how you are feeling. Do you feel smug? Then that is a signal to find the part of you that is insecure and seeks to feel "better than" others. Do you feel off-center? Do you feel tight? Tense? If you are really paying attention, you will begin to notice the constricted energy judgment creates.

Also notice what happens to the energy between those you and those you judge. Do you carry subtle guilt for putting out the judgment? Do you have a sense of self-righteousness, and is this a pleasant feeling? Is there more of a strain between you and the person you have judged? Does this make you feel more judgmental?

There is a significant difference between judging and evaluating. We can develop the ability to see others and their motives clearly without judging them. This allows us to provide people with loving, objective feedback if they are open to it. And it allows us to stay away from unhealthy situations and people who may impact negatively on us. We can do this more effectively when we stay out of judgment.

For example, I can look at how you are dealing with your life and notice that the choices you are making are not likely to lead you to the outcome you say you want. If you are open to it, I can share my perceptions with you. I can do this in a loving way, unattached to outcomes. In other words, I can give you the feedback from my perspective, but I will not feel angry or dishonored, or even sad if you choose not to make any changes. Rather I will have voiced an honest perception so I know you have the information. Then, who am I to judge your choices? Your choices, whether I agree with them or not, are exactly what you need to learn your soul's lesson. If your choices threaten to affect me in a harmful way, I can extract myself from the situation in order to not be harmed. I do not need to be judgmental to do this.

Self-judgment is equally disruptive to our energy field. As I discussed in the section on self-love, when we are hard or cruel with ourselves, we dishonor ourselves and create a destructive reverberation throughout our system. The heart closes, the solar plexus is disconnected from love, and our passion and creativity are either suppressed or inappropriately expressed. Pay attention to when this happens and do your best to transform this. Remind yourself, we are not perfect, nor do we have to be. We move toward harmony, not through perfection, but through love. The more loving our inner and outer talk, the more harmonious our energy field becomes. This creates the loving resonance which can interact with all other life-forms and thus can truly transform our world.

You might want to try the following:

Think of a mistake you made recently or of words you wish you had not said, or of something you believe you should be doing differently. Focus on this for a moment. Then consciously say judgmental things to yourself about it. Now, breathe deeply and pay attention to how you feel. More than likely, your energy will be depressed and weakened. For those of you who know kinesiology you might want to muscle-test your responses.

Next, focus back on the issue you were judging yourself about. This time, instead of saying negative things, do the opposite. Be kind, understanding, loving and encouraging. Say things like: "Oh, there I went doing such and such. It certainly is quite an experience to be human and observe my own failings. How wonderful of me to be able to observe these. How wonderful that being human means I do not have to be perfect – or more accurately, that I can never be perfect. I know I will learn whatever lesson there is in this for me, and the next time or maybe the time after that, I will do better. I give myself credit for being conscious and honest with myself, and I send the part of me who makes mistakes, great love."

Notice how you feel now. You may well have a feeling of being loved and comforted. Your heart will be more relaxed and your view of yourself and the world, more positive.

Right speech is remarkably healing. Imagine what a wonderful world we will have when parents correct their children in this way. Make a commitment to yourself to work on shifting to a more loving internal dialogue.

Other areas to address around right speech include our ongoing cultural practice of withholding truth. We typically do this by telling people, not what we truly feel and think, but what we believe they wish to hear, or what will help us fit in. We reward children for doing this, and may even punish them for not. If I withhold the truth because I am afraid of another's reaction, I dishonor myself and ultimately I dishonor them. This causes blockages in my energy field, interferes with my resonance and creates imbalance in my throat chakra.

It is good to remember there is a fine line between speaking truth, and speaking judgment. I can give my opinion or evaluation of a situation without judgment. This is my truth, and energetically it is right speech. However, if I give my opinion or evaluation as if it is the only truth, this becomes judgment. If we observe our emotional energy while we speak, it will help us to discern between the two. Truth speaks without emotional attachment. Any feelings of hardness, harshness, tightening or anger suggest there is judgment involved.

The fifth chakra is where we communicate our creativity. When our lower chakras are aligned, when they are resonating harmoniously, we are able to access our individual expression. A well-functioning throat chakra aligns this individuality with Divine Will, and allows us consciously and creatively to communicate this out to the world.

Remember however, it is necessary to have our first four chakras balanced because they provide the grounding, passion, power and love to put this forward. Without this, our voice and our truth will be shallow or distorted in some way. And without access to our creativity, we will not be able to communicate authentically.

Aligning the 5th chakra to healthy upper chakras connects our expression to Divine Consciousness. Truth is not fully accessible to us without a healthy alignment of our entire energy system. Our Spirits can only be fully empowered when we can align our energetic field to resonate harmoniously with Heaven (higher consciousness) and Earth (physical consciousness.) This is an essential piece of the evolutionary shift.

Talking Back; Speaking Up

I am continually surprised to hear that teenagers get grounded (or worse, slapped) for talking back to their parents. Usually, that "talking back" is simply a forceful and perhaps tactless expressing of their opinion. The more I understand our energy system, the more concerned I become about this. We all need to "talk back". We need to challenge the prevailing belief system. We need to disagree with whatever feels unfair. We NEED TO SPEAK OUR TRUTH, whether or not our parents, educators, whoever, wish to hear it. Talking back protects our Spirits. If teenagers are speaking in a way that seems abusive, I would encourage adults to teach them ways they could say the same thing, but in a different manner, all the while letting them know that their perceptions count.

Why would talking back be threatening? People who are not repressing their own voice, their own truth, do not have difficulty being challenged. There is no fear connected with others having differences of opinion or questioning the basis of ours. If anything, that challenging keeps us more honest.

A healthy society would welcome and value teenagers who challenge the status quo; who point out adult inconsistencies, etc. This is a teen's evolutionary job. This is also how real learning occurs. My best students typically are the ones who challenge me. My children were respected for challenging us. My husband and I wanted them to think independently. We wanted them to question authority and feel free to voice this. Of course, we also taught them to do this in respectful ways. This gave them great skill to express their perceptions to teachers and school administrators. While this did not get those "unfair" policies changed, it earned them respect, and allowed them to keep their self-respect.

We had only one primary rule in our house about how to express your truth respectfully and that was no name-calling. While we were rather relaxed about swearing (as long as you were not swearing at someone), it certainly is reasonable to make that another part of the rule. Still it is important for parents and other authority figures to not over-react to teens using this kind of language. They hear it so much from their peers and from the rest of the culture that it seems natural to them. So asking that things be restated without cursing is fine, but please do not ignore what they are genuinely trying to express simply because of the manner it is being communicated. Similarly, if you are wanting this teen to speak their feelings more calmly, you might suggest a few deep breaths, but keep your focus on the content of what is being expressed.

If you were not free to talk back, I strongly encourage you to do this now. One of the healing methods I use in my practice is to help clients get in touch with their inner teenagers. I show them how to reclaim and access that teenage spirit. Part of this is to find the angry voice that is outraged by unfairness and hypocrisy; the voice that says "this is bullshit!" or the voice that says "I won't put up with this!" While, as adults, we need to find socially appropriate ways to successfully communicate this in the outer world, our inner teenagers get to be as nasty as they choose in our imaginations.

So Talk Back. Talk back in your head. Talk back out loud. Talk back loudly and lovingly. Clear your throat of those imbalances. Boom out "NO!!" to what does not fit for you, for what does not feel right, to what dishonors you. Then boom out "YES" to what heals, to what feeds life, to what empowers your Spirit. Let your voice resonate with other voices of like-mind. Let it resonate around the globe and back again. Let it resonate into the Universe. The reverberation of your Truth aids us on our evolutionary quest. You need your Voice. Let no one deny the beauty of your Truth ever again.

Chakra Healing Exercise

Rub your hands together until you can feel warmth. Then place them on your throat and allow that warmth to bathe this area of your body. When you begin to feel relaxed, gently place your thumb under your chin at the spot just about the Adam's apple. Then chant or tone a sound which vibrates that spot. The Tantric tradition uses the syllable "ham" and the vowel sound of "eeeeee" (our grammatical long "e") to vibrate this chakra. You may wish to use one of these, or find a chant word of your own. The important part is that you can feel the energy vibrating.

Modulate your voice until the sound you make is full and pleasant to your ear. Breathe into this. See the beautiful swirling energy of your throat center. Feel this energy resonate throughout your entire body, rising to swirl delicately through your head and to vibrate powerfully through the rest of your body. Let its resonance expand your sense of yourself, so you can feel your energy field moving out into the larger world, communicating your unique energetic pattern. Let yourself experience the beauty of this pattern – this is the fingerprint of your Spirit. Notice this pattern can blend in harmony with other patterns, or stand on its own.

Conjure up the person in your life who is the most difficult for you to express your true self. It may be a parent, a spouse, a boss, a colleague, or a friend: anyone who you experience as being defensive, threatened, manipulative or angry when you speak your truth, and who you have therefore allowed to inhibit your expression. See that person as clearly as possible in your mind's eye. If you are not able to get a visual image, hear how they sound when they speak to you, and/or how you feel when you are having a verbal interaction with them.

Now still feeling the powerful resonance from your throat chakra, go ahead and tell them what you most want to say, your deepest truth about the relationship, or simply your deepest truth. Say whatever it is you have been hesitant to communicate, or what you have tried to communicate and have been hurt or disrespected for. Experience the feeling of communicating fearlessly and powerfully. Know in the very depths of your soul that your words come from your source, that they resonate with truth, and must be stated for the well-being of your Spirit (and therefore for the well-being of all our Spirits).

As you speak this truth, imagine loving Higher Beings surrounding you, smiling on you, letting you know what a wonderful thing you are doing by supporting your truth. Feel their protective energy and encouragement. Then allow yourself to imagine this other person's responding to you and that you are able to stay in a positive place no matter how they react.

Experience the freedom of speaking your truth with no fear of the response. Then say loving and encouraging things to yourself for doing this. Once you have completed this, again chant the word which vibrates this chakra. Feel its power resonate throughout your body for as long as you can, then smile and open your eyes.

6TH CHAKRA

This chakra, often called the third eye is located in the center of the forehead about an inch above the midpoint of the eyes. It forms a triangle to the physical eyes. This center is the seat of sacred wisdom. The development of this chakra gives us all the power to be visionaries; to have visions beyond the limitation of the physical senses. It gives us the ability to see through the doors of perception into what mystics have seen as Truth. This is the point of stillness within the mind that connects us to higher thought and the collective unconscious. It is where we develop the ability to witness, to watch ourselves and others with Divine objectivity, and where we obtain inner sight.

As with the 5th chakra, this is a primarily a mental center, and while the throat chakra is ruled by sound, the *ajna* or third eye chakra is ruled by light and brings us Divine information. Imbalances in this chakra can create distortions of reality. These distortions give rise to a distorted self-concept as well as a distorted view of others, and in the extreme, can create psychosis. Our culture asks us to keep this center shut down, making it difficult for us to see beyond the veils of the third dimension. We are encouraged to "live in our heads" and thus develop our intellect. Simultaneously we are taught to impose severe limitations on our view of what is real, and therefore, on our ability to tune in to multi-dimensional, "non-physical" realities.

From the history we have on this planet, it appears that up until now, we have collectively chosen not to use our visionary gift. It has been available only to a select few per generation. Now, as part of the current evolutionary leap, we are approaching a time when vast numbers of us can and I believe, will, choose to open this gate and become visionaries.

The implications of this are awe-inspiring. We will have access to full self-knowledge as well as access to the nature of the surrounding universe. Clarity of vision and thought will bring us unbridled choice. We will know, without doubt, that our mind creates reality and that taking charge of our mind, bringing it to full consciousness, will allow us to create a reality on this earth only dreamed of by a few.

We can truly create an enlightened world. We have the information to do this. We have the ability to teach this information to masses of people. We have a collective stirring all over the globe. We have the technology to create a new paradise. Now we simply must open our eyes – all three of them, watch where we are going, and have the courage to come into our full power: the power of full Illumination.

Consider the idea that the biblical concept of Armageddon may be an internal war: a war we all need to fight within ourselves. Going beyond the simplistic view of a war between good and evil, we can define it as the battle between personal power and powerlessness; self-esteem and self-denigration. It is a call for the acceptance and integration of our shadow aspects in order to become whole. It is a struggle to overcome the limited belief system of antiquity which says we are chained to limited reality and must pray to the benevolent forces outside of ourselves to save us. It is the quest to become a mature species – a species ready to take full responsibility for the reality we have created and will create. It is a quest to break free of the old views which imprisoned us, and replace them with the view that we are capable of creating what we need, we are intrinsically good and lovable, we are able to embody Light and willingly spread that Light to all we come in contact with. The Second Coming is not about one spiritual Being returning grandly to the planet to save us, but rather about all of us becoming spiritual beings, becoming Christ-like and saving ourselves.

To use the power of the 6th chakra for positive ends, it is important to be in energetic balance. If I have a cleared 6th chakra, but a closed heart, I could do terrible harm and have no remorse about it. If I have an open 6th chakra, but my solar plexus is out of balance, I could easily, and for a while happily, misuse power, creating a new illusion that I am a superior being. If I have an open 6th chakra, but my root is not functioning correctly, I will have great vision but topple over with it, for I will have no sense of how to activate this vision in material reality. Our energy field must be in balance to take in the Light, to see Truth, to connect with the Divine and to use this incredible ability for the highest good.

The new paradigm, the coming reality, holds the awareness that we are all Divine; we all have the ability to be Christ; to internalize Christ, to vibrate to the highest levels of our Being. The old paradigm, the reality which is passing away, believes God has produced Christ, but refuses to believe that S/He is us. Consciousness creates God which creates Christ or Beings of Enlightenment. We are in fact, all One.

Once we wake up, life cannot go on in the old way. We need to muster enough courage to face our fear of change and embrace spiritual warriorship. "Becoming conscious means changing the rules by which we live and the beliefs we maintain." (Carolyn Myss, *Anatomy of the Spirit*, p. 262). This is the crux of the inner battle, the ultimate Armageddon: Will we succumb to fear, guilt and doubt, and attempt to maintain the old ways, or will we face our fears, make the necessary inner changes and go forward in faith and inner power? We have eons of conditioning which makes this difficult. Change can be hard. But as an old mentor of mine would say: "Who says you can't do hard things?" The choice is ours and the potential rewards for choosing growth and change are magnificent.

When we choose to see through illusion, to choose the path of illumination and understand the great interconnected web of humanity, we can look at the 6th chakra issue of purpose in a new way. From a Divine perspective, we are each tiny light beams. If we remove the old blocks, we each can vibrate at a particular frequency to create an incredible collective image. We are tiny dots on the TV screen of the Universe, and if we each follow the path of Enlightenment, we will create a harmonious picture of reality that goes beyond our wildest dreams. Each and every dot is important to this picture. Each and every one of us is energetically essential. And it is in this recognition, we find our true purpose.

Often, I will ask my clients, "Why do you think you are on the planet?" When I pose this question, I am asking them to get in touch with their unique gifts and to ponder the spiritual contract they may have made prior to their births. In order for each of us to carry out these contracts, we have to identify and use our gifts. All gifts are of equal importance to the whole. Finding a cure for AIDS or developing technology to counteract pollution is no more important than raising healthy children, raising healthy food, teaching, cleaning, nurturing, creating art. Each gift carries a Divine resonance and a light frequency which will contribute to the harmony of the planet.

There are some people who follow their light simply and intuitively such as women in poverty stricken neighborhoods who take in and nurture the children in their community, or the child who knows he or she is called to a spiritual path of service. These people are not going to a therapist to seek their purpose, they live it. These are the people who managed to stay in inner harmony and never lost the connection to their heart. They are highly developed souls who chose a simple and clear path, and have managed to ignore the unhealthy dictates of the larger culture. But, for the majority of us, the path to purpose is more complex. And opening our inner vision is the way to see ourselves more clearly.

Intuition is one of the highest functions of the sixth chakra. Anodea Judith, in her book ***Eastern Body/Western Mind***, sees intuition as the key to developing our psychic abilities. She recognizes this process as a central function for this chakra. "Without intuition, we cannot grasp the whole or the essence of something. We cannot surrender to the resonance of a more immediate truth and understanding than that which is available to us through the rational, conscious mind. We need intuition to embrace the mystery that opens us to the larger, cosmic world." *(Ibid. p. 370)* In order to follow our path to purpose and to illumination, we must allow our intuition to be the guide. This is not an easy task for us Westerners who have been schooled in the belief that there is no mind but the rational mind.

We heal our sixth chakra as we clear away the blocks to true vision. We then become free to embrace the awareness that we are multidimensional beings, each with a special reason for being here on this planet at this time. If we consciously join together, we can create our illuminated vision on this plane through the combined wisdom of our collective energy centers and the evolutionary leap into the new paradigm becomes complete.

As we surrender to our intuitive guidance, living our lives aligned with this guidance, our Spirits become free to lead the way. Following this path, we become fully ourselves, embodying the vibrational frequency of our souls. This is full power, and the core message of this book.

Chakra Healing Exercise

Begin to focus on the point in your forehead which completes the top angle of the triangle drawn from the center of each eye. When you find this spot, gently press a fingertip there to give your inner self the awareness of its location. Then allow your breath to deepen as you continue to focus on this spot. Breathing deeply and rhythmically will relax you enough to hold your focus. After a while, you will begin to feel an inner sensation here. Your skin may begin to feel tingly, or you will sense an indentation in this area and the swirling energy of this chakra. Hold your focus. Now imagine that you can inhale and exhale through this area. Do this several times until you feel mentally energized. Keep focusing on this spot. Eventually you notice there is a beam or circle of light forming here. Hold this focus. As you continue to do this, be open to unlimited possibilities. Those of you with a highly attuned visual sense may begin to experience visions replete with color and remarkable clarity. This can involve mystical symbols which emerge spontaneously, the appearance of guides and angels, glimpses of the future or distant past, and visions of deeper levels of truth.

For those of you who are not as visual, you may get a sense of guidance around you or even hear messages. You can also experiment with beaming the light from this third eye onto areas of your life – your relationships for instance, your children, your parents, your workplace, and your friends. Notice any awareness that comes as you beam light.

When you feel you have experienced as much of this as you are ready for at this time, go to the heart chakra and send waves of love to this center. Imagine beautiful delicate beams of love moving up to your third eye, soothing and honoring this part of the self. Now take a deep inhaling breath, and allow yourself to fill with gratitude.

7TH CHAKRA

This chakra is located at the crown of our head where the soft-spot is at birth. It is here the Divine enters our body and it is through this center, we experience direct contact with the Divine. Because the energy from this chakra illuminates the Divine within, it helps us understand our souls accurately and profoundly. Imbalances here affect our spiritual body, disconnecting us from our God Source and potentially creating deep levels of inner alienation.

As we connect with the Divine, we let go of our personal desires and needs, and vibrate with the energy of The Great Collective. With the lower chakras in alignment, we still have our sense of individuality and material security, but ultimately we come to realize that the truest beauty of our individuality is how we fit into the larger Collective configuration. Why stay a single grain of sand when you can experience yourself as part of the magnificent, expansive, sunlit beach?

The energy of this center is pure sweetness and compassion. As we open this center and access Universal Wisdom, we are able to become aware of the most exquisite non-ordinary realities and experiences. In this center there is no duality – only unity: "All is One."

In the old paradigm, we have generally been taught that we are not pure enough to directly experience God. That this is to be left to the priests, holy men, gurus. All traditions had their mystics, but typically they were separated from and certainly not embraced by the mainstream of humanity. These mystics could sit in their caves or their mystery schools and experience the Great Oneness, while the rest of the global population struggled in the darkness relying on religion to provide their spiritual life.

The Industrial Revolution brought about an interesting paradox. Religion became less and less important as materialism and scientific positivism gained ascendance, further separating us from Spirit. However, it also brought us an emphasis on individualism and individual authority which allowed us to come to our present awareness that we can move into our own spiritual authority without relying on the external authority of religion.

Carolyn Myss, in *Anatomy of the Spirit*, connects this beautifully to the chakra system when she explains that religion as we know it really operates in the realm of the first chakra: that of the group or tribal consciousness. Religion has kept its followers linked to each other in ways that relate to the needs of the "tribe" rather than one's spiritual development. Since the seventh chakra is connected to Spirit, the group is bypassed here, no longer needed. It is from this chakra that each of us is free to develop our own direct spiritual connection. As Myss says, this gives us the opportunity to become spiritual adults. We are no longer children wanting to be told how we should experience Spirit, and we no longer need the agreement of the tribe, but instead we can take responsibility for bringing in our own spiritual wisdom.

It is ironic, although consistent with the process of new growth, that there has been a strong movement in the last few decades back to religion. On the one hand, many people have become scared as they feel the rumblings of the evolutionary earthquake. They want to reinforce the old structures, hoping if they can just make them strong enough, that they will not tumble. So they have flocked to fundamentalism, or back to the religions of their childhood; "...please, please, please..." they may unconsciously pray, "Let us be safe from change. Let us keep some structures that tell us whether or not we are being good, or instruct us how to live the way God wants." Could it be they are unconsciously saying, "We will do anything in order to NOT have to grow up and learn to trust ourselves?" Others perhaps, are hungry for spiritual community and service and their church is able to provide this for them.

The paradigm is shifting anyway, and we are being given the wondrous, awesome, and to many, fearsome task of coming into what Myss calls "spiritual adulthood." And this, literally and figuratively, comes from opening and healing our crown chakras. When I am connecting directly with the Divine Realms, I come into my spiritual authority. I need no intermediary.

At birth, our crowns are still partially open. This is the soft spot on the baby's head which becomes more and more solid throughout the first year of life. I recently heard a story about a tribe in Bali who view all their children as half human and half God. These children are not allowed to touch the ground until they are nine months old, as a way of symbolizing and honoring their Divine connection. It is interesting that nine months is also the average age for the soft spot to harden.

Our culture has no sensitivity to the sacredness of newborns. If anything, the concept that we are born in sin, suggests just the opposite. We have traditionally not honored the birth process and lack cultural rituals to honor the Divine nature of the child who has been birthed.

As we move more fully into the evolutionary shift, the old view will fall away. Honoring the sacredness of all life forms will be a given. We will be continuously plugged into the Divine through our fully operative 7th chakras.

When the Divine enters, Consciousness enters. And from Consciousness, all else is created. If we allow our fears to control us, we interfere with this process and lose its gifts. If we surrender to it, we live always in a state of grace, facing all challenges with an open heart and an empowered Spirit, which gives us ongoing access to Universal wisdom.

"Opening the crown chakra is not so much about increasing our own consciousness, as it is about expanding our operating system so that it can embrace a larger portion of the universal field of consciousness. ...Sentient beings have the capacity to tap into that universal field of intelligence, where vast stores of information reside, much as a personal computer can access the Internet." (Anodea Judith, **Western Body/ Eastern Mind***, p. 411)*

So here we walk on the planet with an inborn ability, an inborn physical mechanism to maintain constant contact with the Divine and Universal Mind. Here we are able to channel in God and connect the outer Deity to the inner Deity. All levels of guidance exist for us through this mechanism. We simply need to open to it, and to trust.

In order to trust, we need to trust ourselves. We need to have the rest of our energy system working so we can feel what we are channeling. Open channels can attract all sorts of vibratory forces. It is important that we put out clear intention to only open to energies from the Light, and to attune our sensitivities so that we can feel if the energy entering us is loving and affirming or manipulative and fear-based. Not all the energies in the "unified field" are loving and truly have our best interest at heart. An open heart chakra and third eye gives us the capacity to open only to the energy that is connected to the Light and therefore our highest good, and fully healed and operative lower chakras allow us to ground this energy so that it can manifest concretely in our lives. When our spirits are empowered, we have the capacity to discriminate between positive and negative psychic forces, and to send away any unwanted energies. And as "spiritual adults," we are able to take responsibility for the quality of energy we channel.

Chakra Healing Exercise

Allow your breath to deepen and deepen. From the farthest reaches of your awareness begin to intuit the most magnificent light you have ever imagined – a light of radiant brilliance. Allow your awareness to rise higher and higher through the top of your head and into the higher dimensional realms: the realms of pure goodness and love, the realms of exquisite beauty; then slowly, while inhaling, draw this light down through your crown chakra. Feel the warmth and peacefulness as you gently pull this light into you and allow it to wash soothingly through your entire body, lighting you up as it passes through.

Now let this light travel down to each of your energy centers beginning with your third eye. Feel it combine with the energy of that chakra, feel it swirling gently as your awareness opens to the Divine energy of this light. Then draw it down into the throat, the light as soothing and as gentle as a new mother's kiss, stay with that sensation for a moment. Next draw it deeper now into the heart – feel the wonderful experience as the light and warmth of the Divine energy of the Universe merges into your center of love and compassion. Keep breathing deeply allowing yourself to bask in this wondrous glow, this magical warmth. Then bring the light down to your solar plexus, activating the fire in your belly, activating your commitment to move out into the world, and then into the sex chakra, seat of your passion for life; feel the vitality this light ignites, the high frequency energy that pulsates with exquisite pleasure wherever it goes, and then draw it down to the root, the center which grounds and connects us with our Mother Earth, that gives us our physical strength and structure.

Imagine you are standing in front of a mirror and can see yourself aglow. The highest of the angelic beings are surrounding the top of your aura with their hands and pouring out the most loving and refined light for you to draw in. You are truly magnificent. Breathe and enjoy the pulsing sensations. Smile and acknowledge your gratefulness and your greatness. Go to your heart and feel the love so warm and expansive. This is you in your fully aligned state, and you are beautiful indeed.

THE UPPER CHAKRAS

We have five additional chakras which form a straight line above the crown chakra. I see them lined up like an antenna reaching out into the cosmos. The more activated they are, the more capable we become of pulling in phenomena, light and information.

The 8th chakra: Carolyn Myss in her book *Sacred Contracts* talks about the 8th chakra as the place where we gain symbolic sight. It is an energy center of Divine objectivity; free of judgment about any earthly experience. It holds the energy of being fully in the present, of unconditional trust and faith, and of the awareness that the material world is only a symbolic representation of a much deeper reality. From this perspective we look at our life on earth in a new way, realizing we create our physical being in order to work out certain lessons for our soul, and for the collective Soul.

To begin to understand how the eighth chakra can help our transformation, think of a situation from your past that was terrible for you at the time. Then notice if now, after many years, you can look at that "terrible" situation with gratitude for the lessons that going through it brought you both about yourself and about life on earth in general. If this perspective is not available to you, notice if you are still feeling victimized by the situation. If so, spend some time working with the emotions that still need to be validated, expressed and released regarding this experience. When you are able to view this situation without emotional reactivity, but simply as part of the soul's drama in its evolutionary quest, you are now able to bring the 8th chakra perspective into your life. Once you can do this about a difficult past event, you become more ready to bring that consciousness into your day to day experiences.

Chakras 9 - 12 I do not yet have information on these chakras, although I trust we will be able to intuit their energy more as our evolution continues. Still I think it is important to write about them, because simply beginning to realize they exist creates a shift for us.

You might wish to close your eyes for a moment and notice if you can get a sense of those centers. Begin with the 8th which is 8 to 12" above your head, and then let your focus continue up – this is quite a long antenna from what I can intuit, and holds remarkably conscious and loving energy for us. Just stay attuned to any sensation you might get as you allow your attention to rise up this remarkable column of energy.

EMBRACING OUR POWER

Getting in balance and healing those areas which have lagged behind the rest of our development, puts us in a state of total personal power. We quite literally have access to all there is in the Universe. We no longer have anything to fear, for nothing on the Earth plane can harm our Spirits. We understand that all challenges are temporary experiences that our souls have chosen, and that all experience, when viewed from a higher perspective without judgment or attachment, is simply part of the great design. We no longer experience confusion, because we have ongoing access to clarity. We no longer need to search outside ourselves for love, because we always have the ability to be filled with love. We no longer have any need to compete with or outdo others because we know with every cell of our Being that we are all interconnected and my joy sends joyful energy to you, as your joy does to me. The more joy, fulfillment, love and abundance one of us holds in our energy field, the more we all can have. In the next chapter, we will take a deeper look at our individual and collective beliefs which impede our evolutionary progress. We will also look at ways to transform them.

4: GETTING FREE FROM THE COLLECTIVE TRANCE

Our minds are remarkably powerful and complex. They are full of compartments. In some of these compartments live the collective beliefs of our culture, in others are individualized beliefs from our personal experiences. The content in many of these compartments is not easy to bring into conscious awareness. However, until these compartments are entered and explored, the beliefs stored here can create realities totally at odds with our conscious intention.

When we are programmed to believe that reality is made up of disconnected physical fragments rather than an interconnected field, a sense of wholeness becomes impossible. Anodea Judith in her book, ***Eastern Body/Western Mind*** puts forth the idea that we are like children of divorce who have lost our mother, since it is the feminine principle that understands that we are all connected; that we are all "One." In this state of psychic disconnection, we are always feeling torn. Thus, when the original split occurred and the patriarchy gained ascendance, it was psychologically easier for us to "demonize" our Mother, or the collective feminine, as a way of coping with this split. And like children of divorce, if we forsake one of our "parents," we feel guilty and unworthy. If we try to be loyal to both, we feel disloyal to each. It is an intra-psychic double bind.

In losing our Mother, we also lost our connection between Heaven and Earth, our upper and lower chakras, our hearts and our heads. When we disconnect from this wholeness, we become stuck in the polarization of the third dimension. The supreme irony is that our minds have always had the capacity to transcend this, but when we are in a collective trance, we paralyze ourselves from using this capability.

Future survival is no longer possible if we stay in this trance. We have dishonored our Earth to the point where she may not be able to support us as a species. We have dishonored ourselves to the point where we inflict unspeakable atrocities on one another. Still, we have reason to be hopeful. We have developed the technology to daily broadcast this information throughout the world, making it more difficult for people to stay in denial. In addition, quantum physics is redefining our view of physical reality, showing beyond question that we are all interconnected. We are also able to use scientific information to show how decimating Mother Earth can lead to our extinction. Despite the ever-more sophisticated "spin doctors" who are doing their best to keep humanity from observing this, our access to this information has the power to shake us out of our collective denial. We are being bombarded with images which implore us to look deeply at our dysfunctional beliefs and behavior.

We have also developed the skill to support self-examination. Again, this is not just for the select few who are on a deep spiritual or philosophical path, but rather for large numbers of us. Our computers give us access to incredible amounts of information, literally putting it at our fingertips. The awareness that we are all One, all interconnected, reminds us that every atrocity is one we all participate in and simultaneously are all hurt by. It shows us that every time we dishonor the Earth, we impact everyone's ability to survive on the planet. It also shows us that every act of love, every act of faith, every act of kindness nurtures us all, and we have the power to create a collective experience based on abundance, joy and deep love. It is this consciousness that will propel our evolution.

Conscious versus Unconscious Beliefs

Beliefs are thought-forms, and thought-forms build resonance or an energy field that takes on a life of its own. Conscious thoughts can become more powerful when we create intention to amplify their resonance. Unconscious beliefs also have a powerful resonance. If we do not find a way to bring these unconscious beliefs into our awareness, they operate outside of our control. The more people there are who hold the same unconscious belief, the more that resonance is amplified. Since many of these thought-forms have been in place for millennia, they have intensely powerful energy. These thoughts often override our conscious intentions and play havoc with us, collectively as well as individually.

Cultural beliefs tend to form around how a particular group or society believes it needs to structure reality in order to ensure survival. These beliefs resonate intensely in our root chakra, the energy center at the very base of our being where we hold the belief that we need to accept our culture's vision of reality or we will die. Consequently, even when these beliefs are brought into consciousness, there is great fear if we do not heed the message of these inaccurate beliefs, disaster is sure to follow.

Collective beliefs can be divided into a number of categories. There are old limiting ones which I mentioned above, that have resided in our human consciousness for eons, such as "it's dangerous to be different from the group." There are more modern ones like: "there will always be wars;" "you can't change human nature." There are beliefs about our future that range from "we can change the world" and "we are the world" to "we must keep tradition at all costs." There are beliefs which are full of illuminated consciousness and propel the human species forward, such as "all men (people) are created equal," and we all have a right to "justice, liberty and the pursuit of happiness." And there are beliefs which are dark and fearful, and operate to keep us powerless, such as "Men are the heads of the household;" "People are sinful by nature;" "Spare the rod, spoil the child."

These limiting beliefs literally put us into a collective trance where, without focused intent and conscious commitment, we could easily stay. The darker beliefs of this collective trance program us to narrowly define reality and to disconnect ourselves from our awareness of Oneness. While it is awesome and exciting to realize we are now on the brink of a collective awakening, it is also daunting to realize how collective beliefs have limited humankind and caused us eons of suffering.

Somewhat separate from our collective beliefs are our individual or personal beliefs. These are both conscious and unconscious. The unconscious belief compartments are full of decisions we made based on our interactions with our families and from other childhood influences; beliefs such as "I'm unlovable" or "I can't count on anyone." The 70's and 80's were decades when many of us confronted these beliefs through therapy, consciousness-raising groups, twelve-step programs and self-help books. Because of this, there are now large numbers of people who are functioning on a much more conscious and empowered level in their personal lives. Yet the collective beliefs, as well as some deeper personal beliefs, are often still lurking unexamined and therefore unchallenged. An essential part of our current evolutionary process is to locate and take charge of our beliefs – both personal and collective. We need to evaluate which beliefs are positive, illuminated and empowering, and which hold us back, keeping us in the dark.

COLLECTIVE LIMITING BELIEFS

I have two primary goals for this chapter. The first is to help you identify and explore the collective and personal beliefs you hold which keep you from full power. The second is to help you transform these beliefs in order to clear out the compartments of your unconscious which house the thought-forms which hold you back. As we transform these beliefs by bringing them into our awareness, we can reconstruct our personal world and our collective reality.

I have divided our collective belief system into six primary categories, although there are many overlaps. The primary categories are Victim-consciousness, Suffering, Scarcity- consciousness, Competition, Limited Reality and Distorted Concepts of Self. What all these categories have in common is that they promote the views that we are separate rather than interconnected, sinners rather than beings of light, and that we are powerless to effect change rather than co-creators of our world.

Victim Consciousness:

The "victim" thought-form is remarkably powerful in our culture. It is the natural outcome of our old beliefs about power. In the old power paradigm, you are on top or you are on the bottom. No matter which place you find yourself, you are operating out of this victim thought-form. If you are on the bottom, you feel powerless and perceive that you have been victimized. If you are on the top, you may feel powerful, but you justify being on top by believing that if you cannot hold onto your dominance, you will end up victimized.

In 1968, a family theorist by the name of Steven Karpman developed a diagram called the P-V-R Triangle as a visual and symbolic representation of typical family relationships. P stands for persecutor, V for victim, and R for rescuer. Each role has its own corner in the triangle. In studying marriages, families and other close interpersonal relationships, Karpman realized that while each person in the relationship had a favorite corner on the triangle, all the roles were dysfunctional, and all the roles would continually and unconsciously shift.

No matter what role you are generally in on the triangle, you are part of victim-consciousness. The way to overcome this is to learn to stay out of all the corners. This happens as you become empowered and take responsibility for yourself, refusing to engage in the old dysfunctional game. If you can see the triangle as 3-dimensional rather than 2, the point of health is when you are at the midpoint above the triangle observing, (at the top of a pyramid with a triangular base, so to speak) but no longer participating in, the dysfunctional dynamic. This triangle is incredibly operative in our culture. It gets played out in workplaces, in the political and social arenas, and even on a global level with nations having a favored corner.

Any time we adults do not take responsibility for the reality we have created, we are operating out of victim consciousness. Any time we feel like someone has done us wrong, we are operating out of victim consciousness. Anytime we feel powerless to change things, we are operating out of victim consciousness. That does not diminish the fact that people may treat us cruelly or unfairly, or that we may often feel overwhelmed by the challenges of life, but it is how we perceive these experiences that determines if we are in the "victim" belief system or not. And it is not until we are willing to take responsibility for our "victimization" that we are able to become empowered enough to end our participation in the cycle.

While, on the surface, this can be interpreted as "blaming the victim," it is not about blame. It is about a realization that we have created a paradigm, a belief system, that requires that there be victims. And while some people and some groups may be victimized more frequently than others, we cannot break out of this cycle until we shift the paradigm. If we have been harmed, we need to honor our anger about it, and then move on. Simultaneously, we need to have compassion for those stuck in victimization and to work to make things more equitable, but no deep change can occur until we help everyone feel empowered, and people cannot feel empowered while they are viewing themselves as victims; that simply perpetuates their feelings of powerlessness.

As a therapist, I have heard some pretty horrific stories from people who were abused as children. But what is always clear is that once that child becomes an adult and once they break away from the abusers, what is most damaging is not the horrible things they had to endure, but the view they have of themselves for being treated like this. As long as they feel stuck and victimized, they will view themselves as somehow defective or undeserving, and then they cannot heal. It is only when they can connect with their outrage that real change can occur. It is this that can propel them out of the victimization cycle and into empowerment and ultimately into an understanding about why their soul may have agreed to go through such pain. At the very least, they need some way to use that horrible experience for a positive end. We do people a great disservice when we keep them identified with their victimization, because this reinforces their belief that they are powerless to change anything.

I worked in the rape crisis movement many years ago, and one of the things we learned was that when women are raped, it tends to bring up all the other times they felt violated or powerless. Often in seeking treatment to overcome the trauma of the rape, women would find that this gave them an opportunity to work through old wounding as well. Despite the horror of being raped, they were ultimately able to put the experience into a larger context and heal deep wounds from their past that otherwise may not have been accessed. They also emerged significantly more empowered than before the rape took place. To be violated and emerge more empowered begins to free one from the collective belief that we are victims.

Because someone was mistreated and abused, and may have learned to believe that they deserved this from their childhood experiences, does not mean they need to stay a victim. As adults, we all have the power to process the old feelings, and to view things differently. We have the power to take charge of our life, to identify self-defeating beliefs and patterns and learn ways to no longer operate out of these.

I saw an interesting example of this from a news fragment on TV about a young Pakistani woman who was the victim of a gang rape. She lived in rural Pakistan where women are still seen as property of their families. It is not unusual, when a male in one family feels dishonored, for that family to take revenge against the women in the accused's family. When this young woman's brother was accused of sleeping with a daughter in another family, the revenge was to be exacted upon his sister. While many differing accounts of this event have been reported, the story I saw was the following: This 15 year old sister was asked to come into an open field where she was told she would be able to ask forgiveness for her brother's transgression. She went innocently into the field and was raped by 4 men, then made to walk naked back to her home while an estimated 200 people from the village watched. This apparently is not that unusual in the rural parts of Pakistan. It is then expected that the girl will feel such shame that she will ultimately commit suicide, and the revenge will be complete.

In this situation, this young woman decided to report what happened to the religious leader of one of the large mosques in the area. This leader took her side and chastised the men, which gave her the courage to go to the police. Rape is illegal in Pakistan, though rarely proven. If it is proven, the perpetrators can get the death penalty. Ultimately the four men were convicted and then released on appeal. She then went to the Supreme Court and while awaiting their verdict, she was able to get the men rearrested by stressing the danger she was in.

What struck me most about this situation was the transformation I observed in this young woman. When she went in for the first trial, she not only wore her long head scarf, but had her whole face covered. Only her eyes could be seen. I thought about how this would actually make it feel safer to testify. Then they showed her a year or so later. She had been awarded quite a bit of money in compensation by the government, and instead of relocating to a safer place, she chose to use the money to set up a school for girls in that rural community, convinced that education helps people know their rights and therefore helps them better protect themselves. They filmed her in the school watching the students. She had her face fully exposed and she was beaming. There was no victim there. There was only a courageous young woman who used this terrible experience to help make the world a better place.

I kept thinking as I watched this story that this young Pakistani woman is a part of the group of souls who have come in to dramatically change consciousness. Despite the ordeal she went through, her spirit was already empowered and compelled her to work for the change of this cruel tradition and to liberate other women. The reason she was not a victim is that she refused to internalize the shame. She knew what was done to her was abominable. It was over, and she could move on to use the experience for positive ends. That does not mean of course, that she may not be suffering from PTSD. But there are wonderful techniques to work with this, EMDR being one of my favorites. Once we do this work we not only can step out of victim-consciousness, we free ourselves in such a powerful way that no one can enslave us, no matter what the outer experiences.

Self-Assessment around Victim Consciousness

Victim consciousness is derived from the belief that we cannot and do not create our reality. It is derived from the belief that bad things happen to us at random, and that people will mistreat us because that is how people are with each other. This belief system can be prominent in our lives or subtle, and it is important to be able to identify when it is operating.

One obvious cue to look for is blaming others for anything that is happening to us. "If it weren't for _____, I wouldn't have to deal with this, feel like this, etc." If you start to observe this within yourself, you will likely notice these thoughts entering your mind fairly frequently. Since we really are all One, it is impossible for anything to be another's fault, because the "other" is us. This does not mean we do not have a right to feel angry if we are violated by another. It is very important for us to feel angry and to find a healthy, non-harmful way to express and release the anger. This is how we begin to feel more empowered. This is how we send out the message to the Universe that we do not deserve to be treated like this. But we can be angry without blaming others for our experiences because to blame someone gives them power to negatively impact our life.

It is also a sign when we are treated unfairly that the outer world may be mirroring an inner belief. Look inside for a part of yourself that believes you do not deserve to be treated well, and therefore conspires to make this a reality. Typically this is a part that developed when you were treated unfairly or violated in your childhood. These parts become integrated into our unconscious and can be difficult to access; nonetheless, to become totally free, it is important that we do access them.

As a way to assess how free you are from victim-consciousness, focus on an event where you have been violated or harmed in some way. As you recall the event, notice your inner reactions. Does it feel like you are still being affected negatively by the experience? Do you still feel depressed, angry, scared or powerless when you remember what happened? Do you feel any guilt or shame about what happened? Have you consciously worked to release the emotions that were attached to this event?

If this was an extreme violation such as sexual or physical abuse or assault, it is very important to release the emotions in a safe way. A good therapist can guide you through this. Be gentle with yourself and take the time you need. But once you have done the emotional work, to fully release victim consciousness means that you have to find some way to utilize the event for positive growth.

It is also important that we be kind to ourselves while at the same time staying conscious of the fact that everything we experience in our life is something that we have participated in creating. It can be no other way, because everything is One. When we can figure out how to stop creating a reality that harms us, and instead create a reality that encourages and nurtures us, we have empowered our Spirits. This is a process. As humans, we cannot change these patterns overnight. We have to learn techniques to build our sense of self and our sense of self-protection. So when we feel ourselves victimized, or feel ourselves blaming, or find that once again we have attracted a situation that harms us, or we cannot seem to release our anger toward someone, we need to first give ourselves credit for observing this. The act of doing this alone begins to shift our energy field. Every time we can stop blaming (whether the blaming is of ourselves or others), we step into the energy of co-creation.

Another way victimization can be overcome is to realize that the negative events gave us more insight into ourselves and others, or perhaps made us more compassionate and empathic. So look at the negative event you identified and notice what lessons it brought to you which you can be grateful for. When we truly understand that no matter how horrendous the outer event, we have the power to stop viewing ourselves as victims, we are finally freed from a deeply ingrained belief that has kept all of us from stepping into our co-creative powers.

There is a big difference between no longer viewing ourselves as a victim because we have worked through our feelings and have the spiritual development to find the higher purpose in the experience, versus going numb, superimposing forgiveness, and/or building a defensive wall. Often people respond to trauma or more subtle violation by shutting down. They simply learn to not feel. This is not only unhealthy but keeps them from getting free from victim-consciousness. It is the same for those people who become tough or belligerent. They are just covering up their feelings of victimization. Sometimes even forgiveness operates to mask the trauma in a similar way by covering up the deep feelings of anger and resentment that lie under the surface. When we are truly free of feeling victimized, there is nothing to forgive. It happened. We used it for positive end. And when we are anchored in living the life we truly want, and therefore are no longer being negatively affected by what happened in any way, then we are free to feel both emotionally neutral and compassionate toward the person or people who harmed us. Compassionate, because only someone with a damaged Spirit could harm another in the way which we were harmed.

Often we hold on to blaming others because we believe that if we do not, we somehow are saying that they had a right to treat us the way they did. Or we have fear that if we do not stay stuck in our anger toward them, that they will be able to harm us again. This is because we do not realize we have, or can develop, the ability to protect ourselves.

If you have dealt with the painful events of your life in the healthy ways I have suggested above, you are well on your way to getting free. Still, these are deeply conditioned beliefs, and it is very unusual for them not to be around in some form. It may come up subtly. We are faced with certain challenges and we find we are feeling sorry for ourselves. Or we find ourselves telling an old story about how a parent or ex-spouse has been mean to us, and we notice we are trying to get validation and sympathy from others. This suggests that we need to tend to the victimized part within. We need to send that part love, compassion and validation, as a way to continue freeing ourselves from victim-consciousness, and simultaneously make sure that we do not give our victim part any power in our lives.

Being free from this consciousness also means not expecting others to make it better. Certainly we want to have loving supportive people in our lives, but these are our lessons. We have chosen them, and we can develop the inner resources to face these lessons with courage and self-confidence. We have to do this if we are truly going to empower our Spirit and take full responsibility for the lives that we are creating.

The Myth of Suffering

How often we hear phrases like "life is tough" which teach us that life on earth is supposed to be hard, and that suffering is part of the experience of being human. We have even created a belief that being a martyr makes a person spiritually superior, and thus, if one suffers enough, they will be rewarded in the after-life. This culminates in dour religions where dancing and other expressions of joy are seen as sinful and are therefore prohibited.

In the West, our beliefs about suffering can be traced back to Genesis. Before Adam and Eve were evicted from Paradise, they had everything they could possibly desire and lived in harmony, but once they ate from the tree of knowledge and were evicted from the Garden, they were doomed to hardship and suffering. If we look at this myth from an eighth chakra perspective and use our ability for symbolic sight, we can begin to ask just what did the apple represent? Why was it prohibited? Why was the serpent seen as seducing us into negativity and sin?

Since the apple was the fruit of the tree of knowledge which gave humanity an awareness of good and evil, Yahweh must not have had much faith in his creation if He did not believe they could make good choices. He apparently believed he needed to withhold information from them and thus preserve their "innocence." Certainly it would suggest "He" was invested in keeping humanity spiritual children, arresting our development, so to speak, rather than letting us make choices for ourselves.

The serpent is often esoterically linked to the kundalini energy, the spiritual force which, when we reach a state of readiness, travels in a spiral up our spinal cord and through our chakras to bring spiritual awakening or enlightenment. Why would Yahweh demonize this serpent? Why would He want to keep His "children" from enlightenment? A short article by Bob Boyd on the internet notes "the kundalini creates an evolutionary leap in one's spiritual consciousness." (www.Kundalini-support.com, *Bob Boyd, "Kundalini Survival and Support" accessed 3/20/05*) Why was this deemed a bad thing 5000 or so years ago?

Perhaps it was the only way to suppress the feminine principle. Spiritual awakening brings the awareness of the interconnectedness and unity of all things. It allows us to have the direct experience of being part of the Divine, yet the foundation of Western religion is built on the idea that we should be kept in the dark here, and that we should suffer for simply wanting to know about it.

Remember, it is the feminine principle (Eve) that knows "Everything is One" and which connects us to our inner wisdom. Patriarchy could not keep its hold if it did not suppress this feminine wisdom. And one of the primary principles of our present collective awakening is our need to reclaim the Feminine and reinstate her in her rightful place as an equal partner to the Male principle. Without that, we will suffer because we are separated from ourselves, from humanity, and from our Divinity. In addition, this intra-psychic war creates wars in the physical world and therefore supports the collective belief that there will always be war, which in turn deepens our suffering.

Giving Yahweh the benefit of the doubt, I suppose we could view His kicking us out of the Garden as His way of kicking us out of the nest. The problem is that the collective belief which developed says that because of Eve's quest for spiritual awakening, we are unworthy sinners who must learn to obey an outside spiritual authority. Believing this, of course, perpetuates the division in our psyches and therefore causes even more suffering, which we are told we deserve.

Are we ready to individuate from our Parent to find our own spiritual expression and take our place as Co-creators of our world? Are we ready to say, "Wait a minute, Eve was on the right track and true innocence comes from consciously choosing the path of love and connection"? And do you find yourself saying "yes" to this on a conscious level but not able to free yourself from a life that feels hard and does not hold much joy?

Stay conscious of how this belief may still be operating in your psyche. Take time with the following questions:

Do you feel guilty or otherwise uncomfortable if you are not constantly working or struggling in some way? When things are going well, do you find yourself waiting for the proverbial "other shoe to drop"? Do you have difficulty relaxing? Do you have difficulty taking time for fun? Do you have a hard time defining what fun is for you?

Create an intention to notice if you are attached to the idea of suffering. You might want to journal on the subject, asking what suffering means for you, looking at your views of people that go through suffering, etc.

I believe that our souls need challenges in order to grow. But challenge and suffering are not the same. When challenges come our way, we can view them as an advanced course in self-development that we have chosen to take. If we can look at them as opportunities for learning, we will not be suffering and we will likely be enjoying ourselves. I also think that as we release the suffering belief system, our challenges will not bring tragedy for the most part, but will occur inwardly allowing us to meet them before they show up in our external world.

Competition

Our society holds a strong belief we need competition to separate the winners from the losers, the successful from the incompetent, the worthy from the unworthy. It gives us phrases like "it's a dog-eat-dog world," "every man for himself," "only the strong survive." It keeps us guarded and teaches us to measure ourselves by others. Thus if others are richer, better looking, more sought after, hold more prestigious positions, or even seem more spiritual, there is a collective belief that they are somehow better than we are.

Until we have completely healed our third chakra, we remain vulnerable to this belief system. Remember, if this chakra is out of balance, we tend to feel either inferior to others or superior to others, and both are flip sides of the same coin. Once the third chakra is healed, we then become able to release all ego attachments to our accomplishments, and our sense of competition dissolves.

My experience in writing this book provides a good example. If I am motivated to write because I want to create the largest selling spiritual self-help book, make lots of money and appear on Oprah, I am writing this to bolster my ego, my sense of self. I am trying to prove to myself that I am worthy and that my work is worthy through the external validation it brings to me. And I will be comparing my book to other similar books, basing its worth on how good or bad I find these other books to be. I also will not want others to be successful in their endeavors because that might threaten my own position. Unless I recognize and deal with this dynamic, I will be stuck in competition mode.

Spirit, on the other hand, gets excited when we contribute positive energy to better the whole. So if my motivation in writing a book is Spirit-based, then my interest is only in sharing what my soul believes will be helpful to all of us. My joy comes from having fulfilled a spiritual contract that I believe will help change our world, and I will have no attachment to its external success other than feeling a responsibility to do what I can to make people aware of the availability of such a book. Then I am totally Spirit-directed, and I will feel gratitude for, rather than competition with all other books which help people heal.

Though my Spirit is largely in charge of this project, as I take an honest look at myself, I still notice competitiveness that arises. I notice feeling that another's success may take away from mine, or in some other way invalidate me. Of course I know better, but as much as I wish this part were not there, it is. I have to stay conscious in order to not give it power. That is what I mean about inviting the ego to tea. It is not possible for me to erase all the conditioning. But by staying conscious, I can empower my Spirit to help my ego relax and let go.

This can be tricky. If I focus on how much I do not like this quality in myself, I end up stuck in judgment which is just another ego-trick. So what I have to do instead is find that part of myself that still does not feel fully worthy and appreciated, and through visualization send love and appreciation to this part. That releases any ego attachment and frees the way for my Spirit to carry out its work. Notice when you are comparing yourselves to others, or begrudging someone their success. This may be a very subtle dynamic, especially for women. Women are taught that it is important to be loving and supportive of others. Certainly this is an important quality to encourage for all human beings. The problem is that we are taught this from our egos, i.e. being loving and supportive of others makes us a better person. This means that we have our self-esteem invested in always feeling supportive of others, especially other women. So it is very difficult for most women to find the parts of themselves that are competitive, that want to outdo their friends and colleagues. You may have to access your belief system about how bad it is to want to outdo others before you will be able to really see and heal the competitive parts of your own nature.

Conversely, we are often rewarded for striving, and for meeting external goals and diminished for seeking internal goals. Our public education system is a good mirror of this. We typically think that children are smart if they can memorize well and therefore get good grades. Most classrooms separate children by putting them in individual desks set in rows. Many teachers discourage group projects where students help each other learn. Teachers set up this competition from an early age by encouraging students to "best" their classmates rather than to do their best and then share their expertise with each other. Those who cannot "cut it" are put into the "slower" groups, already labeled as not having what it takes to be at the top. Thus, early on, the schools lose some of our most advanced thinkers, often by shattering their sense of self-worth, because their learning style does not fit into the competitive, externally-based model.

Our economic system is also set up on competition. It encourages us to out-do as many others as we can. It typically rewards those who are good at competing with a lot of money and then judges them as somehow superior to those who are not good at competing, without regard for the ethics and compassion of the person who is succeeding at the game. We also have a collective, though inaccurate, belief that everyone starts out on an equal playing field; that everyone, no matter what their "station" in life, has access to the "American Dream." This belief gives us an excuse to look down on people who feel unable or choose not to "play the game."

Besides the damage a paradigm which is based on competition does to our collective self-esteem and sense of self, it consistently belies the awareness that we are all ONE. Simply having these divisions, the winners and the losers, the "haves" and "have-nots," does great damage to our collective energy field. It creates intense stress and perpetuates suffering. It keeps us separated from each other so we miss the benefit of experiencing ourselves as an interconnected network where everyone has something of value for the whole. If we understand that everything is interconnected, we realize that another's success is our success too, and another's failure and pain is ours as well. We also realize if we become externally successful by utilizing negative energy, it is detrimental to the entire world.

Another detriment which comes from this competitive model is that groups become adversarial instead of cooperative. Imagine, for instance, that the purpose of a labor union would be to join with management to set up a fair and cooperative system that benefits all employees including the managers and even the owners. Imagine if, when we have close elections, we elect both candidates and expect them to work cooperatively with each other. Imagine civil court cases where instead of winning or losing, the litigants were made to come to a fair and loving agreement with each other.

To notice where competition is operative in your daily life, you might want to ask yourself the following questions:

- *Do I find myself concerned that I will not be able to keep up or will be left behind?*
- *Do I believe I have to be the best, and therefore end up feeling threatened when someone else is doing better than me?*
- *Do I believe I have to get all A's, whether in school or in life, rather than be focused on the quality of what I am learning?*
- *Do I compare myself with others? If so, notice in what areas.*
- *Am I afraid I might make others feel inadequate when I do my best, and I therefore diminish my true abilities?*

Once you find these qualities in yourself, find the part that carries these beliefs. Ask that part to articulate these beliefs so that you can write them down and then find phrases to change them. For example, a belief that "I'm only good enough if I'm number 1" could be changed to "I'm good enough just because I am. I have no need to outperform anyone else." Then send this part love and encouragement. Doing this frequently enough will transform this part and enable you to let go of these limiting beliefs.

There can be healthy expressions of competition that do not involve outdoing another, but rather involve developing a skill to its maximum – taking on the challenge just to see if you can do it. This stretches us to learn and grow. It stretches our Spirit by expanding the boundaries of what we thought possible. When the feeling you bring to competition is light-hearted, and your attachment is not to winning but to really doing your best, then this is a good thing. If, however, there is any sort of stress or emotional intensity where you feel you have to win or reach a certain standard, then you are caught in the collective belief that you are only okay if you can top someone else.

Scarcity Consciousness

In the book, **Mutant Message Down Under**, Marlo Morgan describes how she trekked across the plains of Australia with a tribe of Aborigines. She accompanied this tribe on their "walkabout," a spiritual journey where they walked hundreds of miles in a desert area that seemingly had nothing to sustain life. They had unwavering faith that they would have what they needed, and always, even in the sparsest conditions the right bird or animal would appear when they were hungry; always they would find enough water. It would never occur to them to doubt that they would have their basic needs met.

Unlike these Aborigines, our collective belief is that resources are scarce. This creates enormous insecurity about our physical survival. Even if we have a lot of money, fear-based thoughts of how this money might suddenly disappear can have an unhealthy hold on our psyches and interfere with our ability to let Spirit lead. When we believe we live in an abundant universe and that our needs will be met, we literally breathe easily. Our inhales and exhales become deep. This, in and of itself promotes physical health and slows aging. Our body will feel relaxed; our energy expansive. If our personal resources get tight at some point, we use our creativity to attract what we need by coming from a place of faith that if we put out pro-active energy, we will magnetize whatever is necessary. This frees us up to focus on our Spiritual purpose.

Until we become free from scarcity consciousness, much psychic energy is used to feed the fear that our survival will somehow be threatened because there is not enough for everyone. Whether these fears are conscious or unconscious, they negatively impact our energy field. This creates the opposite effect of the belief in abundance. From this limited belief, our breathing tends to be shallow and our bodies more contracted or stressed.

The concept of scarcity arises from an ego-driven worldview. Our Spirits know that everything is energy and that energy is limitless. Our egos, on the other hand, believe that everything is finite. This creates a belief that we will need to compete with others to get our needs met. If I hold the view that there is not enough to go around, I will struggle to get my needs met at your expense if necessary. I may hoard things or "over-buy" to make sure that I always have enough. My fear will diminish my generosity, because I believe if I give too much to you, I will not have enough for myself.

The belief in scarcity creates a consciousness of lack. This translates beyond a lack of money and physical resources into a lack of love, a lack of time, a lack of personal power. Our attention is consistently diverted as we struggle with these perceived "lacks." Perhaps, more importantly, this is what keeps us living in fear.

Any time you have stayed in a job, a relationship, a friendship or any other situation that has not felt empowering and therefore has not resonated with your Spirit, you have been operating out of scarcity consciousness. You are limiting yourself out of the fear that if you leave whatever it is, there will not be a replacement and/or you will not be okay. This is so prevalent in our society that we tend to label decisions that keep us stuck as being practical, based on good sense. To break through this I am not suggesting you act impulsively, (a little planning is always a good thing), but rather you act courageously. It is not good sense to ignore the messages from our Spirit.

Messages from our Spirit often come through our intuition. The more connected you are to your intuitive voice, the easier it is to hear what actions you need to take to promote the strongest alignment with who you have come here to be. This often creates confusion for people. We are not used to being able to discriminate between fantasy and intuition and therefore we are often not sure what to trust. If this confusion exists for you, I would suggest you choose a "low risk" situation as a practice run to enable you to become more skilled at noticing when you are getting intuitive messages. Interpersonal issues often are the easiest place to start. Remember as you are going through this that the more we are able to tune into our body and to our emotional energy, the more reliable these messages will be.

Here are some possible scenarios you might choose:

You feel that someone is angry at you, but they are not saying anything about it.

Ask if they can validate any of this for you. Obviously, you will have to choose a person who is both self-aware enough to know if they are angry and honest enough to let you know.

You find yourself unconsciously withdrawing from a friend or loved one or perhaps acting irritable with this person.

This is a message from your intuition. Notice this and ask yourself what you are feeling angry about. Watch if you try to make excuses, for this is an indication of how you generally talk yourself out of listening to your Spirit. Once you can identify your "excuses," it is time to go ahead and take action. Ask yourself what the anger or resentment, or general message is, then listen when it comes to your mind. Usually when we pose that type of question to ourselves, the answer will pop in immediately, but we may have unhealthy strategies that cause us to ignore that information. So be careful. Pay attention. When the message does come, you have to take action, no matter how scared you might feel. This is the only way to support your Spirit and to begin to break through this scarcity consciousness. The more you do this, the easier it becomes and the larger issues you will be ready to tackle.

Many years ago a friend of mine came over with a brochure advertising a weekend conference on Spirituality in Chicago. It looked really interesting to me, but I convinced myself that it would be impossible for me to go. I had 3 young children, the youngest of whom was 10 months old and still nursing. Money was tight. My schedule was hectic. So I told myself and my friend that I could not go. Then I noticed that I became very crabby. After a day of this, I revisited the idea of going to the conference. I decided I needed to go. The crabbiness disappeared. When I mentioned it to my husband, he was very supportive. I realized I could use a breast pump to pump excess milk while I was away. I had a friend to stay with in Chicago as a way to minimize the cost. I listened to the signals that my Spirit was giving, and everything else was easy.

This experience gave me the information that if I find myself feeling out of sorts, it is an important signal that I need to identify and honor whatever is causing this feeling. It might be a signal that I am angry or hurt by someone close to me, and I need to tell them. The reason we tend not to tell people we care about how we are feeling is that our fear of lack makes us afraid they will abandon us. Or it might be a signal that my Spirit is trying to lead me somewhere and my limited beliefs are interfering with my listening and carrying out its wishes. The more practice I had at paying attention to these and honoring my Spirit's needs, the more I was able to trust and empower my Spirit.

Look for examples of this in your own life:

- *What are the signals that you get?*

While mine tend to be "crabbiness" or generally feeling out of sync, yours might be a deflation of energy or even some physical symptom.

- *Are you willing to pay attention?*
- *If you pay attention, are you willing to act on these signals, even if they are triggering fear?*

Make a list of anything that feels unsatisfying in your life now. Then brainstorm fears that keep you from making the changes which will make you feel more satisfied. Now look at your list of fears and see how they fit into your beliefs around scarcity.

Once you have completed this, begin to visualize that you live in a totally abundant Universe.

- *Visualize yourself in a Universe where you will always be provided with enough money, enough time and enough love. As you focus on this, notice the following:*
- *Do you still have the same job?*
- *Do you still have the same relationships?*
- *Do you still do as many of the things you are currently doing that feed your "lack of time"?*
- *Are you able to fully relax because you truly know that there are always enough resources, time and love?*
- *Notice what you are saying to yourself about this while you are visualizing and seeing this new way of being. Then make a mental note to observe yourself when you succumb to the old belief of lack, and always, going gently with yourself, begin to challenge those old beliefs by acting in new ways.*

Limited Perception

The archetypal quote which pops into my head when I talk about limited perception is from the original Star Wars movie when Han Solo says: "I've been from one end of this Universe to the other, and I've never seen no Force." Han, of course, did not realize that what he had never seen had nothing to do with its existence and everything to do with his limited perception.

From the time we are infants, our culture is programming our perceptual abilities. We are conditioned to view reality in a Newtonian or third dimensional way. We assume then that every force has its opposite force and that there is only linear cause and effect. While these laws of physics are accurate from one perspective, they tell only part of the story. It is quantum physics that is now helping us realize that polarities are an illusion of perspective, and that physical reality changes as our perception changes. We have the capacity to see that everything is One and therefore to move beyond this polarization to realize that everything is simply a manifestation of the same remarkable system of creation. If we are not fond of some of these manifestations because they cause unnecessary pain and suffering, then we need to learn to see them for what they are and create something different. As we shift our perception, we begin to see that we do create our reality from our thoughts whether consciously or unconsciously. The energy of these thoughts defines what we focus on in this fluid "reality," and therefore determines what we perceive as reality. From this, we realize that we are creators of our personal and global world.

Notice that even simple day-to-day experiences are presented to us in a limiting way. For example, we say that the sun rises and sets. Of course, the sun does not do this. It is the turning of the Earth that allows us to see the sun for part of each day and then have the sun blocked from our view for another part. We spend our lives on a gigantic Ferris wheel. But it is more comforting to our limited selves to imagine that we are stationary and that the celestial bodies revolve around us. That creates the illusion that it is possible to avoid the unavoidable truth: the truth that everything is always changing – always in motion – always in flux.

We are conditioned to believe that objects are solid; that they are made of some form of molecular building blocks. Yet what we know from quantum physics is that there is no solid building block. Everything in our physical reality, including all the molecules in our body, is made from something that can appear to be either a particle or a wave and will continue to change from one to the other. Everything is made up of energy. Solidity itself is an illusion. Yet how many of us can look at a table and see the energy and all the space that exists in what we have learned to perceive as solid.

From this perceptual illusion of solidity, we then believe that we are made up of dense matter. If we believe that we are creations of dense matter, it is easy to conclude that we are separate from each other. In actuality, we are all part of a vibrating energetic system – an infinite collection of waves which makes up what we call our material world. Quantum physics discovered that when two particles are taken from the same system and separated by large physical distances, a change in the spin of one will cause the other, no matter how distant, to change its spin as well. Like these particles, we are an interconnected system. The more love and enlightened awareness we put into this energetic web, the more love and enlightenment will exist on our planet. As we open to a new perceptual reality, we understand how our thoughts can change our world.

Spend some time pondering how you have been trained to perceive material reality. Then begin to notice if you can alter those perceptions even slightly. Look at a table and let your imagination show you how alive it really is. Do a meditation where you begin to imagine that your skin is melting into all that is around you and notice as you start to feel yourself being part of this cosmic undulation. Play with it. Experiment. But most important, remind yourself as often as possible that you have been taught to perceive a very small portion of what is and that you have the capacity to expand far beyond that limited perception.

Distorted Self-Perception

Just as the material world is so much vaster than we have been taught to perceive, the same is true for us. Our physical bodies are a mere fraction of who we truly are. Our consciousness contains all that Is.

A way to begin to understand this is to think about the phrase "we are souls with bodies, not bodies with souls." In the old Newtonian way of thinking, we hold an image that our soul is something contained in our body. When we realize that our body is just a vessel through which our soul can make contact with this particular part of reality, we begin to perceive who we really are. Our soul is far greater than this physical body and has the ability to be operating in several different dimensions while simultaneously operating on the Earth at this point in time.

We also realize that we are made of the same substance as light; we are just vibrating at a slower frequency. When we see ourselves as light rather than as clay, we free ourselves to intuit our full power. Light cannot be contained. It beams itself everywhere. The boundaries of our body are simply something that we choose to create in order to work through our dramas on the Earth: dramas that come from our experiences in other lifetimes or dramas that develop as our egos attach to the cultural belief system.

Just pondering the concept that we are limitless can be challenging. Our left brains do not know how to "wrap around" such an idea. However, through various types of meditation and spiritual practices, you can experience this. One traditional way is through Yoga. There are breathing techniques in the yogic tradition which, when coupled with asanas and meditation, aid the seeker in experiencing the temporal quality of their physical bodies and of the "physical" world. While I am far from an advanced Yoga student, I have had the experience in a group Yoga meditation where all sense of having a physical body disappeared, with the exception of my legs. When there is no body, there are no boundaries to one's consciousness, and we begin to realize that we are everywhere.

Guided visualization can also help you experience this. You might want to do a meditation where you become a large bird that can soar high into the heavens. Let yourself experience the feeling of being the bird, the feeling of flying and of seeing out of the eyes of this bird. Then let your bird body melt away and notice what happens.

Sometimes when people have high fevers or experience trauma, they find themselves perceiving the world from somewhere outside of their body. Many sexual abuse survivors talk of watching the abuse from a place on the ceiling. While trauma needs to be dealt with emotionally in order to heal, any out-of-body experience helps us expand our realization of who we really are.

Begin to put that awareness into your daily life. Walk around realizing that while your body walks in one direction, your consciousness can go many places. Realize that simply the practice of observing ourselves propels us into seeing from a perspective outside of our body. We are watching our brains function. We are watching our body and our mind go through various motions. We therefore are somehow outside of the body/mind and begin to tap into the field of awareness that can help us see who we really are. Once you are able to observe yourself with some success, you might want to imagine that you can observe the observer. Then note where the location of your awareness of this resides.

Also observe all the telepathic experiences that are in continuous motion in our lives, from knowing who is calling when the phone rings, to thinking about an old friend that you have not been in touch with for ages and then hearing from them that day, to having a flash of some event that is occurring for a loved one miles away. All of these things, which happen to everyone whether they "believe" in ESP or not, support the information that our consciousness is part of a vast energetic web, not limited to some lobe in our brain.

Collective beliefs which limit our access to joy, empowerment and full potential are growing more obsolete with each passing day because they hinder rather than aid our survival. Thus, history has brought us to a point in time when we need to drop these beliefs about suffering, victimization, scarcity, and competition; when we need to begin to see reality and our potential with clarity rather than from illusion. It is time for us to shift out of the collective trance of the old belief system to a more authentic, more loving and spiritual view of reality.

COLLECTIVE BELIEFS OF THE EMERGING SYSTEM

As we release the old dysfunctional beliefs, we have to articulate the new collective beliefs that will support our evolutionary journey. The more these resonate with all of us, the faster our world will reflect this new and healthy way of operating. The following are beliefs I seek to put into our collective consciousness.

- We are all interconnected.
- We are innately worthy and loving.
- We are spiritual rather than material beings.
- Thought creates matter.
- Women are as powerful and intellectual as men.

- Men are as intuitive and loving as women.
- No one group is superior to another.
- We live in an abundant world
- Peace and harmony are our natural state.
- Joy is our natural state.
- Emotions connect us to our vitality.
- Inner development is essential for a loving, fulfilling, productive life.
- We can all create a positive reality for ourselves and the planet.
- There are many paths to the same place and each path makes an important contribution.

All of us are part of a cooperative rather than competitive system and can consistently create win/win rather than win/lose situations for everyone. In the emerging system, the "God" and "Goddess," the "Mother" and "Father," are reunited. This means we can balance the polar sides of ourselves: male/female, yin/yang, right brain/left brain; light/shadow. This is sacred marriage and this is how we return to a state of inner wholeness. We move beyond duality. In turn, this creates a new global society which is mentally, emotionally, spiritually and physically healthy.

UNCOVERING AND TRANSFORMING LIMITING PERSONAL BELIEFS

While our personal belief system has been strongly influenced by the collective beliefs of our culture, unlike collective beliefs, limited personal beliefs are direct judgments we put on ourselves. Generally these judgments form early in this life through our experiences with our families, teachers and peers. Any beliefs we hold about ourselves that interfere with stepping into our full power and/or with fulfilling our sacred contracts need to be brought into consciousness and transformed; otherwise, we will not be able to create or sustain the lives we now intend for ourselves.

We change beliefs about ourselves all the time, although often we are not conscious of doing this. Think about the beliefs you know you have already changed. You may have to go back several years, including into your childhood to remember how you thought about yourself and how you were taught to believe your life would and should be. Typically these beliefs include things like "I'm not smart enough," "I'm not attractive enough" "I'll never make it on my own," etc. They may also include beliefs that you have to follow the dictates or norms of your family.

Put all of these beliefs on a list. Look over your list for the messages your family gave you about yourself, both verbal and nonverbal.

Non-verbal or indirect messages come from how our parents lived their own lives and from the subtle reactions they had to us. If you came into adulthood questioning your intelligence for example, notice if this came from your parents. They may have said you were stupid or not smart enough, for example. That would be a clear and direct message. They may have said another sibling was the "smart one." Again, this is pretty direct. The following is an example of a subtle or indirect message: Your parents let you know they believed people outside the family knew more or knew better than they did. That would indicate a belief that the family was not smart enough, and thus, as a family member, that included you.

As you identify the messages that came from your parents, make a note next to the corresponding belief on your list. Then go back over the list noticing what messages came from teachers or other adults that had some authority over you. Mark these as well. And lastly, look for messages from your siblings, relatives and peers. Go over your list one more time, but now make a note of which beliefs have already been transformed and how you transformed them.

You may find that the transformation is only partial, and that is fine. We change incrementally. Many people, for example, transform the belief that they are not smart enough by going back to school as adults and realizing how successful they can be, or perhaps by realizing that they are highly intelligent in a particular area that was not noticed when they were young. Other people transform these messages through a therapeutic process. When we work to re-parent and re-educate our inner child, we are transforming old, dysfunctional messages. Once you have transformed an old dysfunctional belief, you have a new inner resource to help you transform the others, so pay attention to how you have already changed.

Innate characteristics are core to your soul. This includes both your strengths and your weaknesses. Your strengths are designed to be direct aids for actualizing your evolutionary potential, while weaknesses help you learn important lessons which can ultimately guide you in this process. When our early environment is directly supportive of our development, we get many messages from others that correspond to our true nature. If our early environment is not supportive of our development, we will often get external messages that make it difficult for us to see our true nature. Some souls choose this route because once someone has cleared the inaccurate external messages one develops an unusually clear sense of trusting their own perceptions.

To access limiting personal beliefs that are still operative in your life, make a list of what you believe to be your best and worst characteristics. You might want to do this by repeating the following sentences to yourself several times and writing whatever comes to you. "Some of my best characteristics are..." "Some of my worst characteristics are..." Spend several minutes on each phrase, and write down the first thing that pops into your head. When you complete your list, notice if anything surprises you.

If there are surprises, this would suggest that you have suppressed a level of self-awareness. This often is true for some of our more positive characteristics, but certainly it can point to our weaknesses as well. Next, see if you can identify what has helped you recognize this quality in yourself. For instance, if you see yourself as a loving person, where does this opinion stem from? Is it from hearing people tell you that you can always be counted on or that you always do nice things for others? Is it from your inner observation that you have an open heart? Or is it from something else altogether?

Go through each of your characteristics and identify whether they have come from an intuitive awareness or objective observation about yourself, or if they have come from what other people have said about you and/or how they responded to you. Self-awareness often comes from both sources. *If you find you are not sure how some of the beliefs on your list developed, simply identify these with a question mark. Then state an intention that if it is important, the source of the beliefs becomes clear to you.*

We may have a strong sense about a characteristic being innate but also remember hearing it externally. You may also find there are contradictory beliefs when you look over your characteristics. Understanding how these developed will help you make sense of this paradox.

Look over your list once again, and notice how both your best and worst characteristics are currently operating in your life. What positive qualities do you put forward most frequently and most powerfully? What positive qualities do you still have trouble fully owning? Can you imagine energizing these qualities more in your life? Do you have beliefs that still limit your ability to maximize the influence of these positive qualities?

How about your worst characteristics? Are you able to be self-accepting and loving about these? Spend a few minutes now praising yourself for your courage to identify these qualities and see if you can beam each of them love from your heart.

Sometimes our worst characteristics are innate qualities, which, when channeled differently, are important to our self-actualization. For example, a person who is rigid can learn to use this quality to be well-organized and efficient, while simultaneously learning to relax emotionally and be more open-hearted and open-minded.

Another way to access unconscious personal beliefs is to notice your recurring behaviors or life situations. If you find you always have to deal with a certain type of person in your work, for instance, that person is reflecting something important about you. Either they represent something unresolved from your family of origin, a competitive sibling or a controlling parent for instance, or they are showing you a part of yourself that you may not want to look at. For example, you may have a boss who treats you unfairly. Because we are all part of an interconnected web of energy, this boss is not random to you, but rather you have magnetized him or her for a particular reason. You may carry a belief from childhood that you do not deserve to be treated fairly. Or maybe this person is here to show you how you don't treat yourself fairly. It is also possible you have a message that it is okay to treat others unfairly, and having a person treat you this way can help you observe this characteristic and motivate you to transform this in yourself. Looking at all the external situations in your life from this perspective can provide you with important clues about subtle aspects of your personal belief system.

Besides just demonstrating our more negative beliefs, our external situations can show us positive aspects of ourselves we have not recognized. If you are always surrounded with compassionate people, know that this is a sign of your inner compassion. The same thing goes for any other trait: intelligence, unusual talents, competency, etc. If you begin to notice that you have trouble owning these positive qualities for yourself, this once again points to a personal belief system that is holding you back from becoming fully empowered and, ultimately, fully Spirit-directed.

You can also uncover hidden beliefs by being conscious of your dreams. It is always useful when we have a compelling or vivid dream to write it down, to talk about it throughout our day and to look for its deeper meaning. Once you have made a conscious intention to uncover your hidden beliefs, look to your dreams to give you important messages. If you write down your dreams for a week after creating these intentions, you will notice themes will occur that will give you even deeper information.

Transforming Your Inner Home

Our need to awaken from the old trance and restructure our belief system is similar to adolescents transforming their childhood room. Much of what is in a child's room prior to age eleven or twelve is generally chosen or strongly influenced by their parents, but as a child steps into adolescence, a transformation typically begins.

When my younger daughter entered junior high, she stripped her walls bare, collected all her "childish" possessions, and put them in a bag to give away. These pictures and mementos reflected the way we, as her parents, wanted her to see the world. Up instead went the posters of 60's rock groups and musicians and of the intense, poetic female vocalists of her generation. These posters were an externalization of the changes occurring in her, as were the stickers she put around with various symbols and sayings. The individuality of her room grew as she grew, eventually covering her walls from floor to ceiling and including poems and notes and artwork from friends as well as any magazine images that appealed to her. While many teens cover their walls with similar motifs, there was no other room like hers in the universe; it deeply reflected her experiences, tastes, humor, creativity and uniqueness.

This is a wonderful metaphor for the process we need to go through to develop our own belief system. First we need to observe what is posted on the walls of our psyches. Our parents decorated our minds in the same way they might have decorated our bedrooms. As we grew older, our interchanges with the rest of society added to the decor of our minds. As you worked with becoming more conscious and with transforming limited beliefs earlier in this chapter, you stripped the walls bare, and can now begin to think about what type of room you wish to create for yourself. You may choose to bring some of the old with you if you have discovered it serves you well.

List the beliefs or ways of looking at yourself and your world you wish to empower. Take a moment and breathe into these new beliefs. See your life forming around these beliefs and notice how things look, sound and feels to you. Let yourself experience this as fully as possible. Notice how they change your personal life. Begin to imagine these new beliefs spreading out into the world. Notice how this might change your community, your region, your country and your earth.

If this brings you a sense of peace, empowerment and well-being, you know you are well on your way to creating your most positive reality. Make an intention for these beliefs to grow stronger and stronger within you, and make a commitment to notice how these new beliefs operate in your current life.

Meeting Your Empowered Self

Before we can make the evolutionary leap into being fully Spirit-directed, we need to feel empowered; this in turn empowers our Spirit to lead the way. When we are empowered, we know we are fully in charge of ourselves and our lives. We also feel confident that we can create a positive outcome for ourselves in both our personal and worldly endeavors. This does not mean we will never face tragedy or challenges, it does not mean that we will never feel overwhelmed, but it does mean we will always know that we can deal with and move through these times, observing our process and reaping the invaluable lessons such experiences can bring. Empowered people understand they create their reality and therefore are always able to create positive outcomes for themselves. The more people there are who feel this sense of personal empowerment, the more positive our collective outcomes will be.

For this empowerment to be operating at its fullest, we simultaneously need to be in a state of unconditional self-love and unconditional self-acceptance: the proverbial "loving ourselves, warts and all." Before we can feel fully loved and empowered, we need to give ourselves inner permission to do so. We also need to identify what our unconscious belief system is that blocks this ability. One of our collective blocks to self-love comes from our society's twisted belief that we are only truly deserving or truly lovable when we have no flaws or weaknesses. Since there is no way we can be "flaw-free", until this belief is transformed we typically will not feel worthy or lovable enough. We also need to learn what disempowers us and how to effectively move through those moments of feeling powerless. In the healing exercises that follow, you will have an opportunity to uncover these beliefs, to strengthen your connection to your empowered self, and to experience transforming the dis-empowered or "not-worthy-enough" part of the self.

Healing Exercise:

To do this exercise, you will want to have a paper and pen handy.

Take a moment, relax your mind, close your eyes and deepen your breath. As you become more and more relaxed, I want you to focus on your image of a healthy, whole, loving, empowered person. Let the words, images or feelings just rise up in your mind. Experience yourself in this state of empowerment fully connected to your spirit, totally confident in your goodness, and fully loving, gentle, and non-judging of your flaws, of your imperfections. Breathe into this state. Let yourself experience this fully.

Can you notice the harmony in your energy field as you are in this empowered state? See yourself extend your loving energy to others and notice how they receive you in this state. As different insights and images come to you, jot them down. Feel free to be creative, drawing images rather than writing if this feels right to you. Once you have completed this, open your eyes for a bit and note what your experience is as a whole, loving empowered person. If there are any negatives to this state, make a note of them.

Now go back inside. Close your eyes again, breathe and ask yourself, "In what percentage of my life do I feel myself fully empowered?" Notice the first number that pops in, before your brain has time to analyze it. Jot it down. Using the same process, I want you to go back in and ask for a percentage of how self-loving you are and then how self-accepting you are. Jot those down too. Look over these percentages, giving yourself credit for any progress you might have made over the years, and staying out of judgment of the work that is still waiting.

Next, write the following three phrases down, leaving several lines of space after each phrase. Once you have written down the following phrases, I want you to say each one to yourself, either out loud or in your head, and after each repetition, write down the first thing that pops into your head to finish the sentence. Do this 10 times with each phrase, finishing one before moving onto the next. Do your best to pay attention so you write down your very first thought, no matter how silly or irrelevant it may seem to you.

When I'm in a state of self-love, self-acceptance and empowerment, I......
(Repeat 10 times, writing down your initial response after each repetition.

A fear I have of fully loving myself and being totally empowered is.......
(Repeat 10 times, writing down your initial response.)

Others will experience my empowerment and self-love as.......
(Repeat 10 times/write down initial response.)

Take some time to look over what you have written. Notice your fears. Notice both negative and positive responses you believe others will have toward you when they experience you in full power. Notice what surprises you. Summarize this all in a few sentences.

Often, in this exercise, people realize they are afraid to be fully empowered because they fear others' envy or they fear being all alone. Yet it is from full empowerment that we are able to really experience that we are all One and therefore never alone. In addition, like attracts like. Our energy field magnetizes people with compatible energy, so the more empowered we become, the more empowered people there are in our lives. We also cease to feel vulnerable and therefore scared of others who may be envious or angry and project negativity onto us.

If we do not shift our fear-based beliefs, they interfere with our flow of energy. They create blocks which keep our energy fields from being in alignment, and make it more difficult for us to allow Spirit to lead. As we identify and shift these blocks, we clear our field and move away from the constraints of our ego. When this occurs, all our cells actually start vibrating more quickly, at a higher frequency, bringing us literally closer to being light-beings. In this state, our spiritual purpose can unfold with ease.

To finish this exercise, do the following:

Rub your hands together until you can feel warmth and then put them over your heart area and breathe deeply. Feel the warmth of your hands and imagine that warmth being poured into your heart, and allow that whole area to just relax... to just let go. You might want to imagine when you exhale you push the breath out through this area in your body. Keep breathing deeply and allow yourself to bask in the warmth from your hands feeling it melt all the tension around your heart. When you feel this area relax, when you feel it let go, I want you to imagine that you can send this feeling of warmth, this feeling of love, out from your heart in a beam of light. Let this beam of light wash over your whole body, bathing you in light and warmth and love. Then spend some time sending this beam of light to everyone in your household, in your community, and ultimately let it extend out to our entire globe. Bask in the good feelings and notice what happens to your energy field as you do this.

Go back now and visualize yourself again in your fully empowered state. Hold that image in your mind's eye. Next to that image, see yourself when you are depleted, deflated, dis-empowered. Let these parts of you stand side by side.

Now imagine them dialoging with each other. You may want to continue this in your head or you may want to write down the dialogue. Continue in whatever way works best for you.

Once again go inward and focus on both your empowered and disempowered parts. Go to your heart chakra, putting your hands over your heart and beam light filled with love to both parts. Now breathe deeply, feel yourself become your fully empowered self, and with your breath draw the dis-empowered part of yourself into you. Notice how your empowered self is able to contain the part that holds self-doubt and fear without losing energy. Send love once again to strengthen this experience.

Use this visualization to help you stay in a state of empowerment. Whenever feelings of powerlessness begin to stir, see both parts and beam them love from your heart. Then become the empowered self and draw in your dis-empowered self with your breath. Feel the healing. Eventually this will become reflexive and you will find yourself consistently operating from an empowered state.

RECLAIMING YOUR SOUL CONNECTION

We are born with a particular energetic pattern encoded in our DNA. At birth, and to some degree at conception, our own energy field began to interface with the energy field of our parents and the energy field of the environment we were to live in. More often than not, this new field was not in full harmony with our own energy. As we grew up, we had to interface with influential energies outside our families. Some of this influence resonated with our Spirit; when this happened we strengthened our connection to our essence. Other influential energies invaded or dishonored us, pushing us to disconnect from our Spirit and to form beliefs about ourselves that limited our ability to see ourselves as co-creators of our reality. It is in this way that the collective trance gets passed down from one generation to the next.

As we awaken, we reclaim the integrity of our own energy field, which then allows us to live with clear intention and full creative power. As we awaken, we know at a deep level that all loving creation is a partnership with our individual spirits and the Divine.

The following story is a way for you to identify clearly how this has played out in your own life, and will help you reclaim your ability as conscious co-creator. Before you begin, take some deep centering breaths and put yourself into a relaxed state. You might want to play soft, somewhat dreamy music. Say the words out loud or have someone read them for you. Then write down whatever comes up for you, doing your best to allow the information to arise spontaneously.

LIFE PATH STORY

Once upon a time, I, a radiant being full of love, light, and innocence came to the Earth. When I go back and I feel myself at my birth, I can experience the sweetness and harmony of my energy field. (take a moment and allow yourself to feel your sweetness as newborn being.) I realize the purity of my soul.

The mother I chose in this life was named_____. After my birth, when I think about it now, I realize I experienced her energy as_____

The father I chose in this life was named _____. After my birth, when I think about it now, I realize I experienced his energy as _____

I chose these people with the conscious hope that:
_____
_____
_____

The energy field, or general feeling, in my household was:
_____
_____
_____

As I grew older, the following things happened which seemed to change my field, making me question my light and feel more disconnected from my Spirit and from those early feelings of love:

___

When these things occurred, I began to form the following beliefs about myself:
___

These beliefs have impacted my life in several ways: These include:
___

This has caused me to make certain decisions or to hold myself back in the following ways:
___

I have already done things to help myself break through these blocks. Some of the things I have done include:
___

I have learned many lessons from going through this. The lessons which come to mind are:
___

As I have learned these lessons, and as I am more conscious of both the strengths and weakness of my parents, I understand some of the deeper reasons my soul made these choices. The reasons that currently come to mind are:

_____
_____
_____
_____

If I still have unresolved issues with these people, I ask that these come into my mind now. The issues that come are:

_____
_____
_____
_____

Things I can try to help me resolve these issues are:

_____
_____
_____
_____

The ways I will benefit spiritually from my resolving these issues are:

_____
_____
_____
_____

Issues that still need to be resolved with other important people in my life are:

_____
_____
_____
_____

I will benefit spiritually from this resolution in the following ways:
_____
_____
_____
_____

As I feel the energy that comes with all of these resolutions, I am now free to write the next chapter of my life. I am free to experience myself as the radiant, loving light-being I truly am. As co-creator of this next chapter of my life, having reclaimed my true self, I see the following occurring or beginning to occur:
_____
_____
_____
_____

I am getting a stronger sense of the contribution I have come to the Earth to make. What I know now about this contribution is:
_____
_____
_____
_____

I see my empowered self carrying out this new chapter in my life. As I feel a strong connection to this empowered self, I allow a color to surround this part. The more I see this color in the coming weeks, the more empowered I feel to carry out the dictates of my Spirit.

Now look over your responses and give yourself love and praise for all the work you have done up to now. Then list what you still need to resolve and the action you need to take to do this. Make a commitment to yourself to move forward toward this resolution. Notice how empowering it is to know that you are truly the author of your life.

In this story are many of the elements we have been talking about in this chapter. As you identify both the belief systems and what happened to your energy field when you were operating under these old beliefs, you become empowered to shift them. As you write out what you have already done to heal, to awaken and to empower yourself, you are then ready to discern what is left to do. The more you realize that this is your story and you have the right to consciously add to or alter it in any way you wish, you can begin to create the future life you envision -- for yourself and our world.

5: CLAIMING OUR BIRTH AND BIRTHING OUR VISION

Our souls have made the choice to return to Earth at this time. Before our birth, we made many choices that included our soul contracts. We agreed to these contracts for our personal development and for the betterment of humanity. The more conscious we can be about these pre-birth contracts, the more likely and the more effectively we are able to fulfill them.

These contracts contain our life purpose. They include our unique contribution which may or may not be grand in any way, yet each contribution which is made from our heart is equally important to the well-being of the planet. Every action, every decision, every feeling has an energetic imprint that affects the whole. While you may be operating behind the scenes in a small milieu, the ripple effect from your contribution may change history. Since we are all part of one energetic web of being, any action can contribute to shifting the world.

On the other hand, your Spirit may have chosen to make a more public contribution. If this is the case, it is vital for you to face and clear whatever fears and doubts exist from your ego so that you may express this sacred contract. It is equally important to clear out any ego attachments to having what may seem like an "important" job. No job is more important than any other job. Having an influential job, however, does ask that we come forth and accept our authority, influence and leadership.

Remember, purpose is not simply one thing; rather it is often a process or a series of things. For example, all of us have the purpose of learning to live more consistently from a loving heart. Developing this is often our first priority. Awareness and acts of service only support Spirit when they come from love. In order to fully open our hearts, we need to become more conscious and self-aware; this allows us to heal the wounding that has disconnected us from unconditional self-love and unconditional love of others. Other aspects of our purpose typically combine our innate propensities or talents with our passions. This can be anything from creating a loving family and learning to bring mindfulness and creativity to all activities we perform, to carrying out some inspiring and overtly spiritual work that directly benefits humanity.

Living "in purpose" is living a life that is consistently connected to higher consciousness and deeper meaning. It is living the non-ordinary life in the ordinary world. This is the art form mystics throughout the ages have perfected. Now we have large numbers of people who have chosen to live this way as well. When Spirit leads, we always choose this connection, for this is the way we "walk with the Divine."

Sadly, mass culture is constantly inundating us with powerful messages that meaning comes from achievement and the accumulation of material goods, that the more luxurious our vehicle and the more beautiful our home, the more valuable we are. Despite the fact that we all know better, and despite our intention to free ourselves from the collective trance, our consciousness gets re-invaded every time we turn on our televisions, go to the movies or look at a popular magazine. To stay on the path of our higher purpose demands constantly attuning to our day-to-day life and noticing when we are pulled away from Spirit, away from meaningful connection.

As we become more conscious and more skilled at self-observation, we are able to protect ourselves more effectively from the ongoing onslaught of the larger culture. We can pay attention to when we are aligned with Spirit and when we are disconnected from it. Remember to watch this as you go through your day-to-day life. Notice how your life looks, and the profound sense of inner peace and well-being you feel when you are in alignment. Notice what you are saying to yourself and what you are saying to others. Often our choice of words unconsciously reflects whether we are resonating authentically with our souls or whether we are operating out of cultural conditioning. So pay attention to what comes out of your mouth. Notice, too, when you are in a state of disconnection, how you feel, what you are thinking and what words you find yourself using. Keeping a daily journal can really help this process. As we empower our Spirit, we become able to hold the resonance of our souls in every action. This is the deepest meaning of being in our purpose.

To live the non-ordinary life means to continuously stay aware of one's inner life and to understand that since this is the life of the Spirit, this is the life which is more real. The outer world is ephemeral; the inner world, timeless. When we chose to incarnate, we chose a journey to travel on both the inner and outer dimensions. Those of us here in the West also chose a culture which tends to deny the existence of the inner dimensions. This is a fascinating dichotomy which only self-understanding and self-trust can help us resolve. It is the modern challenge and an exciting one.

THE DARK NIGHT OF THE SOUL

As we go through the process of living in alignment with our purpose, we go through cycles in our growth where we are pulled away from feeling our spiritual connection. These are times when we feel distracted from being "in purpose"; times where either old feelings or beliefs are surfacing to be dealt with and transformed, or new information is coming to us which throws us off balance until we learn how to integrate it. By understanding these cycles, we have the opportunity to use them to our advantage. The mystics called this "the dark night of the soul". It is a fertile time when seeds planted in the underground of your psyche are being energized, but are not yet ready to sprout. At this point, they exist beneath conscious awareness. These are times when we feel disconnected from faith and these are times when we have to rely on trust in order to ride them through. Because our souls have chosen this current life of accelerated growth, we generally go through this cycle with some regularity. The more conscious we can stay of these cycles, the deeper in purpose we will find ourselves.

Think of times when you have gone through the "Dark Night of the Soul." For some of you, this experience lasted for several months or even longer. Usually, we experience this for the longest duration when we are shifting from a life based on the outer journey to a life based on the inner one. Sometimes the "Dark Night" follows some spiritual awakening and development which has excited and inspired us, and then seems to screech to a halt. And sometimes the "Dark Night" precedes, and ultimately motivates, our spiritual awakening. You might want to journal on these experiences. Notice what seemed to precipitate them and what lessons you learned. Notice what occurred inside you as you made your way through them. If any significant and lengthy "Dark Night" for several years, then you have learned to speed up the process and now find these periods will likely last for only a few weeks or days, or even hours. This is the way we progress: not in a linear fashion, but cyclically, each time shortening the length of the cycle. So notice now if you are now handling these experiences differently, using your inner resources to move through this cycle more quickly.

WHY WE CHOSE OUR BIRTH

Spiritually, there are no accidents. We all make pre-birth choices that determine when we are born, to whom we are born, and what attributes we are born with and will choose to develop throughout our lives. As we understand this, we then understand that we pick our family based on what our soul needs to develop and to ultimately express its purpose. If we come from a loving and relatively functional family, it is somewhat simple and painless to come to terms with why we chose the particular souls we did to be our parents. The more painful our childhood, the more challenging it is to understand why we would make such a choice.

If you have come from an abusive family, I strongly urge you to heal from the abuse on an emotional level before you embark on the spiritual dimensions of your experience. Otherwise you may avoid doing the necessary emotional work to fully clear your energy field. What I can assure those of you who were abused is that you did not choose that situation because you deserved this type of treatment, but rather because your soul believed this experience could ultimately be used for its evolution. Our family of origin, simply by being human, was not perfect. In addition, they were part of our culture which is neither psychologically or spiritually healthy. Most, if not all of us, have faced life challenges which developed from difficult experiences in the family where we were raised. The more we understand these connections and how to use them in their most positive form, the more aligned we become with our Spirit and our spiritual purpose.

We also choose our generation. Each generation has a particular purpose in carrying out the collective plan, and therefore groups of souls enter with common traits and often common goals. We see an interesting evolution when we track the generations of the last century.

The parents of baby boomers typically came of age just before and during World War II. In the United States, this was a generation that believed they were fighting for freedom and justice. The 40's were also a time when women had more status and freedom since so many of the men were overseas fighting and women then had access to work and activities that had generally been for men only. Once the war was over, I suspect that this group of souls believed they had then earned the right to material prosperity. They also tended to exhibit blind faith in the government. Simultaneously, this generation of women had a taste of equality which they could pass onto their daughters, the precursor perhaps for the Women's Liberation Movement of the 60's and 70's.

Their children, the baby boomer generation, were notorious for rebelling against the material complacency of their parents and for challenging the status quo psychologically, politically, sociologically and spiritually. The 60's and 70's brought in a new level of consciousness and those souls who came in to participate in this, had a sense they were here to transform the old ways. This shook up the society and created imbalance. This imbalance was necessary for change.

The souls born during those decades, the Gen X group, often experienced unstable childhoods because of the disruption of the traditional family unit. Gen X children often search for security through a return to material stability, but also tend to carry a great deal of political cynicism. So the old ways have fallen and this generation, as they are getting through their young adulthood and beginning to approach their 40's, may well seek to carry out a new vision of what security really means. They will ultimately have to look inward for this.

Groups of Gen Y children have been born to older baby boomers: those of us who matured and established loving partnerships before bringing children into the world. These are the children born from the mid-1970's to the mid-1980's. Many of these Gen Y children came into healthier, stable families with parents who were more self-aware and more conscious. But the Gen Y generation also mirrors the polarization which exists in the larger culture which was almost equally divided between constructive and destructive forces. There are the empowered Gen Y young adults who are committed to being true to themselves, carrying out their spiritual contracts, and healing our planet. Then there are the others in this generation who seem to have lost all connection to themselves. They are the first group to be massively medicated and to act out violence in socially astonishing ways like the school shootings of the late 90's. I believe the Gen Y group is here to lead us through the transformation and that their polarization is a part of this. Some will be involved actively in bringing in the Light, and others will loudly display the shadow of humanity as it is currently represented on the earth.

You might want to ponder why you decided to come in as part of a particular generation. In what ways are you similar to others in your age range, and in what ways do you feel different? What coming-of-age experiences have you had that were unique to your generation? Be aware that the music, movies and books that were popular when you were in your teens and young adulthood gave everyone in your generation important common experiences. While each individual will relate to these differently, there clearly is a group experience that has an influence on our collective soul development.

Your soul has also chosen the particular date and time of your birth because this gives you a unique energetic configuration which matches your soul's intention in this lifetime. Astrological natal charts are a blue print of this. While we always have free will, your birth chart shows the characteristics, gifts and challenges that you have chosen to manifest in your current life.

Think about the circumstance of your birth. See if you can look at the various aspects of your family's life from a higher, more objective perspective. ***Did you choose parents who were unusually young or unusually old to be having children? Did you choose parents who were struggling financially or who would provide you with material security? Were they married and if so, was the marriage based on love or on convenience? Did they treat each other with warmth, civility and respect or were there arguments, tension and general hostility? Was it something in between?*** Take a moment and ponder why you might have chosen that particular type of environment from the perspective of what you currently know about your soul's purpose.

Then spend some time thinking and writing about the following questions, noticing how you have been affected by these characteristics of your parents.

- *How self-aware were your parents?*
- *Were they conscious of their gifts and talents?*
- *Did they understand their flaws?*
- *Were they able to accept themselves for these flaws?*
- *In what areas were they in denial?*
- *Did they have an authentic connection to Spirit?*
- *What kind of relationship did they have with their bodies?*
- *Did they take good care of themselves physically?*
- *Were they respectful of their bodies?*
- *Were or are they in good health?*

- *How developed was their ability to have close relationships?*
- *How well were they able to provide you with stability and material security?*

You might want to make a chart where you assess each parent in various areas of their lives including in their ability to be loving and conscious. Look closely at their underdeveloped areas – the ones that caused you the most discomfort or pain when you were growing up. Notice what you learned about love and about yourself from experiencing your parents' deficiencies. Remember that often it is the hardship or challenges within our families that propels us into a deeper search of self. The more you are able to view your parents from a higher perspective, the more you will understand why you chose these particular people.

When my father was dying, I went through a very enlightening process. My father was 89 years old, and had been in good health until he contracted pneumonia and was hospitalized. It soon was clear that my father's health was deteriorating rapidly and he was not going to live much longer. I lived 1,000 miles away. By the time I arrived he was no longer conscious, but stayed alive for another week.

I had a lot of time and solitude during that week to reflect on my relationship with my father as well as to grieve that he was leaving. As I remembered how attached to him I was as a little child, I became overwhelmed with my feelings of love for him. What was most interesting to me was when I began to remember how disappointed I had felt through my later childhood and especially my teen years that my father was not like the fathers my friends had, or like the "good husbands" that my mother would critically compare him to. He did not make a lot of money. He was not family oriented, and was pretty closed off emotionally although he always treated me with affection.

The other men in the affluent Jewish community where I grew up, were very focused on providing well for their families and taking on the role of the kindly patriarch. Not my dad. He made enough money to pay the mortgage on our two-family home, and to provide us with food, clothing, even college educations for my brother and myself, but making money was never high on his list. He was in sales and often would spend the afternoon out in the neighboring hills, or reading by a lake. He had not come from a close family and had no idea how to be close. My mother's ongoing disappointment and ultimate hostility pushed him away even farther.

Growing up, I always thought that I wanted a father like my friends had, but now as my father was dying, I realized how even in his "failings," he was my perfect father. Unlike the fathers of many of my childhood friends, there was no family money to ease my passage into adulthood once I finished college. This helped me be able to feel more resourceful and independent. Also I loved the fact my dad was not ambitious because it modeled positive values for me: I never made choices in my adulthood to sacrifice my Spirit for financial security.

Because my father was not family-oriented, I did not get stuck in the pattern of family loyalty that many of my childhood friends seemed to. I was free to go off and explore my world. If he had been the warm, loving and family-focused patriarch, it is unlikely my parents would have divorced, and I might have felt compelled to stay close to home and live by the norms of the sub-culture I grew up in, norms which would have been stifling to me. His free-thinking and somewhat cynical attitude toward life separated him from his community, yet modeled a larger way for me to see the world. What struck me the most, however, was the awareness I had that since he was the perfect father for my spiritual development, it also meant that my mother was my perfect mother. That demanded a lot of growth on my part.

My mother was highly critical of me, especially when I began to go off on my own path. She typically accused me of being a bad daughter because I had not followed the adult script she had raised me for, and she made it continually clear to me that my life choices, my work included, were not worthy ones from her perspective. No matter how much work I did as an adult to stay out of this dysfunctional dynamic, and I worked on this for years, she would do her best to create yet another way to negatively engage me. She became slightly more respectful of me when I published my first book, and when it was clear that I was raising loving, bright and healthy children, (I was almost 50 by this time), but there was always treacherous emotional territory that I had to traverse in order to have any semblance of a relationship with her.

While my mother had many wonderful characteristics -- she was a highly intelligent, attractive, independent woman who liked to have fun and was blessed with many dear friends – she was extremely difficult to have as a mother because of unhealed emotional issues which she projected onto me. Her positive qualities provided me with a great model and with inner permission to be a strong, smart independent woman. I am also enormously grateful for her ability to have fun which also made this easy for me. Conversely, she would say cruel, insulting things, and then act like there was something wrong with me if I gave any indication that this was not okay. While, I had learned ultimately to keep a safe emotional distance and still fulfill what felt like my familial obligation, I began to realize that on a deep-seated level, I had an inability to fully trust and fully love myself. This slowed down my stepping into more public roles where I could be more influential. Yet it was the very challenges she continuously provided me with, that kept showing me where I was not fully healed. Every time she insulted me, I had to deal with an inner child that believed she could be right. That kept me peeling through layers of negative self-beliefs, and allowed me to heal at continuously deeper levels. That was a wonderful gift, without which I could not as effectively be actualizing my soul's purpose.

Think about why you might have chosen the parents you did. You might want to start with the challenges you had to face because of their dysfunction. Then look at what you gained from going through these challenges. Perhaps you became unusually resourceful. Perhaps you became an outstanding parent by your insistence on treating your own children differently from how you were treated. Perhaps you had to hit bottom before you could reclaim who you have come here to be. Or perhaps, you were being shown that despite how you were treated, you are still a loving, compassionate person. It is easy to be loving and compassionate when we have only known love and compassion. But to be able to be loving and compassionate when we have not been shown these things is truly the sign of a great soul.

Even the most abusive and dysfunctional families have strengths. Clearly we chose our parents for their strengths as well as their weaknesses. Notice what positive qualities you have received from your parents, even if your expression of these qualities is quite different from theirs. This can be anything from inherited intelligence, to the ability to handle money or simply to be able to work hard. Or maybe it is creativity or artistic ability. Sometimes our parents may not have viewed certain qualities they had as positive, but you can use them in a positive way. As an example, often the most dominating and cruel parents were very sensitive as children, but were punished and insulted for being this way. So while this parent may have then treated you with great insensitivity, you still inherited the ability to be sensitive. You then were free to use this ability in a positive rather than a negative manner.

To give you an even clearer understanding of why you have chosen the parents you have, try the following:

List what you liked best in your family and list what the worst or most awful things were about being in your family.

The more information you put in the list, the broader picture you can gain of why you chose these people to raise you. (If you were not raised by your biological parent, do separate lists for all parents and parental figures.)

Once you have completed your list, notice how what you liked best has helped you in your life.

As an example, two positive things immediately come to mind for me in my family. One was the belief that just because people had external authority, it did not mean they knew what they were talking about. I was thus taught to think independently and not put blind trust in "so-called" experts. This led me to trust my intuitive knowing rather than external information, obviously a very significant gift for me in my development. Another thing I deeply appreciated in my family was the focus on eating healthy food and taking care of one's physical body. Both my parents exercised daily, even if it was 5 or 10 minutes, and I remember my mother saying to me when as a child I did not want to eat my vegetables, "if you only knew how good these are for you…" While that meant nothing to me at the time, the message began to filter in. As an adult, I love healthy food; it makes me feel good physically and I like the taste and texture. If I eat junk food, I do not like the way my body feels; therefore, I am not attracted to it. My mother, in her phraseology, gave me a strong message that I would come to like foods because they were healthy for me.

Go over each of the things you listed in the "liked best" column, and see how they have positively impacted your life. You may find that you have grown to appreciate these things more as you have gotten older, and that they may have taken on new meaning depending on what you were going through at various stages in your life. Make a note of this. Then notice how these positive things have inspired or in some way supported what you know to be your deeper purpose. Write all of this down.

Next put your focus on the "liked least" column.

Understanding why our souls would choose parents who treated us poorly, even abusively, is essential if we are to become truly free from all feelings of victimization. Only then is the Spirit able to become fully empowered. The first glitch in this process is that if we were treated poorly as children, we internalized a belief that we deserved this treatment. To shift out of this internal and often subconscious self-blame, we need to become an advocate for the hurt child within. This means we have to come to the full awareness of just how unjustly this child was treated, and then release all the rage and resentment that comes with this realization. The tricky part is that when we realize the unfairness of this, it is a human tendency to then translate this as victimization. Certainly children are victims when they are abused, whether the abuse is brutal or subtle. This needs to be acknowledged. The key is to do this without continuing to see your adult self as a victim, since that would continue the bondage in a new form. Freeing oneself from this is a complex and demanding process. There is a cognitive shift which needs to happen, as well as an emotional shift and an "energetic" shift.

While these are unlikely to happen in an orderly way, here is a procedure to give you a general outline of how to go through this process:

1. *If you have not yet dealt with the things which were most painful for you in your family, get into therapy and do it.*
2. *Learn to recognize the feelings and beliefs of that hurt child inside of you.*
3. *Learn to help this hurt inner child express and release those feelings and beliefs while you are being nurturing, loving and supportive to him or her. Visualization is a good technique to use for this. Realize this is not a finite process – i.e. you do not just do it once and that is it. This is an ongoing process, for as long as we are in a state of growth, the energetic configuration which coalesced from these family experiences will come up over and over again to get healed more deeply. So have realistic expectations, and go easy on yourself.*

The repetition inherent in this healing is a process of peeling off layers. Looked at holographically, each piece of healing we do to the original pattern does not change the configuration; it simply makes it fainter and fainter. One's life can be very much in flow; one's Spirit can be very empowered, yet still there will be vestiges of these patterns. What happens over time and through healing work is that the electro-magnetic charge of these patterns becomes weaker and weaker and eventually will not significantly affect your energy field or your life.

4. *Take a deep, objective look at why your soul chose to experience these hurts. Realize how these experiences have deepened you and have prepared you for your higher purpose on the planet.*

Our souls chose these challenges. Without challenge, there is little stimulus for growth. Our souls may even choose horrendous abuse. Again, this can be tricky psychological territory. It is possible that this is a way of burning off negative karma. Perhaps in other lifetimes, we have perpetrated harm to others, and our souls choose this suffering to help us understand how that might have felt to those we harmed. However, I feel strongly it is not the suffering that burns off the guilt, but rather being able to experience the suffering and to still be, or to become loving, compassionate and caring. Since we are all interconnected, people who do this, do this for us all.

There are other reasons for choosing these abusive situations. If your highest purpose in this life is to lead those who have been abused to health, imagine what a beacon of light and hope you can be if you have gone through this yourself and have healed. If the deepest desire of your soul is to overcome old feelings of resentment and victimization, imagine what deep levels of healing will occur if you have survived monumental abuse and become free of its symptoms. It is important to look at all experiences with a creative eye. We do not choose to experience pain and betrayal because we deserve it or because this is the human condition. There is always a higher purpose for our pain which, when we are able to move into this purpose, will add more love, compassion and healing to the whole of humanity. Our job is to find this higher purpose.

Go back to your lists and decide what the worst things were that you listed in your "least liked" column. Ask yourself what positive reason your soul may have had for putting you through these painful, challenging and perhaps traumatic circumstances. In order to find your answers, focus on how you can utilize these painful situations to enhance your own development and to enhance your ability to better our world. This will increase your ability to carry out your purpose.

When I worked with the ongoing criticism my mother directed at me, I was able to understand it in a much deeper way. My mother was a person who was deeply disappointed in her life, and consistently gave the message to those in her immediate family that they did not measure up. While I was a good child with a loving disposition who did not get in trouble, did well in school, was well-liked by my peers, she managed to often find fault with me and compare me with children of her friends, putting me in a negative light. This created a sense of self-doubt for me. When I graduated from college and began making life decisions that differed from her expectations of me, not only did the criticism escalate, but the implication that I made those choices as a way to hurt her incorporated itself into our relationship. My choices were based on what I needed in order to be on my path, (although sometimes that was more obvious in retrospect,) but my inner child was still vulnerable to my mother's judgments. This made it hard for me to trust I had a right to make these choices. Because I was carrying a great deal of guilt – guilt for going my own way and thus not making my mother's life better – it was also difficult for me to fully love myself.

    I believe I chose this life situation for two primary reasons: feeling this self-doubt has caused me to hold myself back from being more public. This was my soul's way of protecting me and helping me notice fears I have been carrying from other lifetimes: fears that speaking my truth and in turn, challenging the commonly-held norms of my society, would end in me and/or my loved ones being harmed. In order to overcome this fear, I had to empower my Spirit more strongly and activate unconditional self-love so that external responses to me would not matter as long as I was carrying out my purpose. To go through this process successfully, I had to get to deeper levels of self-realization, strengthen my spiritual connection and identify and disconnect from my ego. Because I have a spiritual commitment to speak out, my Spirit keeps pushing me forward until I overcome any identification with the self-doubt of my ego.

    This self-doubt also kept me from becoming arrogant. I have a tendency to be very attached to my view of things and without this self-doubt to balance me, I could have lost perspective and in so doing, lost the ability to inspire and empower others to follow their true inner direction.

    Once our old wounds are fully healed, we will be able to feel appreciation for the lessons this wounding brought us. As we do this, we begin to feel compassion for whoever inflicted those wounds. This compassion, this deeply open-hearted response, is what is meant by true forgiveness. This in no way means excusing abusive behavior. It is rather to free ourselves and our energy from all old pain. An essential part of the evolutionary shift on our planet is to end its long history of treating others cruelly and unfairly. When we reach this level of forgiveness, we have empowered our Spirits to align with our purpose. My mother, despite the pain she caused, was only playing out her role in a larger picture. Could it have happened in less painful ways? Perhaps. But this is the way it did happen, and every piece of the experience, no matter how painful, has been ultimately useful for me.

    Remember however, you cannot bypass the anger. Even after my mother passed away, vestiges of anger still arose and still arise. This allows me to heal this wound at a deeper level because I have to process this anger in order to feel compassion and to truly forgive her once again. This becomes an even more complex process when you have been dramatically abused as a child. To be grateful for the experience of being abused is unthinkable; however, we can be grateful for our ability to survive and our capacity to remain loving despite how we have been treated.

Releasing all Blocks to Resolution

As I have already said, before we are ready to fully resolve the wounding we experienced in our families, a psychotherapeutic process needs to be completed either with a therapist or in some other way. And this process needs to include identifying and safely releasing the fear, anger and sadness our inner child has been holding. We need to have a strong sense of well-being already operative in our lives before a complete release of our wounds can be successfully undertaken. It is when we reach this point, that it is time to take care of any traces of the wound that are still around.

While I am going to suggest a process here, do not limit yourself. If you get a sense that you need to handle this differently, by all means trust your own guidance.

To identify and list any traces you notice inside, you may want to do the following.

1. *Ask yourself what feelings you still carry of being treated unfairly.*

Realize that feelings are very different than thoughts. Thoughts of being treated unfairly may simply be reflections of what happened, but as soon as emotion becomes attached to these thoughts, we are being given a signal of the cleansing that needs to occur. Anything that creates an unpleasant emotional charge for you is an important signal from your physical and emotional body that needs to be honored.

2. *Ask yourself if there is more you need to be doing to stand up for yourself.*

If you are not feeling empowered in a relationship in your life, this is likely a mirror of the emotional dynamics that occurred in your family or through some traumatic encounter in your youth with people outside of your family. If you are still giving your power away in any of your relationships, it is important to identify this, and create a strategy for change.

While it may not always be possible to have our truth heard in these situations, we always have the option of setting better boundaries. If these relationships include parents or others that had some authority over you when you were small, notice if the dynamic is simply residual, in other words, the only reason it has not changed easily is that you have been afraid to speak your truth, or if it is chronic. By chronic, I mean that the people involved still are unwilling to hear how their behavior affects you and are likely to blame you in the process. Remember you always have a right to be treated with honor. In a residual situation, there is some possibility that the "offending" person will take responsibility for their behavior, or at least be open to change. In a chronic situation, communication is likely to be distorted and therefore speaking your truth, while it may be necessary for you to do, will not resolve the situation. Creating stronger boundaries will.

3. *Strategize on how best to protect yourself. Put your observations about your negative treatment in a letter. If this is a person that you have a close emotional connection to, wait a few days and then decide if it needs to be sent.*

If you decide to send it, be prepared in a chronic situation to ignore any blaming or disrespectful response. Simply know that you have accomplished part of your mission through speaking/writing your truth. Start pondering how you can set better boundaries for yourself, even if it means ending the connection, at least for a while.

When I went through this with my mother many years ago, I found that I needed to cut off contact. I wrote her a letter saying that I was resigning as her daughter until she could treat me respectfully. While I still wanted to treat her kindly, I could find no other way of keeping myself out of a dishonoring situation. I still acknowledged her by sending her things on Mother's Day and on her birthday, but I had no personal contact. By doing this, I gave her no opportunity to show me disrespect. Finally she went into therapy and when she heard that I was planning a trip back to my hometown, she asked if I would attend a session with her. While, after the joint session, she overtly refuted everything the therapist said since it was not what she wanted to hear, the process had an impact on her, as did my refusal to play the old game. Part of the old pattern was broken. Simultaneously, I had much stronger boundaries and had become considerably more skilled at self-protection. I had released all expectation that she could be a loving mother to me as an adult, and coming to terms with that reality allowed me to feel safe enough to reestablish a relationship with her which was never as close but was considerably healthier.

If the dynamic between you and the other person does not change, in addition to honoring, expressing and releasing your anger, it is important that you extract yourself from any dishonoring interaction. To allow this to continue is a sign that you are still replaying old childhood beliefs of unworthiness. This interferes with being Spirit-directed because the old ego wounds will still have energy. Ultimately, you may have to cut off contact if this person is unwilling to modify their behavior in any reasonable way.

Often people hold a belief that if their security will be threatened e.g. if the offending person is a boss or a spouse, or even a parent that you have relied on for financial help, that it is smarter to put up with the negative dynamic. This is never the case. To sacrifice your Spirit for material security can never provide you with what you truly are seeking.

4. *Look honestly at your beliefs about anger and victimization.*

If you find that you are holding onto your feelings of anger and victimization, it is likely you hold an inner belief that a need will be met by doing this. Often we hold onto anger because it helps us feel safer. If we have feared being hurt by someone we love, holding on to our anger insures that we will keep our emotional distance.

Owning our anger helps us to feel empowered and to begin to heal the ego. It is no wonder that once we have learned to identify and express our anger, we run the risk of getting stuck there rather than completing the process by releasing it. Until our ego is healthy enough to surrender to the wisdom and guidance of our Spirit, it becomes very difficult to release the anger and still know how to feel safe.

If this is a theme for you, there is a two-fold process you can use to break through this:

First: Find the part of the ego which is still afraid. Usually it will be a hurt, scared child. Send love, nurturing and protection to that part. Keep reassuring that part, over a period of several weeks, that you are grown up and now able to protect him or her.

Second: Strengthen your connection with your Spirit. Prayer or meditation will likely take you there. Feel yourself connect to the energy of the Divine. Notice the sense of both security and empowerment this brings. Use this experience both to transform the fearful ego part and to move you forward in your path.

If you are holding onto feelings of victimization, you may still be looking to have someone outside of yourself validate the pain you have been through. An additional possibility is a part of you is still hoping someone will rescue you. Do your best to bring your motivation into consciousness. You can do this through journal writing, meditation or a therapy session.

If you do not feel validated for the pain you experienced, ponder what you need to feel this. Do you need therapy or will an understanding response from someone you trust work for you? Ultimately, you will need to validate yourself. Take an objective look at what really happened to you as child; how you were victimized. Watching what happened to you as if it were a movie and noticing your responses, can help you give yourself permission to trust your perceptions, to honor and release the old feelings and validate your right to these feelings.

The rescue fantasy is slightly more complex. It also involves a child part of us. To work effectively with this, you need to check whether you hold a belief that being a responsible adult will be neither fun nor fulfilling. Or perhaps you are still holding a belief that it is someone else's job to love you into health, because you feel sad and angry that you have always had to do this for yourself. When you find this child part, you can begin to show him/her the rewards for being in charge of one's life and therefore for able to own your creative power, rather than being at the "mercy" of a benevolent "prince," or parent or fairy godmother.

Men with a rescue fantasy may at first glance, find this dynamic is reversed. You may always seek to be the rescuer in your relationships with women. However, unmet emotional needs from childhood are at play here. It is likely that you believed your mother was being victimized which created a subconscious pattern where you feel you must rescue women who you love, hoping in return, they will emotionally rescue you. If this is your pattern, you will often feel "victimized" when you are unable to successfully rescue these women. We can never rescue anyone; that is a task that must be done by the individual. Again, noting this dynamic and taking care of your inner child's own needs will free you from this pattern.

If you are having difficulty locating this part of your inner child, you can try visualizations where you ask this part to show up. You might want to try the visualization to access the inner child found in my book *Journey to Wholeness*. Or you might now want to do the following:

Close your eyes and take some deep centering breaths. Imagine you can go back in time and into your childhood home still being the adult you are now. See yourself at the front door of this home knowing that when you enter, only your child will be able to see you.
When you feel ready, turn the knob and walk into this house, going from room to room until you locate your child. Introduce yourself as their future, as who they became when they grew up and let them know that you have come back to help. Also let them know that you are visible only to them. Spend some time with your inner child. You know what they have been through and may well notice what is unhealed for them emotionally. Let them know that now that you have found them, you will be there to support, affirm and nurture them. Invite them to come and live with you where you are "magically" able to add on a wonderful room for them filled with all the books, toys, music, art supplies etc. that they love. And if they are willing, see them relocated there.

Then you need to follow through by checking in with this part twice a day for three weeks, even if it is for only 30 seconds each time. Whenever feelings of victimization or feelings of wanting to be rescued surface for you, go back to this visualization and give that child love and nurturing. Remember, visualizing beaming love to this child from your heart chakra is always an effective technique, and once you locate the child, this might work in lieu of your ongoing 30-second check-in. My recommendation is to do both.

Another method for working with this part is to write out a dialogue between you and this child using the non-dominant hand to provide the child's responses.

You begin with your dominant hand asking your inner child why she or he believes they have been treated poorly. Then respond to the question using your non-dominant hand. Then ask the child what they need now to feel safe and loved, and then respond again with your non-dominant hand. This is a way of accessing your unconscious, and for most people it works surprisingly well. Continue the dialogue, tailoring your questions to meet the child's responses and to ultimately reassure the child that they never deserved to be treated unfairly, and that you are now there to take good care of them.

If you try the accessing techniques suggested above and are still not successful at identifying this part, journal on why you may not want to locate this piece of yourself. There is likely a piece of work you will need to do first before you are ready to try those techniques.

Once we are able to be clear about what our pre-birth choices were and how to best utilize them in our lives, we become free to be in full alignment with our soul. We have released all our resistance and can now fully commit to manifesting our optimal purpose. Feelings of victimization, indignation, old rage, guilt or shame embed themselves in our energy field and thus can interfere with our pure manifestation of intention. Watch yourself closely. Lovingly observe these patterns, even the traces. Remember to send them love from your heart. Use prayer to ask that they shift, that they be released, and watch to see what happens.

OPENING TO PURPOSE

While our purpose can be more about the qualities which we bring to all aspects of our life, many people have signed on for more specific reasons and for specific jobs. To fully manifest our Spirit's intention in this incarnation, we need first to identify it.

Sometimes it is necessary to go beyond the obvious. I would have said that I was living out my purpose by being a therapist. After all, I had helped numerous people and many of these people have gone on to make significant contributions in their communities and beyond. Yet I would have readings from spiritual intuitives, who kept saying I was not using my potential and that I had signed on to have a larger field of influence and that I would be teaching before large groups of people.

The truth is I was always thinking about writing a book. I also liked presenting workshops even though for many years they were very stressful for me to prepare. Finally I had to admit to myself that to fully use my soul's potential, I not only had to write, but I needed to find ways to teach more people the material I was writing about. While this was not easy for me, I knew in my heart that this was accurate information and I kept feeling the inner push to carry it out.

You may have a similar experience where you have become content with carrying out a smaller piece of your purpose, while avoiding or being unconscious of a larger piece. Or you may feel confused about why you have truly chosen to be here. A good way to begin is simply to write down what you already know of your purpose.

After you write what you know of your purpose, notice and list the attributes you need in order to carry out this purpose, and how those attributes are likely to relate to experiences or lessons you had in your early life.

Write down how the strengths and weaknesses in your family of origin contributed to your developing these needed attributes.

For example, as a young child it was clear to me that my mother was unhappy. After pestering her quite a bit to tell why she was crying so much, she finally started to share all the problems she had with my father. I would listen and try to help her. I was barely in first grade and already discovering my therapeutic skills. She found my responses to be so sympathetic and pleasing that she continued this throughout my childhood. The difficulties later on in our relationship also helped me learn how to keep good boundaries, and of course, how to understand and help others with difficult their parental issues.

Next, look at any gifts you had as a child that stood out to others.

When I look at the "writing" component of my purpose, I realize that as soon as I was able to read, I began to write stories and essays. I also remember how I won several essay contests as a child, even though I would wait until the last minute and often turned in a very sloppy final draft.

If you may have vague feelings about your purpose like "I know I am here to help others" or "I know I have some connection with healing the Earth." You might want to try the following:

Write everything that comes to mind about these feelings. List your talents; include all the things you do well. Then list your passions; anything which grabs your attention, which holds your interest because this gives you important clues. Your purpose will have to incorporate these.

Then create a purpose statement from this list; a clear, concise pronouncement of what you believe to be a primary expression of your mission on the Earth.

Now read this out loud and notice how it feels. Do you get a sense of excitement? Do you feel your energy being activated? Do you feel scared?

If your statement is a close reflection of your true mission, you will probably feel all of these feelings. While occasionally there are those who pick a clear, unobstructed path to purpose, this is rare. More often we enter this lifetime with unhealed wounds from being ridiculed, shunned or persecuted in the past. This leaves an energetic imprint on our souls. Growing up in our present life's dysfunctional family generally undermines our ability to trust ourselves, our self-esteem and self-confidence. Because of this it is common that when we deeply connect with our birth vision, with our purpose, it is often a double-edged experience. On one hand, we can feel our Spirit's responding, yearning. On the other hand, problems from other lifetimes, as well as self-esteem and self-doubt issues typically surface. So, carefully observe what is activated in you as you read your purpose statement.

If you write a purpose statement and upon reading it feel no emotion, then it is likely you have not really come upon your true *raison d'etre,* your true reason to be here at this time. So try again, until you feel some passion whether that passion is excitement, fear or both.

Once you have written your purpose statement, assess how much you are actualizing your purpose in your life by answering these questions:

- *Does the way you make your living allow you to carry out your purpose?*
- *Does the way you live your life allow you to carry out your purpose?*
- *Is the quality of your relationships in harmony with your expressing your soul's mission?*

Look for what is working. Also look for the contradictions, for example you may have a gift helping others feel safe, yet tend to be fearful yourself. The more aligned you are in all areas; the more you are living in purpose. When you heal the old wounds, overcome the old fears, and shift the old limiting beliefs about yourself and your reality, there is nothing to stand in your way of fully actualizing this birth vision.

If you feel what you are doing in your life is not aligned with your birth vision, look at the broadness of your purpose statement and at your ability to flexible. My youngest daughter began the essay on her college applications with the following statement: "I want to help and enlighten people." She was barely seventeen. While she did not identify this as such at the time, it is clearly a purpose statement and therefore part of her birth vision. It is also appropriately broad. Think of all the ways we are able to help and enlighten people. We can do this in every conversation, every decision we make, every relationship we have. So design your statement so that it optimizes your ability to carry out your purpose in numerous ways.

If after broadening this statement, the work you are currently doing still seems to exclude your life mission, play around with different possibilities. Be careful here because there is a tendency on the one hand for us to not want change because it is too frightening, or on the other hand to seek change somewhat blindly, feeling that anything different has to be better. Ultimately you will have to trust your intuition to lead you; however here are some tips and techniques to facilitate this.

Imagine going into your workplace and with every act, every word infuse the environment with something which reflects your deeper purpose. If you feel your deeper purpose is to inspire people, walk in and hold that image. See what happens. Can you imagine people responding to you differently? Can you see a deeper meaning to the work you are assigned to do? Does your energy field feel more harmonious because you are being more authentic?

When you actually enter your workplace, take a careful look at yourself. What type of attitude do you bring? What happens when you go into your place of employment with a totally open mind? Try walking in with flowers, a sacred object for your desk and a heart beaming with love. Does that change your experience? If you work in an environment with negative energy, "seal" your energy field with white light before entering the building. Then you are likely to be more effective bringing in something new.

Notice if any of these changes creates openings which allow you to manifest your birth vision? Be creative. Remember there are many ways to manifest purpose. You may be carrying out your purpose to heal others, for instance, by having a casual conversation about positive changes you have made in your life with someone who needs to hear new ways to create a healthier life for themselves.

If using this new imagery and creativity do not seem to open possibilities for you to be "in purpose" where you work, then look carefully to see what is going on. Are you holding anger and fear for the people you work for or with? If so, what do you need to do to resolve this and how do you imagine you would experience your workplace if this were resolved? Even if it is impossible to express your purpose through your current employment, I recommend you look at all unfinished emotional business you may have there and make sure you shift any feelings of victimization you may be holding before you move on. Otherwise, you are likely to recreate this after you leave your current job which will interfere with your ability to manifest your birth vision, even in a better setting.

There are certainly times when the nature of one's job and the reality of the organization one works for are simply not harmonious with what one needs to make their contribution. Then courage is called for. Let go of your paycheck and move on. ***The Purpose of Your Life***, by Carol Adrienne, gives wonderful examples of people creating intention to be "in purpose" and following the synchronicities that ensue. Look for this to happen in your own life. Remember to create your intention in such a way that you are open to numerous possibilities. An intention such as "I want to live in harmony with my inner nature and earn my livelihood expressing my deeper purpose," is an example of an open-ended intention which gives the Universe plenty of room to work with.

Once you create the intention, two more things are called for. First, bring to light and transform all unconscious intention which might interfere with manifesting your desire. For instance you may have a belief that it is more important to be safe and secure than to actualize yourself. This belief would create an unconscious intention for you to opt for material security and could keep you stuck where you are. One of the ways to bring this into your awareness is to write on the following: "

What beliefs do I have that could undermine me?

Keep asking the questions over and over again, and write whatever comes into your mind. You can then set an intention to shift this belief. Several of the techniques I talk about in Chapter 4 will also help.

When you feel you have brought your unconscious beliefs to the surface, restate your initial intention and make a commitment to stay focused on the "signs" that come to you. Sometimes the synchronicities may be subtle, so you need to pay careful attention. It is better to follow what appears to be a synchronicity and which does not pan out (at least not in the way you believed it would) than to overlook a possibility because you are not sure if you are really being led.

If you create the intention and nothing happens that seems connected to your intention, you may not be finished preparing. This means you have more personal growth to do before you are ready to fully manifest your birth vision. Some people come into this life with all the preparation they need; others of us come into this life with eons of "baggage" which needs to be released before we are fully ready to step into our soul's potential. The rest of us are somewhere in between. When you create an intention to move into purpose, it is as likely synchronicities will unfold to help you get ready, as to help guide you to direct action. So notice all the signs, and stay open to both possibilities.

Remember how important it is to be mentally flexible. We have to utilize our creativity in order to make the most use of what is being presented to us. Here is an example: if you have just created an intention for a new job which is aligned with your Spirit, and that day you meet someone who mentions how tight the job market is in your field of interest, this is a very important sign. If you think about it too rigidly, you might believe it to mean that your intention has no power and you will not be able to get a job in this field. If you think flexibly, you will see there are numerous possibilities this conversation could be bringing to your attention. It may mirror some limiting beliefs which you are running unconsciously. It may be a challenge to not get hooked into pessimism and/or a lack of faith. Notice the general attitude of the person who gave this information to you. If they are generally positive, as well as open-hearted and open-minded, then it may be safe to take their statement as a suggestion to expand your intention. If they tend more toward fear-based thinking, then it is more likely a message to clear your own fears and limited beliefs. The latter is an example of a synchronicity to help you develop clear the old so your ultimate intention can manifest.

In addition to staying conscious of the synchronicities and interpreting them correctly, another key to strengthening your connection to your birth vision is to stay conscious when you are "in purpose". There is an effortlessness that accompanies being in harmony with who we really are: it feels good! This does not mean that we will not be required to struggle through fear, to feel challenged and maybe even overwhelmed by the demands we might see connected with our tasks. What it does mean is that while you are in the midst of it, it flows from you with ease. In turn, this elicits feelings of deep satisfaction and well-being. When we are "in purpose," people are responsive and generally appreciative of what we are putting out. We integrate the larger meaning of our existence into our daily lives as we step more fully into our sacred purpose.

One last thing to stay conscious of as you step more fully into your purpose: I have just finished reading Paulo Coelho's introduction in his book ***The Alchemist***, where in 2 short pages, he addresses much of what I have written about in this section. He lists 4 things that keep people from staying on their path. The first is the limiting beliefs we learn as children: beliefs that our dreams are impossible. The second is the fear that we will have to leave those we love and who love us, or that we will hurt them in some way. The third is facing defeats once we actually make the commitment to move forward. And the fourth, which I want to emphasize, is that often just as people are about to achieve their goals, about to step into great success, they back off and undermine themselves because they are carrying the belief that since they are no more worthy than anyone else, they do not deserve this type of success. This is a very common issue, and one that I address in many ways in this book. But as Coelho says at the end "… if you believe yourself worthy of the things you fought so hard to get, then you become an instrument of God, you help the Soul of the World, and you understand why you are here."

CHOOSING OUR PRESENT/CREATING OUR FUTURE

When we are fully resonating with our birth vision, our life is in harmony. We feel empowered and infinitely resourceful. We feel fulfilled in our daily activities and have healthy, loving relationships because we have opened our hearts. We bring a great deal of creativity and joy to whatever we are doing. Our view of our present lives as well as of our future is optimistic. We trust there is a deeper meaning in everything that happens. We honor ourselves and feel honored by others. We treat all living things with respect.

This does not mean we have overcome everything, nor does it mean we never experience the "dark night of the soul," but now when fears or issues surface, our lives are not thrown out of balance. We know we have the inner resources to carry out whatever challenges arise to their positive resolution, simply by becoming proactive and taking care of whatever needs our inner attention. Because we now feel confident in our ability to do this, we are able to keep an overall sense of wellbeing no matter what comes our way. That means that we are always able to turn external challenges into experiences that support us rather than drain us.

I have learned that as soon as I am able to shift into a positive and appreciative attitude about whatever I am confronted with, the Universe will work with me to ease my way. This has happened for me over and over again. I know in my heart I am no different than anyone else; this is available to all of us. When we are living in inner harmony, when we are allowing our Spirit to lead, we continuously and consciously fill our lives with blessings. It is not our outer circumstances which matter.

In 1968, after I graduated from college, I worked for a Head-Start program in a poverty-stricken African-American section of Boston. I developed a deep and loving connection not only with the children in my care, but with their mothers and my co-workers, many of whom were from the same area. Being with people who had few external resources and who were consistently faced with the racism of our society, people who easily could have caved into their "victimization," I learned that there were still many who were choosing to experience joy and well-being despite the outer circumstances of their lives. These were people who had open hearts and inner permission to have fun. These were people who cared about others and would give of whatever they had to help others. Conversely, I have known well-to-do people traveling in the top echelons of our society, who had unlimited opportunity, and were quite miserable. They were so wrapped up in their misery, they were unable to open their hearts and so their existence was joyless.

Despite our cultural brainwashing, it is quite clear that outer circumstances ultimately play a small role in our ability to experience a joyful harmonious life. It is our inner circumstances that are the true detriment. I certainly do not intend to diminish the reality of poverty or the fact that material prosperity can give easier access to resources that help people connect with their authentic selves, nor am I naive enough to believe that growing up in the inner cities, currently ravaged by drugs and hopelessness, does not create deep beliefs about oneself, one's future and our society which makes it difficult to enjoy a positive inner life. But I do know that experiencing a purpose-filled life is something that is possible for each of us.

Noticing what is Right with Your World

Pay attention to this simple truth:
"A joyful person lives in a joyful world; an angry person lives in an angry world."
Like attracts like. When we shift ourselves inwardly, we shift our energy field. This magnetizes new experiences. There is a powerful irony here: To live the life we want, we have to love and honor the life we are living. When we focus on what is missing or not good in our lives, we amplify that energy. When we focus on what is good in our lives, we amplify that energy as well. If we want our lives to improve, we need to stay focused on our blessings.

Understand that it is one thing to stay focused on the positive aspects in our lives; it is another to be in denial of the negative. When we are healed, we know what can be improved and we certainly know if there are areas of our lives, or relationships in our lives, that dishonor us or those in our care. We are not living in denial; we are not in fantasy-land. Rather, we learn to see things honestly and choose to do what we can to change things and to keep a positive focus.

There was a beautiful article in *"The Sun"* magazine some years ago about a young woman who was hospitalized for a lung ailment. She was on a ventilator, unable to eat and in an enormous amount of discomfort. After going through the very human experience of feeling sorry for herself, which was intensified by having a roommate who would consistently watch cooking shows on TV, she began instead to focus on each moment. As she totally immersed herself in the present and achieved the state of mindfulness she was seeking, she no longer felt miserable, but rather was able to notice each and every sensation with both objectivity and grace. What a powerful blessing that is, and it is available to all of us at all times.

St. Francis of Assisi was able to enter ecstatic states of consciousness while he was locked in a dark dungeon for over a year. He must have been able to be grateful for each breath he took, for each sensation he had, for each thought and awareness that passed through his mind. Perhaps he was appreciative of being removed from the day-to-day life he had lived. Prior to his incarceration, he had lived a life of wealth and privilege which did not support his spiritual awakening. Thus, in what we consider to be some of the most unpleasant of circumstances, we have the capacity to be in a state of gratitude and to remove ourselves from internal suffering. When we know with our entire being that all experiences can be used for our spiritual development, then we can be grateful for all experience.

To put ourselves in this state we need to add gratitude to our daily practice. You might want to list several things each day that you are grateful for, and thank the Divine for these things. Stop at different points throughout the day and notice when you feel good, when you feel loving and/or loved, and express gratitude at that moment. You will begin to notice a significant shift in your mood. One of the ways I incorporate this into my life is whenever I notice myself feeling love and joy, not only do I put out gratitude for having these feelings, I go to my heart and send loving energy out to the world. If I am in my car or in a public place where I can see others, I beam this loving energy from my heart to the people around me. Large numbers of us doing this will truly change our world.

Besides noticing the positive parts of your personal world, notice the collective world as well. If you hear, read or witness an act of kindness, put out gratitude. Pay attention to all the positive things reported in the media, from inspirational books and stories, to deeds that help humanity and all other living things. When a politician does the right thing, something that supports the peace and well-being of the planet, feel the energy of gratitude and send it out. When an enlightened view influences public policy, send out gratitude. Tell others about it. We all need to model this for each other.

This is not a magic pill. People who are extremely depressed may simply not be able to stay focused on what is good in their lives until they deal with their depression. People who have a deep sense of unworthiness may carry a strong unconscious intention to not allow themselves to live a positive life. As a general rule, however, this will work. And the longer you do it, the more joy you will experience in your life. And the more joy you experience, the more joyful energy you will put out into our world which will help us all.

IDENTIFYING OUR PRE-BIRTH CONTRACTS

When you are activating positive loving energy the majority of the time; when you find yourself often in a state of gratitude; when you have a sense of why you are here, why you chose your family and why you are leading the life you are presently leading, you are ready to fully activate the vision you held before your birth. Most of you are already activating this to some degree. Some of you are beginning to get inklings about it. The more you develop, the more energy you have for your purpose. As we stay committed to our growth, focused on our inner life and on letting our Spirit lead, our purpose will evolve until finally it becomes fully aligned with our pre-birth intention.

Our psyches have the ability to go back to this experience. There are also people who are trained to take you back to your pre-birth existence to see what contracts you actually made. Michael Newton wrote a wonderful book called **Destiny of Souls** where he recounts the hypnotic regressions he has done with numerous people. Through hypnosis, he is able to take them to the realm they were in and to the consciousness they had just prior to incarnating in this life. He has trained others to do this as well. For now though, you might want to let your imagination take over.

As you let yourself intuit why you may have chosen the family that you did, you might want to remember the story of the **Horse Whisperer**. This is a movie based on a man who travels around the country healing traumatized horses. This man uses gentleness, compassion and telepathic communication to heal these horses. It is my understanding that as a child, he had been treated brutally by his father. He also grew up around horses and saw his father show the same brutality to the horses that he showed to him. His soul may have seen that while he was going to have to endure such violence in his childhood, what he would learn from that experience could help him manifest his destiny and help shift peoples' consciousness around the globe.

Below is an exercise to help you connect with and understand your pre-birth choices.

Breathe yourself into a relaxed state and let yourself imagine you are in a pre-birth dimension. Feel yourself as that pre-incarnated soul. Your pre-life body, while being a glowing representation of human form, may feel like a collection of etheric cells vibrating frequencies of joy, love and enlightened consciousness. Notice, in this state, that the primary motivation of your soul is to activate the joy/love/enlightenment frequency more strongly in order to expand its influence in the web of life. From this perspective you can scan the Earth in order to see the perception you had of your parents prior to your birth. Notice how you view them from this perspective. As this soul, what do you feel you might bring to them by incarnating as their child? What lessons will living in their care bring to you? (If you were adopted, first visualize your birth parents. Then notice the intricate connections which led you to your adoptive parents and how all of these souls provided you with lessons for your development.)

Pay attention to the challenge or challenges you chose in your family when you were considering honoring them with your birth. These often are a direct link to the sacred contracts you have made.

See if you can put your own story in these terms, connecting your primary lessons and challenges as well as the strengths in your family, to your own mission. Write this down or speak it aloud. Tell it to a trusted friend and see how that feels. Add details. Play around with various scenarios and see where they take you. Begin to focus on what you are already doing to fulfill these contracts and what you are still being called to do in the future to serve all of humanity. Notice as well, what challenges you have completed that support this vision, and what are still to be completed.

As you make peace with your choice of parents and your early life, as you become clear about your pre-birth vision, you become ready to look at all beings on Earth as your family and to see how your birth vision fits into the larger pattern of global healing we are currently embarking on.

6: REINCARNATION & OUR MULTIDIMENSIONAL SOUL

The concept of reincarnation has interested me for over 40 years. The idea that our soul goes through numerous experiences in different bodies in order to ultimately re-merge with the Divine Source, instantly made sense to me. At the same time, I began to meet people who I felt I had known in other lifetimes. Sometimes I would get flashes of the lives we had led together. I saw that many of my close women friends have shared lives with me in Catholic convents. Most of us were nuns, although some were priests that interacted with us. This was an interesting awareness since I was brought up Jewish in this lifetime. I would also get story lines from these lifetimes which gave me important information about myself and gave me clues of how to heal old fears and dysfunctional patterns.

Strong feelings of where I have lived geographically also have come to me. For instance, I am aware of having early Native American experiences on the continent; however, I sense I was never in the United States as a pioneer; it simply does not seem to be in my soul configuration. I feel I was in Russia around the time of the Revolution. I spent a fair amount of time in Europe. I do not have any memories of Africa outside of the Northern desert. I also have no memories of the Far East. This could mean several things: I may not have had lifetimes there; I may simply have not accessed those memories or perhaps, and this one makes the most sense to me, I am only accessing the memories that are relevant for my soul's purpose in this lifetime.

My intuitions here may also be metaphoric. Instead of literally being in these places, my soul might have picked up holographic fractals of various experiences. We do know scientifically that we are holographic, in other words, each part of us contains the whole. Ancient wisdom such as "As Above, So Below" teaches us that the Universe is a hologram, but now science gives us tools to understand this cognitively rather than just through faith. Because holograms contain the whole in each part, every cell essentially contains the universe. I contain parts of everyone on Earth and beyond, and everyone contains parts of me. Because we all have unique energy configurations of this larger pattern, each of us is also an individual. We contain fractals or pieces of this larger hologram, and these fractals when they are in us, illuminate certain parts of the hologram more brightly than others. So part of my unique energy configuration, as contained in these fractals, may emphasize the collective Native American experience for instance and not that of an American pioneer.

The right hemisphere of our brain can grasp the concept of multidimensionality and reincarnation with ease. It is from this side we process emotions, inspirational awareness and telepathic communication, and it is from here our creativity flows. This hemisphere is activated from practices such as meditation, prayer, yoga, dream interpretation, art, creative writing and music, as well as through Holotropic and Shamanic Breathwork®. Part of our current evolutionary process is learning how to tap into the astounding abilities of this right hemisphere, while using our brain's highly evolved left hemisphere to interpret and organize this information.

Unlike our brain's left hemisphere which operates in linear or 3rd dimensional time, the brain's right hemisphere operates in higher dimensional consciousness where all time is perceived as occurring simultaneously rather than sequentially. Because currently many of us are choosing to access our "whole brain," we get to live in a portal of time where we not only have the capacity to experience the past, present and future concurrently, we are developing the ability to integrate the high levels of awareness this brings into our daily lives. The potential this gives us is remarkable. Learning from the "past" takes on quite a new meaning when we realize the "past" is still being experienced by our consciousness as if it is occurring in the present. Seeing into possible futures and understanding that we are totally empowered to decide which one we want, could become as normal as choosing which restaurant to go to for dinner.

While time travel still carries a science fiction label, our quest to become fully conscious could make it a common place occurrence. We are learning how to recognize and ultimately to use the vast amount of unexplored potential remaining in our minds. This potential holds both information and wisdom that our soul carries from other lifetimes.

Our concept of linear time is a product of the left hemisphere of our brain which can perceive time only in sequence: this happened first, then this happened, etc. This is the time/space relationship of the 3rd dimension. When we go beyond this concept to a larger understanding of time, we realize that what we call past lives is happening now in these other dimensions. As an example, suppose I become aware of a lifetime I spent in ancient Egypt. Looking in on that lifetime, I might notice it occurred around 2500 BC on our third dimensional time line. This could be important for me because our history provides us some information about how things were in Egypt in that era, and my soul may need this specific information. However, when looking at time from a higher dimensional perspective, that lifetime is still going on. And any change I make in the present will, in some way, affect that lifetime.

To truly understand multi-dimensionality, we need to expand our ability to perceive non-linear time and be willing to delve deeply into the mysterious. We can utilize the concept of past lives as a linear way of searching for some of the dimensions of our soul – to understand them in a certain context – while at the same time keeping in mind that what we uncover is still going on.

While, these concepts tend to strain our brains, understanding them furthers the evolutionary process. We do not need to change physically to make the leap into expanded consciousness; our brains already contain the ability to do this. What needs to change instead is the limiting belief system that has prohibited us from using our whole brain. Spirit communicates to us through our right hemisphere and as more of us follow the dictates of our own Spirit which is urging us always to become more conscious, we will collectively make a shift into multi-dimensional consciousness. This is an interactive process between both sides of our brain.

Scientific development has brought us to the point where science can explain and support our full potential. Since culturally we have been taught to trust only that which can come through the left brain, this scientific information allows us to understand cognitively what prior to this point, we could access only through intuition. Science can now prove that we are energy beings. It shows us how our brain function has been unevenly developed and how to rectify that. It also provides us with information about time/space coordinates with mathematical theories that support multi-dimensionality and more expanded ways to look at time. Thus, we are given a wonderful bridge to travel from the limits of the old paradigm to the vast frontiers of the new.

Technology has also brought us to the point where the qualities we need to survive on this planet are profoundly different from what was needed before. The old model of competition which kept us separated and focused only on the goal, is dangerous for us now. To survive we need to cooperate with each other and to honor our interconnectedness. We know that whatever happens on one side of the globe will affect us all. We know polluted waters and polluted air do not remain at their source; they threaten all the air and water of the entire planet and this is a metaphor for all that happens on our Earth.

The skills we need in order to develop these new qualities and heal our planet cannot come from our left brains alone; we need to equally honor the right hemisphere's functions. Accurate interpretation of information relies not just on our logical abilities, but on our intuitive skills and our emotional acuity because information is easily manipulated. Moreover, as Dr. Larry Dossey points out in his book **RECOVERING THE SOUL: *A Scientific and Spiritual Search***, as we come to realize our minds are non-local, i.e. they are not limited to a physical location in the body but rather they are consciousness and thus part of the collective mind, "the world becomes a place of interaction and connection, not one of isolation and disjunction." Dossey understands that this awareness creates the potential for a new foundation for modern ethical and moral behavior, which calls for "a radical departure from the insane ways human beings and nation-states have chronically behaved toward each other." (p.7)

Physical strength is no longer needed for survival. A highly developed ability to understand and interpret information is. And not just verbal or written information, but symbolic information as well such as the information gleaned from others' energy fields. The right hemisphere of our brain intuitively understands this information, so it is essential that we strengthen our connection with this side of our brain. Then we need to be able to take our awareness and translate it through our left brains into effective communication. As we become more skilled at reading energy fields, speaking authentically becomes an even higher priority for survival. The most effective way to do this is to be able to speak from the heart. And in order to speak from one's heart, one must develop ways to know one's heart.

As we understand how energy works and as our understanding of our interconnectedness deepens, we realize how all parts affect the whole. Every one of us affects the overall energy field of the planet. The more we empower our Spirits, the more the human energy field on our planet will honor all living things. The less we empower our Spirits, the more at risk the planet becomes, both energetically and physically. Remember, the physical is simply a denser manifestation of energy. To clear ourselves energetically, we need to understand and have access to the multidimensional layers of our soul. In order to fully cleanse our energy field, we need to do more than clear our issues from this lifetime, because our energy field holds all other lifetimes as well. We are multidimensional beings, and therefore to fully heal we need to be working on multidimensional levels.

THE CLEARING

If you understand we are multidimensional, then it will make sense to you that we have numerous unhealed soul experiences in our energy field that need to be healed. Accessing the most highly developed aspects of our soul can allow this clearing to happen rapidly. Using the concept of fractals as explained in quantum physics, we have scientific theory to understand that there are mirrors of ourselves which exist simultaneously on numerous other planes. We can tap into the wisest and most loving of these fractal parts to help us with this process.

In my first book, ***Journey to Wholeness***, I provide a detailed method for clearing out emotional trauma from our childhoods and reclaiming our sense of self and Self. While any intervention helps the whole, this form of healing is primarily centered in our third-dimensional reality. The next step is to recognize the more complex journey. Our Self goes far beyond what we might have dared to imagine at the beginning of our healing path. We may have known there were wise parts, often called the "higher self," that needed to be integrated once the emotional healing had occurred, but few of us realized the depth of experience held in our souls. As we have become more conscious, we can see how these experiences impact our present lives, and we can also see that understanding their multidimensional nature is a primary step in the evolutionary process.

As we make the evolutionary leap, we are beginning to develop the ability to bring these experiences into conscious awareness, heal what needs to be healed and thus fully integrate our many parts. Fragments of our soul are scattered throughout the time lines in the universe, with each fragment having its own consciousness. To become fully conscious is to learn to be aware of the fragments, the magnificent parts as well as the unhealed ones. Then to embrace all of our parts emotionally so we feel them to be us. This will amplify our soul nature exponentially.

As we learn to understand time from a multidimensional perspective we realize the past, present and future happen simultaneously. There are an infinite number of timelines and so any future that we can imagine already exists somewhere. When we clear past pain and become fully empowered, we can choose which future we will live. Our job is to create the conscious intention and assert our conscious will to tap into that desired future.

When we allow ourselves to connect with our highest expression, we can go about the business of reclaiming the pieces of us that are dispersed throughout the time lines. As we do this, we can harness the helpful energies to strengthen our positive intent, while transforming or neutralizing the disempowering ones. **We have to do our emotional healing from this lifetime for this to be successful**. Then we can go on to reclaim and heal each disempowered part we hold in our soul which is impacting our present. As we reclaim these parts, we are able to identify what needs to be healed. This chapter teaches techniques that enable us to connect more deeply with our personal power to carry out this healing. We also need to claim the parts of our soul which hold the wisdom, beauty and talents which we need in order to fully carry out our sacred contracts.

The following exercise, Radiant Beings of Light, will begin to connect you with your highest potential: Remember to use your breath to take you into a meditative state.

Imagine for a moment that you become aware of living on another planet or star system. You realize this is place where social harmony has been achieved, personal empowerment is a given, and each individual knows the unique purpose they have to help the less developed parts of the Universe "catch up." Breathe deeply for a moment and experience yourself as this being; a radiant being of light, fully secure and therefore fully loving, who has immediate and continuous access to Divine wisdom. Let your breath flow through you, calming and centering you to move into this image. Keep breathing deeply until you begin to feel yourself as this radiant, fully conscious being.

Ask that anything in your energy field that is not congruent with this Higher Being, be cleared. If fear comes up, do your best to breathe through it, assuring yourself this will not bring you to the brink of insanity nor will it bring you to the brink of arrogance; rather it will fill you with love and clarity.

From this vantage point, you see that many people on the Earth are operating out of harmful extremes and are undergoing needless suffering. You may feel very sad as you notice this, because you know without a doubt, their pain is unnecessary. Because they have allowed themselves to be tricked into believing they do not have the power to create their reality, they have unconsciously created a reality where they allow themselves to be manipulated by forces that surround them. You can see the deepest work for these humans is to open their hearts, fill themselves with light and embrace their creative power. This, in turn, will serve to re-balance the earth and allow the Divine spark to be in ascendance. You can see with deep clarity that change needs to occur and that the time is ripe.

Realize that you have a human counterpart you can communicate with, a part of yourself who lives on the Earth. Because your Earth self is likely to be caught in the duality of the third dimension where so many are entrapped in fear, and because your Earth self is also likely to have become attached to some of this fear, you have an interesting dilemma: How do you communicate to your human self that not only is it safe, but deeply in your Self-interest to get out of the entrapment and open to this higher aspect of your soul?

As you as this higher dimensional being ponder this, you begin to send light, warmth and love to this human part of yourself. See this light, warmth and love begin to melt that part's resistance, relax that part's fear, and open the energetic field of your Earth self to horizons of unlimited possibility. Keep seeing yourself beaming this light filled with love to your human self. Notice how this feels. When you feel that this part of you is accepting the love and consciousness you are sending, imagine that you can breathe this human part into you, and you both can operate from that time forward from this higher place of co-consciousness.

This exercise can be used with each unhealed part of your soul that you uncover. The more frequently you can experience yourself as this radiant being, the more quickly you will be able to heal and integrate your soul fragments.

OBSERVING OUR RESISTANCE

The more I understand the human mind, the more amazed I become. It is an incredibly intricate and complex system. Ironically, it is based on very simple principles. Like computer language which is composed entirely of zeros and ones, our minds can take the source of creation, light (consciousness) and love, and far surpass the intelligence of any computer designed on this planet. We literally can create anything. Why then have we created the mess on Earth? What keeps us from activating our marvelous creative potential to create peace, abundance and harmony? Why are we so afraid?

As we understand the wondrous qualities of light, we also have to understand that light is contained by darkness. It is the dynamic of the Universe, the Yin/Yang: darkness contains light, light contains darkness. It is all part of the Divine hologram. In and of itself, this darkness will not be harmful. It is simply shadows, shadows which are a natural bi-product of light when it intersects with the material realms. But when we either fear the dark or seek to solidify and therefore magnify the world of shadows, we can create crystallizations of dark energy which we call evil.

Why would we choose this? What purpose does this serve? There are, of course many theories, but from my perspective, it is more like the story below.

Playing With the Dark

Once upon a time, a long time ago, we were very curious and wanted to explore more of life: the beautiful things in life and the dark or cruel things in life as well. We wanted to experience what power over others felt like. We wanted to become a malevolent God just to see what it was like, just because we could. In our innocence, we did not realize what we could potentially set in motion. We did not realize that some souls might get stuck there. They would disconnect from their Divine essence and become addicted to power, not caring who or what they harmed. Like alcoholics, the high they would feel from that power would become more important than anything else. Perhaps these souls became unstoppable since they would use any method to exert their influence.

Other souls became afraid of these Dark addicts. They felt it was their job to make it clear that Darkness was bad and was to be avoided at all costs. They then lost the ability to understand and truly recognize the dark. They could not integrate their darkness with their light because they had learned to believe their darkness meant they were bad. Instead, they projected it onto others.

This fed those addicted to the dark side of power. It actually made them stronger because when people who espoused to be of the Light became afraid of their own shadow and therefore denied their own shadow, they not only projected their shadow onto groups they did not understand or feared, they projected their shadow onto the Dark Seekers as well. People of the Light became very confused because without being able to see their shadow, they could not truly know themselves. This gave the dark forces more power.

As the Light Seekers became more afraid, they created little rituals to try to make them feel safer. Organized religion was used to help this process along. While there were people who knew the truth that is inherent in all religious paths, there was a belief that the masses would be vulnerable to this "dark" addiction. Like the temperance movement, all sorts of prohibitions were created. When these prohibitions were given more power than true prayer and/or meditation, people became even more removed from their Spirit. Those who focused on these prohibitions believing they were protecting the Light were actually creating more Dark. They were crippling their innate ability to create positive reality. They developed the belief that if they owned their true creative power, they would automatically misuse it. (to be continued)

This fear still exists in our collective consciousness and keeps many people from exploring their true abilities. It also keeps people in self-doubt and struggling with self-esteem issues because they are disconnected from their inner truth. The time is ripe now for change. We must write a happy ending to the story above. This is our evolutionary challenge: we must reclaim and integrate our power, knowing by doing so we heal ourselves and our world.

As we engage in this process, we periodically hit walls of fear that must be scaled if we are to successfully own our creative abilities and therefore come into full purpose and power. This is another reason self-observation is so essential. Take time to observe yourself. Experience yourself again as the evolved entity in the above exercise, and ask the following:

- *How and when do I allow myself to be drawn back into less empowered states?*
- *Do I give other people the power to deflate me like a balloon?*
- *Do I have a powerful/albeit unconscious system of putting negative judgments on myself?*
- *Am I afraid if I really see myself as this empowered multi-dimensional being, I will be ostracized, locked up or drugged into oblivion?*
- *Do I trust myself to put up clear and appropriate boundaries?*
- *What healthy ways do I have to protect myself?*

Spend some time pondering the above questions. Journal on them; dream on them. Clear your mind and meditate on them, then jot down what comes to you. If you do not yet feel empowered enough to set clear boundaries and in other ways protect yourself from others' judgments, there is some foundation work for you to do before you can go much further in this process.

More Shadow Work

As we learn how to notice when our hearts are open, and then learn how to keep them open even though we may feel angry, scared or sad, we will not misuse our power in a destructive way. This is the true difference between serving the Light and serving the Dark. We may inadvertently misuse power just being human, but Divine Consciousness will be honored as long as we are motivated by love.

One way to practice being openhearted is by thinking of a person who emotionally triggers you. Perhaps it is someone you feel anger toward and/or judgmental about. I suggest starting with someone easy who you might find irritating or who you feel competes with you, rather than someone who you feel has deeply wounded and /or betrayed you. Notice if you can literally soften your heart by placing warm hands over your heart chakra and beaming them love. Continue this process over a period of weeks or months. Once you can easily soften your heart to "irritating" people, find someone who has angered you more deeply, and practice this until you feel you have succeeded in being openhearted to them as well.

Once you have this skill well-developed, you are ready to do this with someone who has deeply violated you. This is to be done only after you know, on all levels, you are protected from them. From this place you can feel compassion without ever letting them violate you again. When we are able to do this, we begin to master the art of openhearted living and therefore minimize any likelihood of misusing our power or being the target for someone else's misuse of power. Be aware this must be an ongoing process. It is a well-known metaphysical reality that the "higher" you go, the farther you can fall. If we do not fully know ourselves but think we do, if we do not have ways of objectively observing ourselves, our egos may lead us astray.

It is important to stay in a state of gratitude, faith and love. Incorporate this into a daily ritual. Whenever you notice you feel openhearted; whenever you co-create more abundance, joy and opportunity, acknowledge your gratitude to the Divine. Gratitude flows from our hearts and incorporating this into our daily lives helps us stay attuned enough to our hearts to notice whether or not they are open that day. Be aware, as humans, this will fluctuate. If you notice that your heart is more closed down for a while, create an intention that you reconnect with love, and use whatever means you have at your disposal, whether journal-writing, prayer, yoga or any other technique that works for you, to shift this. We also need to stay aligned with Higher Guidance: that resonant state where we are plugged into Divine Source.

Think about what would help you stay in gratitude and Divine Resonance. Realize, of course, that we are human so this certainly does not mean we never have a nasty thought or angry feeling; rather we can observe them, keep our sense of humor about our own contradictions and send those thoughts and feelings, love. This is our shadow; we must learn to love it as much as we love our purity. Staying in gratitude is a simple process of looking for all the gifts we have in our lives and acknowledging these daily.

The same goes for surrendering to the wisdom of your Spirit or Divine Guidance. This can involve direct contact with other dimensional light beings or angels, or it can involve noticing who you bumped into the day before and what they said to you. It is through your awareness and attitude that you keep the resonance of the Divine humming in your life.

Keeping a journal on your process is another way to amplify your growth. It is important to record your resistance as well as your moments of gratitude, moments of ecstasy and moments of doubt. Write down the shadow areas you see and remember to send yourself love for your courage in facing your shadow. Then remember to beam love directly to your shadow.

Ask your fear to step forward and to speak to you. Remember that courage is being afraid and doing it anyway. Go ahead and do what you are afraid of. Speak your truth and see what happens. Share your desires and perceptions. Be a pioneer of the new world.

Going Places You May Hesitate to go

Part of our resistance to going into other dimensional parts of ourselves is the same resistance people have to going back to heal childhood trauma: sometimes we will tap into nightmarish experiences. While I do not believe we have to relive the nightmare to heal, there are some instances where we need to travel into the old experience in order to reclaim and heal those lost pieces of ourselves. To do this as painlessly as possible, I would suggest having a guide. There are many people, both professional therapists and alternative healers, who are able to do past life regressions which are a form of hypnotherapy, that take you "back" in time to other experiences your soul has had. Once you have the information from the regression, it is then necessary to release the old feelings and shift old beliefs. The help of a skilled therapist can be invaluable here.

As we work with and shift the themes from these other lives, we begin to profoundly change our current situation and current soul configuration. This healing changes the electro-magnetic charge of our aura so we can begin to create a much different reality. As this occurs, the "past life" also changes because it is occurring in the present as well. While again, this taxes our brain, what is most amazing to me is to realize the effect this transformed energy will have on the entire universe.

In preparation for accessing "unpleasant" experiences from other lifetimes, you might want to imagine your "worst nightmare." Look within yourself by meditating or journaling on what would be most difficult for you to integrate. What if you find yourself abusing children? How will you handle this? What if you participated in Nazi Germany? What if you were a cruel slave owner?

Conversely, what if you are that child who is being abused? The concentration camp victim? The slave? What if you were a passive bystander who, while horrified by the cruelty you saw, did nothing to intervene out of fear of retribution? What if you were a parent who allowed your child to be sacrificed to save your own skin? What if you were that child?

These types of themes exist for all of us. The older our soul, the more likely it is that we have had these experiences. It is essential to understand this in order to be ready to reclaim disparate parts of the Self. There is a tendency for people to want to explore "past lives" because they believe they were someone special, maybe even someone of historical significance. That may or may not be the case, but ultimately it is only the themes, beliefs, feelings and talents that are relevant. We are all part of each other, and all humans have the capacity for deep love and service as well as horrible cruelty and tyranny. The choice is ours. If we are not able to look at ourselves dispassionately both as perpetrators and as victims, then we are not ready to be fully whole.

It is not easy to give unconditional love to parts of the Self that are harming others, yet this is the energy needed to transform the negativity both in ourselves and in the larger world. Remember we are holographic. We contain the whole, all of it. Sending compassion and love to the cruel parts of ourselves, will shift the collective energy so that all of us who have perpetrated abuses begin to have the option of changing. Part of what keeps people stuck in a cycle of cruelty is a deep belief that they are unlovable. We need to send love to them. In no way does this justify their behavior; it simply gives them the opportunity to love themselves. When we really love ourselves, we become incapable of doing intentional harm. I believe this is the only strategy to eradicate cruelty from our world.

Sending love and compassion to the parts of ourselves that have experienced victimization is equally transformative, and for some just as difficult because self-loathing often accompanies victimization just as it does perpetration. As we learn to hold this love and compassion, we will experience a much greater degree of tolerance and compassion for all living beings.

Once we develop a level of comfort with the likeliness that as a soul, we have experienced the whole gamut of human possibilities, we are then ready to go into more specific experiences. The experiences we are most likely to access will be directly related to challenges that we have faced or are facing in our current life. If you have done a great deal of personal healing already in this life, and you feel stuck on something that no matter how much you work on it simply does not release, then this is an indication that going into other lifetimes may be necessary for a full resolution.

I had an extremely illuminating experience after I published my first book. I was in my late forties, had been working on personal growth for almost 30 years and had pretty well cleared my emotional field. My life was going well. I was in a loving long-term marriage, raising three wonderful children, and had a career that allowed me to serve others, help the world and make a substantial contribution to the economic well-being of our family. I was surrounded with good friends and a supportive community of like-minded people. Yet as soon as I published ***Journey to Wholeness***, I began to experience something I had never known before: fear of going out into the world, especially fear of public speaking.

I had given numerous workshops and presentations throughout my career, and had taught regularly at a community college always feeling very confident about my speaking abilities. But suddenly something shifted. When I was asked to do a short presentation at a local holistic fair which coincided with the publication of my book, and an even briefer presentation at Barnes & Noble for a book signing, intense fear arose. It became hard for me to prepare and the nervousness lasted right up to the time I began to speak.

To make things even more bizarre, when I went back to teaching that next fall, I could feel my gut tightening with anxiety as I neared the campus. It became very clear to me this fear was not about any experience I had in this lifetime.

I had been conscious of nervousness whenever I was with religious people who might see my spiritual views as heresy. I would joke with my friends about the "being-burned-at-the-stake" fear that so many strong women experience. One of my friends intuited part of my nervousness might have to do with fear that people who did not agree with me would project negative energy onto my family, and that my children, still young, might not know how to protect themselves. She suggested I could be holding myself back from going out in the world for fear of bringing harm to them.

A great irony here is that *Journey to Wholeness* is hardly controversial. While it is obviously built on a spiritual "new age" perspective, it is a self-help psychology book aligned with widely accepted psychological theories and based on years of successful practice. Nonetheless, it represented a potential beginning for me: one where I could go beyond my comfortable range of influence and open up the option of inspiring large groups of people into a healthier and more conscious way of life and I was terrified. Here I was, aligning more fully with my life purpose, and I was feeling paralyzed with fear.

Fear like this was a new experience for me, and it took me completely by surprise. While I am not likely to bungee jump or sky dive, taking personal risks to promote my inner growth had been easy for me. I had never taken the path of choosing safety or security over growth, and deeply valued this in myself. I also credited my ability to create such a positive life for myself to this quality. So what in the world was going on here?

Two things became obvious to me: first that it was time for me to learn about this type and intensity of fear, thus enabling me to help others with fear more effectively; and second, I realized if I was going to break through this fear, I would need to look beyond this lifetime. I was certainly open to looking at the influences of other lifetimes. I had explored them in many ways, including processing my memories with friends to help identify their psychological significance and see how their themes were showing up in my current incarnation. But this was different because the emotion was so strong.

I created a conscious intention to remember, and began to intuit a relevant lifetime. I had a sense that it originated in the Mediterranean: I saw myself speaking out and being thrown in a dungeon. I could feel my outrage. I also felt that I was ultimately executed and probably not very humanely. I worked on this on my own for a while. I began to feel more hopeful although the fear had not diminished. After a few months, I went to see a woman who was a spiritual channel. I had consulted her before and felt that she was bringing in high quality information. During the channeling, I asked for more information about that lifetime. I was told that this took place in Greece just when the city/states were beginning to form. I had been speaking out against the government or powers that be and ultimately was arrested and executed. It was suggested that I have a past life regression so I could resolve what remained unhealed from that lifetime.

In the regression, I realized the following: I was born into a peaceful, loving and spiritually evolved village in the hills. My family was well-respected in that community and I had an important place as a poet or seer. As a young woman, I journeyed with my husband to one of the cities. I became appalled at what I witnessed, feeling that the political group in power was intent on disconnecting the people from their own inner wisdom in order to politically dominate them. People were falling for it. I told my husband we had to move there because my mission was to help counteract this influence. I can almost see the house we lived in. It had a rather large front yard. For the next 10 years, while I gave birth to and was raising our three children, I would regularly go out into my yard where large groups of townspeople would gather to hear me speak. I was appreciated and felt myself loved by them. The government seemed to turn a deaf ear.

Then one evening, just after my husband had left on a visit to our old village, the authorities came for me. They ripped me away from my children, including a young baby that was still nursing, and threw me into this dungeon. I was livid. I was also sick with worry about my children. I was afraid the neighbors would abandon them out of fear of reprisal, and for some reason I did not trust that my husband would be able to get to them without being harmed himself. I railed and cursed and screamed until I collapsed in a state of resentment and hopelessness, feeling total powerlessness and deep guilt for jeopardizing the well-being of my children.

I was executed fairly quickly and have a memory of looking into the crowd of people who had gathered, trying to make eye contact with them while feeling betrayed and accusatory. No one would look me in the eye. I do not remember how I died. I do know, however, that after I crossed over, I was still in a state of fury and guilt. I was convinced that I had traumatized my children and had endangered my husband because I believed he would be killed if he tried to return. I also believed I should never have taken on this mission. Best I could tell, my emotional state was so distraught that I was not able to really observe what happened to my family after my death. I had left my physical body still harboring a belief that I had done great harm to those young souls entrusted in my care and I feared ever speaking out in public again. In fact, I made a vow that I would hold myself back from then on.

While the experience in the dungeon was not pleasant to return to, I was able to see the emotions while feeling them at the same time. Because it was not the lifetime I was currently in and because I knew in the deepest reaches of my soul it was absolutely necessary for me to go back there in order to move forward on my Path, it was not really a painful experience. However, without the knowledge and the option of releasing my pent up feelings of rage and guilt, shifting the beliefs I had formed from this experience and breaking through the terror that had developed about speaking my truth, it would have been next to impossible for me to utilize my full potential in my present life. So while it is natural for us to hesitate reliving old pain in this life or others, when we go back with the intent of reclaiming our full selves, any difficulty we encounter is more than compensated for.

The fear has not fully disappeared for me although I have a much greater handle on it. Since uncovering that particular lifetime, I have uncovered many less dramatic lifetimes where I was harmed or scorned for speaking and writing spiritual truth. It is interesting that this intense fear remained hidden until I published my first book. It took something that concrete for me to realize on an emotional level that I had the potential for reaching large numbers of people. It was then that I could face and begin to work through my feelings of vulnerability when confronted with those who disagreed with my world view. The very act of publishing was a sign, on a deep soul level that I was ready to deal with and transform the old wounds in order to fully resolve them in this lifetime.

I encourage you to uncover and resolve similar experiences of your own soul. Notice as you walk through your day-to-day life if intense feelings surface which you cannot track to the present situation. These are invaluable signals. As you notice them, first explore the possibility that they are from experiences which occurred earlier in your present life – remember we are holograms so any lifetime intervention affects all the others. If you cannot find anything in this lifetime, or what you do uncover does not release the feelings, then it is likely you will have to go to other lifetimes.

The exception to this is repressed memories from trauma, especially sexual abuse. While it is beyond the scope of this book to delve into this, be aware it is common to repress memories in traumatic situations. If you suspect childhood trauma, if you have gaps in your memory from your childhood, it would be a good idea to explore this possibility first, rather than looking into other lifetimes for the source of any emotional turmoil you are experiencing. If after examining your current lifetime carefully, you cannot find anything of substance which would explain the intensity of your emotional response, then I urge you to explore your soul memories from other lifetimes.

Remember, the important signal is your emotional response. Once you notice it, you can go deeper to examine what is triggering this. In order for this to work, your emotional field needs to be cleared enough so you are in touch with your feelings. If you are numb from your childhood, skilled therapy can help you to develop the ability to feel deeply. Once you can feel deeply, then you can trust your feelings to direct you in the process of reclaiming and transforming wounded aspects of your soul.

Other signals that you may need to look into other lifetimes are the themes which have followed you throughout your life. For instance, a client of mine was dealing with a lifelong struggle of feeling different and excluded from whatever groups she was participating in. She was a bright, attractive young woman with good social skills and a pleasing personality. There was no obvious reason for these feelings. Her family of origin, while not perfect, was reasonably healthy, but placed a high criterion on intellectual banter. As the youngest child, she was not able to engage in conversation like her older siblings could, and being more of an emotional than intellectual person, she began to feel alienated in her family. Other events in her childhood solidified the belief that she simply did not fit in. This began to repeat itself in adulthood. As we went into a deeper analysis of what was going on, it became clear to both of us that certain experiences from other lifetimes were at play here because her childhood experiences were simply not intense enough to be producing the degree of alienation she often felt.

Through our process and through information she was given from other channels, we began to piece together how this theme materialized in her psyche. We realized that she secretly and unconsciously used these "exclusionary" experiences as proof of some sort of moral and spiritual superiority directly related to experiences she had in other lifetimes. Once awareness about this surfaced, she now was empowered to shift this deeply ingrained soul pattern. Without the benefit of knowing the other lifetime scenarios, it would have been extremely difficult, if not impossible, to truly break through this pattern of alienation.

Remember, the important signal is your awareness of having an emotional response which is not congruent with actual events in your life and is not an accumulation of unexpressed emotions from prior experiences in this lifetime. Once you recognize the signal, the next step is to discover what evoked it and then set about finding ways to heal it so you can be free of the pattern.

Another example of people getting signals of past life trauma comes from a member of a training group I was leading. This man mentioned that he would often get a strange sensation near his throat. This sensation seemed to occur spontaneously but was linked to feeling tense. Whenever the sensation occurred, he felt compelled to put his hands or his collar up around his neck to calm the sensation. When asked when he first developed this, he told of reading a Prince Valiant comic strip when he was twelve. In this particular strip, people were ambushing the Prince and had shot a poison arrow directly at his throat. Prince Valiant was wearing a necklace with a gold coin and the coin protected him from being pierced by the arrow. This left such an impression on this man, that from that moment on he would periodically experience the throat sensation.

When he told this story, I immediately felt this had to do with a past life experience. This group was not made up of people who I knew to be particularly open to that idea, so I kept my intuition to myself. As the discussion continued, however, this man first joked and later confided that he felt there might be a past life connection. In fact a psychic had told him he had been a Viking and had been hanged. It's interesting that Prince Valiant was Prince of Norway. While there were issues going on for this man at age twelve that made it difficult for him to express his truth and therefore could have created some constriction in the throat chakra, I suspect he will only get free from that sensation once he has worked through his other lifetime issues.

If you have worked hard in therapy with a good healer and still have not shifted your life, this may be another signal of your need to explore other lifetimes. Remember, we are connected energetically to all parts of our multi-dimensional soul. All of these parts are currently existing somewhere in time and space. If there is intense and negative energetic entanglements which parts of you are concurrently experiencing in other dimensions, breaking these entanglements could demand going to the source. A skilled and trustworthy energy worker can be invaluable here, as well as a psychic or channel who has strong abilities to see what other lifetimes may be currently impacting you.

TECHNIQUES FOR HEALING OUR MULTIDIMENSIONAL SELVES

It is difficult to heal parts of ourselves we do not know exist. There is somewhat of a paradox here. Since we are holographic, any healing we do helps all parts of ourselves whether we are conscious of them or not. On the other hand, it seems what remains unconscious gets only a bit of residual healing. If deeply wounded parts are still operating outside of our awareness, then the residual healing is not going to have much of an impact; certainly not enough to empower us to make that evolutionary shift. Therefore, to fully heal, we need to collect information about ourselves in other lifetimes or dimensions.

There are many ways to do this and I suspect utilizing a combination of different methods is optimum. I have mentioned several in passing. Besides our own intuitive flashes, getting readings from psychics, intuitives or channelers who are skilled in this area can be very helpful. As with any guidance or advice, I would encourage you to take it seriously only if it resonates with you. Let your intuition guide you. People skilled in reading the Akashic Records also are a good resource. Many with this skill advertise, especially in big cities; however I would rely more on the experiences of friends, acquaintances, recommendations from healers you have worked with, and synchronicities. An example of a noteworthy synchronicity would be if you are feeling a desire to consult with a channel or intuitive to collect more information about other lifetimes, and just after deciding this, you run into a friend or acquaintance who spontaneously refers to a person with this skill. Pay attention to experiences like this. No doubt, it is a sign this is the person for you to see.

You can also find a good hypnotherapist or other healing practitioners who do past life regressions. In these regressions, you are guided into a mild trance state and led "back" to pre-birth experiences. There are numerous ways to do past life regressions and they are relatively easy and generally successful. The problem is, if you do not have a focus on a particular lifetime or at least on a particular issue, you may hop through the timeline to something less important. So it is good to begin the regression with a clear intention if you want to get the most relevant information.

Another way to gather the information is a technique I use with my clients. I generally use this when we are working on an issue which has a large resonance – larger than anything we have uncovered in this lifetime. If the client is open, I will ask them if they have any sense or any flashes of a story from another life which might relate to our work. I stress that it is not all that important to be 100% literal. What is important is to be metaphorically accurate. This means having the wrong place or time period or name is considerably less important than uncovering an accurate psychological dynamic which corresponds to what is going on in this lifetime. The psychological dynamic would be primarily made up of two parts: The challenging emotional content involved in the experience: fear, rage, guilt, shame, joy; and equally important: The belief system created or reinforced from this experience. I have included the feeling of joy because even though our focus right now is to seek out the still-wounded parts, we will soon be talking about multi-dimensional parts of ourselves that hold beauty, talents and gifts to which we not yet fully connected.

Sometimes I have clients create the "story" while in session. Other times, I suggest they go home, write it out, and then bring it back and we explore it together. When they tell me the "story," I will have them do so in the first person, present tense as if they are currently experiencing it. Because I am clairsentient, (in other words, I get kinesthetic sensations about other people's emotions,) I pay close attention to the feelings being transmitted during the retelling of their experiences. This gives me an indication of the authenticity of the story because I can directly observe if the feelings are congruent with what is being shared. It also shows me what feelings need to be identified, expressed, released and transformed. Once that is done, we can then look for the belief system inherent in the experience and work at transforming it.

As an example, if a client is in touch with a lifetime where they were victimized, and I sense they are feeling guilt, this is an immediate sign to me they need to get in touch with their rage at being violated in order to release the feelings associated with self-blame. It also shows me they need to transform the belief they are bad or unworthy. This is the same method one would use to work through an early trauma in this lifetime; in fact, working with and healing one's inner children is essentially no different than healing other dimensional parts of the self. Other dimensional selves will have to express their anger at those who treated them unfairly and/or disrespectfully, just as abused or traumatized inner children need to do. And just as wholeness is achieved in this lifetime when we are able to glean the "gift" in all our experiences no matter how terrible they may be, a more profound level of wholeness is achieved when we are ready to glean the soul growth from the experiences of our multidimensional parts.

Once the feelings are expressed and released, we feel empowered rather than victimized. This releases us from victim-consciousness at a deeper level, and opens us to understanding the deeper meaning of the experience from a new perspective. It also allows us to identify any inaccurate beliefs that might have formed from these experiences so that we can transform them.

Another step in resolving other-dimensional trauma which corresponds to resolving trauma in this lifetime is the need to recover complete memory. Renee Frederickson, author of ***REPRESSED MEMORIES: A Journey to Recovery from Sexual Abuse*** speaks to the necessity of recapturing the entire memory of the experience for full healing is to occur. By "entire memory," she means what happened just before, during and just following the abuse. She explains the reason for this is "the unconscious always operates in present tense" (p.117). This means if you do not get to what happened after the abusive episode, the client unconsciously feels as if the abuse is still happening. I believe this is true of other-dimensional experiences as well. In the past life I spoke of earlier, I was stuck in the millisecond following my death, and it was this which was negatively affecting my ability to speak out publicly in my present life.

An interesting thing happened during my own past life regression. The intuitive I was working with was not a trained therapist, nor had she ever heard of Renee Frederickson. Still she knew to ask me what happened after my execution. When I went forward on that timeline, I was surprised to find that my husband did indeed return for our children and got them to safety. The news had traveled to our village while he was visiting. He was able to locate our children and sneak into the city in the middle of the night to take them safely back to our village. I still well up with tears when I see my children back in the loving energy of my old community. There they are loved, comforted, protected and healed, and while I know they miss me terribly, they are able to lead good lives. The emotional intensity of this vision astounds me. In my present lifetime I have never known a place which resembles the energy of this village, and yet I can feel, see and hear exactly what my children are experiencing there. Though, during the regression, I could still feel outrage at the way I was treated and the potential harm which could have befallen them, I could now work my way through the stuck feelings more effectively.

Was this "happy ending" real? I can only guess. I trust that it was because of the emotional response I had. I feel that my husband in this lifetime is the same soul as my husband then. Certainly, his nature and the feeling in our relationship are the same. When I told him about this part of the regression and my interpretation, we both laughed because it was typical of me not to realize he would come through and figure out a way to save our children. Even after more than 20 years together in our current lifetime, I would feel surprised each time he would come to the fore whenever the children or I would need him, even though he always did. I had carried a theme that I could not count on men, amplified by the messages I received from my mother this time around. While my experience in my marriage was shifting that theme, I do not think it fully disappeared until I recovered these memories.

If the ending had not been happy, reclaiming consciousness of what ensued would still lead to a resolution. Remember, the primary issue is not just remembering the occurrence, but to process the emotions and transform dysfunctional beliefs from the traumatic event so it no longer feels like it is still going on. Bringing the story into awareness allows the crisis to end. Even if my children had not been rescued, the crisis would eventually have passed. They would have managed on some level to cope or to cross over. Either way their souls would have survived.

To fully empower our Spirit, we need to be able to find the parts of ourselves till stuck in our old wounds. Obviously, as multidimensional beings, this means intervening at various points in a timeline which expands far beyond the scope of our present life. The more we are able to find these parts of our soul, the freer we can become to create a positive reality in the here and now.

We cannot clear our energy field completely if some part of the soul is still operating within a paradigm based on wounding. Wounding promotes feelings of victimization which if not worked through, attract more victimization. So create an intention and begin the process to get "unstuck" in all dimensions. Remember to stay open to allowing your own creative and inner healing process to provide you with additional ways to do this.

More Suggestions for Multidimensional Healing

If you are already in touch with experiences from other lifetimes which still need healing, you may wish to write them down. Leave space under each of them for additional writing. If you know of several, choose the ones that feel most relevant. Next go over what you have written, taking time in each lifetime to breathe into character and feel what it is like to be there. Use the present tense whether you are writing or doing this in your head. As an example, if you have uncovered an ancient Egyptian lifetime, you might begin with something like:

"I am now in Egypt at the time of the ___ Dynasty. As I look around, this is what I see....... The people who are with me are .... They are responding to me in the following way:....... My relationship to these people is....... Presently, this begins to happen to me........... I am feeling........"

Continue this process, going through whatever scene you can remember. Then write about what happens just before the scene and what is happening just afterwards. If you do not know exactly where you are or when, just skip that part. Remember to focus on how you are feeling, as well as on what beliefs are being developed and reinforced from this experience. Once you have finished with each lifetime, jot down what you have discovered. Include the nature of the wounding, the feelings associated with the wounding, and what conclusions you are drawing about yourself, other people, life on this planet, and the nature of reality.

Depending on how much information you are already privy to, you may wish to spend several weeks processing the feelings and beliefs for each lifetime beginning with whichever one you are most drawn to. As you process these different lifetimes, pay attention to who you were. These are parts of yourself you will need to reclaim. Visualize going to these parts, validating their feelings, and then help them express and release the feelings they are still holding.

Work with each part until you feel you have helped them transform the wounding experience. Remember to continuously send love while you are going through this process. This is true for "abusive" parts as well as "victimized" parts: they are both wounded. When you feel a sense of completion, imagine putting your arms around each part that is now healed and open to your loving energy. Envelop them with love and allow them to become a part of your present self. Go through this with all the significant "remembered" parts. If you get stuck or simply want a guide, see a transpersonal therapist and/or a skilled energy worker to help guide you and clear your field.

Again, I would strongly recommend you first heal the wounds you have from your current life. Once this has occurred, you are free to move into deep multidimensional healing. The danger of working multidimensionally before you clear this lifetime is falling into illusion and emotional avoidance. The pain of one's present life is generally more pronounced and therefore it is tempting for some people to go into more metaphysical realms as a way to avoid the important emotional work of the here-and-now self.

Once you have completed the process of transforming these wounded selves from this life and others, the energetic resonance of your Divine Self can shine through far more congruently and far more brilliantly. You have completed the shamanic journey of calling back the traumatized parts of the soul. The next step is to call back the multidimensional parts of ourselves which hold the higher resonances of love and enlightenment. Until we do our current life healing, we have less access to these parts and less ability to bring them into our consciousness and integrate them in a healthy way. Once we have done our healing, not only will our access to these parts be more authentic, we will have also created a vibratory field that allows us to magnetize and then integrate these parts in profoundly exciting, satisfying and globally enhancing ways. We will be activating the energy which can bring untold joy into our lives and simultaneously help raise the resonance of the entire planet, drawing in more light for every living thing.

Welcoming Our Magnificence

One of the most profound ironies of human existence is how difficult it is for us to accept our own Divinity. In the West, we have been programmed to believe that we are sinful and therefore if we accept the "God" within, we will use this for negative ends. Through this religious perspective, we are conditioned to want to stay children, dependent on an external God who we like to see as stronger, wiser, smarter, and infinitely more pure. We believe that if we do what we have been told God wants us to do, and refrain from what "He" does not want us to do, we are good. If not, we are bad. We are thus free from thinking and taking responsibility for ourselves.

Those who do not "buy into" the religious control often like to imagine they are pure intellect – negating the spiritual as superstition. In both these scenarios, we stay disconnected from our essence and therefore unable to claim our true magnificence. This creates a collective self-esteem issue, because we are not able to trust our intuitive guidance. This dynamic also sets us up to be easily controlled. As I have said in many different ways in this book, people who are connected to their Spirits, to their core, cannot be manipulated; people who are disconnected from Spirit, can.

As we reconnect, we embrace self-responsibility in a new way. Rather than viewing it as something that will make us feel over-burdened, we now can see responsibility as the ability to take charge of our life and rely on our inner resourcefulness and creativity. As we do this, we actually are able to have more fun and to take life less seriously. When we are taking full responsibility, we can simply visualize how we want our life to be. What is asked then is that we do the inner work to clear any blocks that prevent us from creating this and that we transform obstacles into challenges, which we then meet.

Be aware, however, that we need to commit to being accountable in order for this to work. That means we have to keep our commitments to ourselves and to others. If I tell myself I will exercise daily, then I need to take this seriously. If I find I am not able to follow through, then I need to look at what is going on and what will help me do this successfully. Even if it takes a year, I need to stay true to this commitment I have made for myself. Carolyn Myss says in ***Anatomy of the Spirit*** that we do harm to our solar plexus chakra, the seat of our personal power and integrity, if we do not keep our word, and that includes our word to ourselves.

Becoming fully responsible also means that we stop hiding our power and wisdom by acting like others know more than we do when intuitively we know this is not true. We need to be willing to make mistakes and then learn from them while giving ourselves credit for being able to take risks.

We are ready as a species to bring in all the parts which will let us be fully in charge of ourselves, including our God/Goddess part, the part that holds our creative magic. We are well-informed and well-aware. If we stay true to ourselves, we will always choose the commitment of doing no harm on any level because we know that not only are we all One, but that this commitment keeps our heart open, and there is no better feeling than that. As we make this consistent in our lives, we become infinitely trustworthy.

In order to insure that we do not inadvertently cause harm by becoming unconscious or by going into denial, I encourage you to focus on the following:

1. ***Pay attention to your heart and to how loving you feel at any given moment.***
2. ***Look at the outer world as a mirror of what is occurring within and if you do not like something, work on shifting it inside yourself (more about this in the next chapter).***
3. ***Stay committed to on-going self-observation to detect when your ego is starting to take over, and then do what you need to reverse this.***
4. ***Know that you are not perfect; you are a work in progress and if you mess up you always get another chance.***
5. ***Sometimes you just have to take the leap and jump out of your comfort zone.***

The more we do this in our lives, the more empowered and hopeful we become. While fears come with the territory when we are engaging in this type of growth, they can co-exist with our magnificence; we just need to not let them hold us back.

Each of us has many magnificent parts floating around in the Universe. They are the creative and Creator parts of us. They may be artistic geniuses or master gardeners or ingenious scientists. They may be wise parts, parts which know the answers to many of the questions about the mystery of our existence. There are awesomely loving parts of ourselves; those radiant beings whose hearts overflow with the sweetest love imaginable. There are wonderfully efficient and effective parts of us who strategize and implement with ease. There are the inspiring and healing parts of ourselves, whose transformative energy resonates at frequencies we can barely fathom. They exist in many dimensions and on many timelines. The complexity of our true nature defies the ability of our logical brain; in order to comprehend these concepts, we must instead look to the gifts of our intuitive mind.

The exercise which follows will help you access this.

Breathe deeply and allow yourself to enter a meditative state. Begin to call in each of these special parts: First ask for your genius self, that cleverest part of you who can create brilliant innovations and solutions. Let your consciousness rise to your higher chakras and extend out into the Universe enabling you to find this part. Notice what s/he looks like, sounds like, feels like. Maybe this part will have fragrance as well. Just let images float into your mind. Your genius self may be a different gender, a different age, even a different species than your human self. As this part appears, notice what areas this part excels in. If this is not clear, then ask. Notice the flair with which s/he expresses those wonderful ingenious talents. Then ask this part how they can best help you in your life. Visualize this happening, and jot down the information you are gathering.

Next, call out to your wisest part. Let this part appear to you from wherever s/he is presently residing. As with the genius-self, see, hear and feel this wise part. Notice what it is like for you to be around this kind of wisdom. Then allow yourself to realize this is a part of you. Notice how it feels to have such easy access to this wisdom. Ask this part a question. Listen and watch for your answer. Jot down your experience.

Go on to claim that loving-self which is also floating out somewhere in the Universe. This self radiates the most incredible unconditional love, love that emanates from its entire being. Feel this part shining love on you. Breathe this in through your heart and feel it expand. Take a few minutes and exchange love with this being, with this part of yourself, still breathing in their love and breathing your love for them through your expanded heart. Feel yourself bathed in this love. Then begin to bring this being into yourself and see yourself walking through your life with this loving heart.

Next call forth your strategist – the most masterful part of yourself, a part who knows how to accomplish any task with skill and ease. See, hear and feel this part. Give this part an example of something you wish to do, and let them explain to you the most effective way to do this. Realize again, you can integrate this part within you and utilize this infinitely skillful approach to accomplish anything you seek.

And finally, call in your transformer self – the part of you who can activate the highest levels of healing or transforming energy. This part might take your breath away once you locate him or her. This part is God-Light, able to permeate any level of matter and create radiant health and well-being. He or she will carry a unique set of techniques which you will soon be able to access once you welcome this part as you. Collect as much information as you are able to about this part. And then allow yourself to feel him or her work on you and activate more health throughout your body, mind and spirit. Some of you will feel this vibrationally; others will see the radiant waves and healing images and still others of you will hear the resonant healing tones. After the healing work, ask that this part begin to integrate into you as well.

Understand, of course, that while a simple visualization will not bring full discovery and immediate integration of these special parts, it will set this process in motion. Also know you may identify other parts; parts I have not thought of. Use your own creativity and inspiration here. For some of you this process of discovery and integration may feel easy; for others the concepts may currently be too foreign to work with. Let yourself be where you are. Remember we are all magnificent, and all those amazing parts of ourselves do exist somewhere in the Universe. They are waiting for us to call them home. Any feeling or inkling you can get of this begins to bring you closer.

THE JOY OF WHOLENESS

In addition to these magnificent parts, we all have a High or Divine Self: the fully awakened part of us. This is the part Jane Roberts called the oversoul in her ***Oversoul Seven*** books. The evolution which is now at hand gives us the opportunity to become our Divine Selves. While I do not know if we will be able to sustain this continuously, what I do know is we have the ability to see out through the eyes of this Self and to observe and transform the other parts of ourselves from this new perspective.

Earlier in the chapter I suggested seeing yourself as a Radiant Light Being and looking at your life from this perspective. This is a good metaphor for your Divine Self. This Self contains all the parts from the "magnificence" exercise and more. So, return to that image.

Imagine you are observing yourself through the eyes of this radiant being as you get up in the morning, as you go about your daily activity. Notice how you interact with people in your life. Notice if you feel your earth life is aligned with your soul; notice if you feel your activities are aligned with the well-being of the planet. Pay attention to what you love about yourself; Notice where you feel dissatisfied with yourself. As this Radiant Being, go into your heart center and beam your Earth self with unconditional love and acceptance.

Observe yourself in other lifetimes. Imagine lifetimes when you are behaving cruelly and/or ignorantly and then beam love to those parts with that radiant heart love. Imagine lives when you were victimized or cowardly – again repeat the process. If you have no conscious recollection or information, imagine your different parts in different historical times acting out the full spectrum of human experience, and then send them all this love.

Notice how joyful it is for all your parts to feel this love... let yourself bask in this feeling.

Now begin to see those lifetimes where you developed marvelous abilities: where you knew how to heal others, where you could communicate with the trees, where you could sing like the angels and create poetry that opened the hearts of all who heard it. See the parts who dedicated their lives to Spirit; the parts that were remarkably courageous, the parts that were brilliant and innovative. (if you have no conscious content, you might want to take time to write out 6 or 7 "fictional" parts of yourself.) Let your imagination run wild; whether you actually uncover literal lifetimes or simply metaphoric selves is not really important.

Breathe deeply and strengthen your connection to your Divine Self, to this Radiant Light Being. As this Radiant Being, create a beautiful hall, a magnificent wooded grove or some other setting that you associate with beauty and well-being. Call in and greet each of your parts, from the most undeveloped to the most remarkable. As they step forward, one at a time, show them your love and appreciation.

Remember even the most negative of your parts has redeeming qualities – qualities which you can now use in a positive way. A brutal torturer may have creativity. A child abuser may have a way with words. No matter how horrible a part is, if they are an expression of you, they have some aspects of light within them. So as you greet each part, honor something of good in them. Imagine doing this with the sweet gentle firmness of the all-loving parent. Let the negative parts know you are there to help transform them. You can help them take responsibility for any harmful behavior and then to really change.

Fill that hall or grove with your radiance and notice how it affects all the parts who are there. Imagine that you can spread your great arms and draw them together in a loving embrace. Breathe in this feeling. Let your being vibrate with the sweetness of this love. As you embrace all of your multi-dimensional parts, as you feel that unconditional love and acceptance, notice how this vibrates through your radiant light body. Notice how this vibrates through your Earth body. Notice how this vibrates through every cell in every piece of you. Feel this ecstasy.

DAILY LIFE

We are all capable of living with intention. This means we are all capable of living the life we want. The more we have integrated the multidimensional parts of our soul, the more able we are to magnetize and energize our intentions. When we are in alignment with our soul, it is natural for us to create intention that serves the greater good rather than the needs of our egos. If what we consciously desire is not aligned with our soul's optimum development, we will not feel fulfilled and may have to face difficult challenges. This is because the intention of our Spirit and the needs of our soul will ultimately win out. Thus, if I have a conscious intention to be wealthy, but do not stipulate that it come to me aligned with my soul's integrity, I can draw the money, but might have to go through a challenging illness, or experience losing people or things I deeply value, or find myself in ongoing relationship struggles. These experiences are my Spirit's way of waking me up to the growth that is still needed.

We also need to remember the power of unconscious intention. When consciously magnetizing, we need to ask that any part of our unconscious which might have a different agenda, come forward. As stated earlier in this book, any intention which comes from negative beliefs about the self or from unexpressed pain threatens to undermine our highest good. It is therefore important to always "check in" with your unconscious to see what still needs to come into awareness. Realize you are, and always have been, fully in charge of your life. Now that you have access to heretofore unconscious territory, you can utilize this power by allowing your Spirit to lead in a way which promotes individual as well as collective well-being. The following visualization will help.

Envision your Spirit fully in charge of your life. Can you allow yourself to know with every cell in your body that everything you are experiencing is a choice of your own creation? Take a moment and breathe into this. Let this concept come through your breath and reach and energize all your cells. Let yourself tingle with this energy. Feel the empowerment from your solar plexus and the joy from your heart. What do you notice? Are you calmed? Are you scared? Are you relieved? Are you excited? Do you have several contradictory responses at one time? Do you feel empowered to utilize your magnificence, to shine your Light? Do you feel empowered to encourage others to shine theirs? Jot down your responses.

See your life exactly as it is at this present moment. Do you now understand why you have created it to be this way? If there are some things in your life that still do not make sense to you from this perspective, write them down. They are signals to you that there is still unconscious intention to explore. As you understand why you have created difficult situations in your life, you can become aware of what you need to do to meet the challenges of these situations and shift the beliefs which create them.

Now, see your life exactly the way you want it to be. Take some time and go into detail. Notice how you feel when you wake up in the morning. Notice what your surroundings look and feel like. Notice what you are saying to yourself about your day. See yourself going through a morning ritual of self-care, prayer and exercise. Create this any way you wish. See yourself connecting with Divine energy and projecting your magnificence forward into your day. Notice your activities and your interactions with people from this perspective. How do you feel? How does your life look to you? How does the world look to you? What are you saying to others, and what is the energy behind your words? How does your energy field affect those around you?

Notice yourself in the evening. Bask in the serenity of having lived your day in alignment with your Spirit. Feel gratitude for all that has happened and all you have learned. Experience yourself as fully peaceful and relaxed, and imagine sending this energy out to the entire planet.

In looking over your day from this perspective, you begin to anchor your ability to integrate the full power of your multidimensional soul into all your relationships and activities. You begin to operate out of a higher dimensional vision. You raise your frequency as well as the frequency of the planet. We all have the capacity to do this. It takes clearing, focus and practice. So do your best to put this into operation in your life.

The well-being of our planet, the well-being of our species depends on our activating courage and utilizing our full abilities. As we understand and accept the multidimensionality of our soul, emotionally as well as intellectually, we understand the remarkable amount of potential we have. The more we integrate this, the more we step into this next stage of our evolution.

PART TWO

7: CREATING EVOLVED RELATIONSHIPS

Evolved relationships are relationships based on unconditional love and mutual respect. These relationships feed our spirit and promote our growth. They help us to hone our ability for honest self-assessment and honest expression. They appreciate and honor our uniqueness and nourish our essence. They ask us to change only when that change promotes positive personal growth. Evolved relationships, by their definition are beneficial to all involved.

As we heal our individual emotional issues enough to open our hearts and shift our energy field, the quality of all our relationships begins to shift. However this is not a linear process. We may have made a quantum leap in our personal growth and find ourselves still attracting and engaging in relationships that are reflecting our old dysfunctional patterns. This is both the beauty and challenge of creating intimacy with others. It is through these connections that we get to refine our growth and dig out deeply hidden parts of ourselves that need transforming because some aspects of ourselves will only surface in the context of close relationships.

Anything unhealed in our own energy field will draw its unhealed complement in an outer relationship. This manifests most dramatically but by no means exclusively, in romantic relationships. In rare cases, people who have not healed old wounds are still able to manifest a fairly healthy primary relationship, but they will find themselves working with their wounding in other forms: work, siblings, friendships, etc. Usually though, it is close family relationships, our sexual partners, our children and parents, where we magnetize our most challenging lessons.

Therapists have long known that any unmet emotional need within one person is likely to draw to them a person with the same unmet need. Typically that need is operating in an opposite and complementary way. Thus, if you have one person who holds the belief they are unworthy and can only be okay if they are care-taking someone else, they will be drawn to another equally insecure person who believes they will only be okay if they can get their partner to take care of them. Since beliefs of our unworthiness can only be healed from within, both partners will ultimately feel disappointed and find that instead of healing through this relationship, they become entangled in a deeply painful dynamic.

As we develop a deeper understanding of the way our energy field interacts with another's, we begin to understand how and who we magnetize into our life. This transforms our view of relationships and gives us more power to advert, or at least shorten the duration of unhealthy entanglements. It also shows us areas where we need to take responsibility for ourselves and heal at a deeper level. Since we are all energetically connected, there is nothing accidental about who we draw to us, or who puts us off. Rather we see how we are continuously getting and responding to electromagnetic signals sent out from another person's field. We also see that our response to those signals is connected to what is going on in our own energy field. This is true for all of our personal relationships: we choose friends, lovers and life partners based on the interconnections and interactions in our energy fields.

The way this works can take several forms. There are many people who we may think are nice, attractive, and intelligent for instance, but we are not drawn to them as friends or romantic partners. This is because there is not the magnetic resonance needed to draw us closer together. It may be we are put off by some disharmony in this person's field; or conversely, we may have unmet needs that are not complementary with this other person; or there simply may not be a strong enough energy connection so our fields respond neutrally to each other and there is no attraction.

Sometimes there may be people who initially elicit an intensely negative response from us, yet we end up in relationships with them. Several clients have reported that their unhappy marriages resulted from relationships that initially gave out negative signals, but became overridden by something more compelling. Upon reflection, they often concluded that the connection felt like "unfinished business" from other lives. The more conscious we become, the more we are able to recognize when we have "unfinished business" with someone. This will allow us to assess these relationships more objectively. If there are lessons here, we can ask the other person to participate with us to complete it. If the other person refuses (which is generally the case in the type of marriages I have mentioned above), then we will be free to clear our own field by learning our part of the lesson. We can then move on before linking any more of our life with another who will not participate in clearing the old hurt and negativity and thereby transform the old pattern.

If we are picking up a negative vibration from a new person, we need to first look within to see if this person is activating unhealed parts of us. Then we need to create the necessary inner shift to realign our energy. When we do this, we are then unlikely to have to engage with this person. This does not mean we are avoiding challenging experiences; it means we get to select only those challenges which are necessary for our growth. This is an ongoing process of responding to any disharmony which comes from the outside by looking within; then identifying and transforming any negative energy we find, thus cleansing our auric field. As we do this, we may well save ourselves a lot of pain and suffering.

If I meet someone I get a negative feeling about, my first response is to not invite them into my life. If, through other people or events, they still end up connected to me in some way, I then realize it is time to look inside myself to see why I may still be drawing this to me, and what my lesson is. Often I will be shown that the negative qualities which I am sensing in this other person, are areas in myself I need to attend to. Because I have access to numerous techniques, I typically do the inner work myself. Often it is as simple as finding the part of my self that holds these qualities and sending that part love; then going to my heart and sending this other person love as well. This releases me from any emotional pull around this person, and there is no longer a negative charge. At that point, this person usually disappears from my life because I have no need to draw them in. The goal then, is to learn to pay close attention to any time an external experience causes our emotional energy to be charged or out-of-sync, then look within for what issue needs to be cleared or what wound needs to be healed.

As we understand how interactions between human energy fields really work, we also become aware of larger social and political ramifications. Our energy is not restricted to physical proximity. Quantum physics has shown us that energy interacts without regard to distance. The energy field of someone speaking from our TV has the power to affect us. People who are charismatic have a strong magnetic resonance in their aura. We will be drawn to them if our energy field holds a similar electro-magnetic frequency. If we become manipulated by a charismatic personality who is not operating from the heart, be it a politician, a self-help guru, or an evangelical preacher, this shows us there is a configuration in our own field that reflects an unresolved need or issue that we unconsciously believe this person can fulfill. As with personal relationships, this charismatic figure holds dysfunctional energy within their own field that complements our own.

As an example, an evangelist who is insincere collects his "flock" from people attracted to his outward presentation. These people are drawn into the illusion that this preacher is loving and nurturing, and has a direct connection to the Divine because this is the quality that they are missing in themselves. While this evangelist certainly has a strong resonance, what is being transmitted unconsciously to these people may actually come from this preacher's own inability to have or sustain the faith he professes. Remember like attracts like. This evangelist may be hoping unconsciously to heal his own heart and Spirit through convincing others he is sincere, and he may actually believe his own pretense. Or conversely, he may be truly jaded and therefore intent on wielding more power and making money. Either way, the energy configuration which is transmitted will have the same effect: to make his followers more disempowered and disconnected from faith and Divine Guidance.

If you grew up in an authoritarian family where you were conditioned to follow parental injunctions without questioning them, and you were programmed to believe you could only be a good person if you complied, you learned to consistently give up your personal power and sense of self. This would have created certain energy patterns in your aura. Those patterns could make you feel comfortable with a public figure who, like Hitler, explained it was your duty to your country and to save your race by following him. If you went against his dictates, you might feel the same guilt you would have felt going against your authoritarian father. Psychologically, of course, you would have great rage against that father, but since it was unacceptable to feel this rage, you could easily be convinced to project this anger onto whomever this "father" identified as the "evil enemy."

This is a profound psychological phenomenon. Without the necessary collective energy configuration, how could Hitler have had such an impact? He was not the German's father. He was no one they knew. In order to be drawn into following him and hating who he told them to hate, there had to be a stronger invisible force. This force developed because large numbers of people in Germany had been psychologically wounded in similar ways and had developed the same destructive energy patterns from this unhealed part of their psyche. Hitler was able to use these people to amplify this energy of fear and anger.

As we become emotionally and spiritually healthier, we will find ourselves repelled rather than attracted to this kind of energy. We are only vulnerable to a spiritual or political leader of this kind if we are disconnected from our essence. It is in this state that people cannot discern when they are being deceived. This is why it is so important to seek answers from our inner wisdom rather than outer authority. Those who are too afraid to rely on this guidance create disharmony or holes in their energy field which then magnetize people to them whose energetic configuration projects a false ability to do so.

CODEPENDENCY & THE SEPARATION MYTH

Because it has been the norm in our culture for people to be emotionally wounded, romantic relationships have typically been based on two people trying to fulfill their own unmet emotional needs, essentially the unmet emotional needs of their inner child. We will always have unmet emotional needs as long as we are separated from our essence, because this separation makes wholeness impossible. No wonder we often hear phrases like "your other half" or "your better half" when referring to someone's spouse. Because this lack of wholeness creates an inner emptiness and loneliness, people often seek partners expecting that romantic love can and will fill this void.

From the early Agrarian societies where Patriarchy first began to take hold, until the end of the Industrial Revolution, our world became more and more left-brained. The wisdom of the Feminine became more dishonored and repressed. This created our disconnection from Source, which intensified as time went on. Because the collective belief systems held that being separated from our essence was normal, we believed we had to seek an external solution to our unhappiness. Romantic love, or more aptly, romanticized love, was a "logical" way to go.

This romanticized love was actually not love at all, but rather addiction, or what we now call co-dependency. Co-dependency, by definition, means we are looking for another to make us whole; therefore, we come to believe our well-being depends on our partner's love and approval. People put themselves through all sorts of hell simply hoping to keep the other person tied to them. As a culture, we have fully embraced this addiction. Our songs, poetry, plays, movies have all presented images of co-dependency in place of love.

Whenever we have an emotional connection with another person, there are energy cords that come from our aura and attach to theirs, and vice versa. In a healthy relationship these energy cords transmit heart energy and in no way bind people together. In co-dependent or other forms of dysfunctional relationships, these cords become entangled. People knot themselves up with another and then wonder why they feel so stuck or trapped. While I am not yet able to see the details of a person's energy field, I know through my intuition the co-dependent's energy field is a tangled mess. I imagine that visually, the connecting cords look like badly snarled hair. Imagine how challenging it then becomes to disentangle oneself from this.

The energetic configuration in an evolved relationship is flowing; each person can easily extract their energy to flow somewhere else when feeling called to do so, and then return with more energy to bring to the relationship. The combined energies of the two loved ones vibrate easily and create a sense of warmth, a glow like sunlight, and these configurations magnetize even more light. The heart energy of each expands and both are enfolded, enlivened and nurtured by this energetic caress. The energetic bond created through their loving sexual connection is sacred and powerful. There are no knots or tangles. There is total freedom to shine the warmth of their light on others and to seek whatever experiences are needed for each partner's soul growth without fear of being hurt.

Many people now are in a transitional process. I have met and worked with people who are able to stay in a positive love flow with others in their lives as long as they do not have a romantic partner. Once they allow a partner in, they have difficulty maintaining this flow and staying out of the tangles.

In the next section, we will look at ways to assess the configurations in our energy field, and learn how these configurations are affecting our relationships. You will learn to identify what needs to transform in order to get free from any knots and tangles and thus how to keep yourself in the flow of love. We will take an in-depth look at five types of important relationships: romantic/sexual partners, parents, children, sibling & friends.

LOVING PARTNERSHIPS

I use the term loving partnerships to define a committed sexual relationship based on love between two adults. This includes marriage partners, couples living together, couples who are not living together but are serious about their connection, and of course, includes both heterosexual and same-sex relationships.

Loving partnerships are formed through synchronistic occurrences or connections. Often people are not conscious of this, but if they trace the inception of the relationships, the synchronicities will unfold. When we look at this electro-magnetically, it is quite simple: each person puts out a particular frequency which attracts another. Depending on the inner development, the emotional health, and the level of conscious awareness of each person involved, a story is contained that will develop between the two of them.

These stories are as varied as people, and like people, share some common themes. Some of these stories are quiet, subtle. Others are high drama; loud and intense. Some become tragedies, some inspirational, some merely boring. Because of the likelihood that the people in these stories have known each other from other lifetimes; these stories are often deeply compelling. All stories can have a happy ending if both people can become conscious and take responsibility for themselves, whether they stay together or not. But, while the themes of the connections are contained within our energy fields, we always have free-will in terms of how we work with these themes; thus whether the outcome is positive or negative remains fully in our hands.

If two people who are magnetized to each other have not worked out old hurts and are not conscious of the need to do this, it is likely the story which unfolds will center on recreating these old hurts, usually through hurtful interactions with each other. Once this occurs, there is free will for both parties to use this information to heal; however, by this time the energetic enmeshment has generally been created and needs to be dealt with since these entanglements keep people knotted up with each other rather than bonding them in love (the emotion emanating from an open heart.) Even if there was love at first, the enmeshment and the emotions the enmeshment elicits operate to extinguish this. The extreme of this type of relationship is people who have been married for decades, are extremely dependent on each other, even spend a lot of time together, but have no love flowing between them and habitually treat each other with animosity.

Sometimes people are drawn to each other before their emotional healing occurs, create some entanglement, but keep the love, affection and friendship flowing. This story can create a decent marriage where old hurts may come up but are not seen as being created by the other. Here, there is genuine fondness which grows through the years, but the entanglements may hold back deeper soul growth unless one or both breaks free enough to create healing.

Since all relationships are magnetized from the frequency of our energy field, they all have an important purpose. If we know from the start that anything hurtful or negative from our partner can be used as a sign of some inner work for us to do, we will not become entangled. We will continue our growth, and if our partner chooses not to grow, we will leave each other. The disengagement then can be relatively painless, because little or no enmeshment has occurred.

As we grow to understand ourselves at this deeper level and we understand how and why we magnetize others to us, we are free to deeply explore and heal our relationships. When we are committed to transforming our inner wounds, taking responsibility for our life, and watching for all lessons, we create an opening for the best story to occur. We no longer need the deficiencies or wounds of our partner to mirror our own in order for us to learn what we need to heal. Now we are free to attract an entirely different scenario, and to create a relationship where we enhance each other through the flow of love that encourages and supports each other's soul growth.

Assessing and Overcoming Sexual Wounding

Loving partnership is the most profound of the relationships available to us because of its sexual connection. Through healthy sexuality, partners can experience the Divine together. In joining our bodies which joins our earth vehicles with the etheric, we are able to ignite and share the deepest form of ecstasy. In order for this to happen at its fullest, there must be a deep shared love and no entanglement. This allows our love making to be energetically pure because there are no hidden needs, or ego agendas; the cells in our bodies vibrate faster which means we are filled with more light: we become "light beings" literally.

Typically however, when we look at sexual connection, we open up a potential Pandora's Box of wounds and inaccurate beliefs. A multitude of people in our society have been sexually wounded. Vast numbers have been sexually abused as children. All of us were bombarded with messages about sexuality that have been formed by our society's collective sexual wounds. Males have typically been raised with the idea that sex is a way to assert one's manhood. Many females were conditioned to believe that sex was bad or they were bad for having sexual feelings. Others were conditioned to believe that sex was to be used to manipulate men. Still others came to believe that sex was about marital obligation.

The 60's were generally a time when people reclaimed the right to experience sexual pleasure, but often sex became promoted as adventure and pleasure-seeking without a sense of loving connection. All of these beliefs have kept people out of sexual alignment and have hurt us deeply. These beliefs have also kept people disconnected from themselves and from each other.

No matter how much love may exist between two people, any old wounding or dysfunctional beliefs still are likely to interfere with making that full sexual connection. So healing our wounds and transforming our beliefs is important. The first step is to identify them.

If you were sexually abused and have not sought help to heal, I strongly urge you to do so. On rare occasions survivors, even before doing their healing work, are able to keep their wounds from interfering with their sexuality, but it is far more likely for the opposite to occur. One of the most important parts of healing from sexual abuse is to reclaim one's connection with one's body and with one's sexuality because this is what is ripped away from a child during the abuse. Both therapy and energy work can facilitate this healing.

If you have experienced sexual connections that were exploitive and/or manipulative, these too need to be processed, healed and cleared. Begin by identifying them. Many times we overlook the more subtle versions of sexual wounding, so do your best to make these conscious. Think back to your early sexual experiences. Ask yourself the following questions:

- *What was your motivation?*
- *Was there love and passion?*
- *Was there deep connection?*
- *Did you feel good about yourself before, during and after? If not, why? What was out of sync?*
- *Were you sexual for the wrong reasons?*
- *Were you already wounded sexually so you were not able to be yourself?*
- *Was the other person dishonoring of you?*
- *Were you dishonoring of yourself?*
- *Did you have rigid beliefs that created guilt or shame because you did not know someone "long enough?"*
- *Was there fear?*

Make a list looking at each significant sexual partner using the above criteria.

To do this process successfully, it is important to not judge yourself. I realize this can be a tall order. We need to remember we were doing the best we could at the time no matter if we were exploitive or manipulative, exploited, dishonoring, dishonored, guilty, scared or ashamed. We consciously or unconsciously choose experiences to help us develop. If we learn from these experiences, if we take responsibility for our choices while still being open-hearted with ourselves, the needed healing can occur and we can move on.

Be aware also there are no hard and fast external rules to determine the energetic quality of our sexual connections. We can make love with someone we barely know but feel a deep affinity to and have a pure and loving connection with them. We can make love with a partner of 30 years and end up dishonoring ourselves and/or our partner. What is most important is to allow your heart and intuition to lead, not the old repressive views of our society or the sensationalism that touts sex as an easy "high."

Here are some more questions for you to ponder:

- *What are your beliefs about sexuality?*
- *What were you taught as a young person about sex?*

- *Did you believe what you heard? Why or why not?*
- *What was your parents' attitude towards sex?*
- *What impressions did you get about sex from popular songs, books, movies, TV?*

Now that you understand that you can unconsciously believe something that you do not believe consciously, ask yourself how these old beliefs might still be affecting you. Look deeply inside for the answers and be open to uncovering contradictions. Write down everything that arises. Now look this list over and note which negative beliefs still remain that need to be transformed.

Because there is an intense exchange of energy in sexual intercourse, you may still be carrying the energy of the sexual partners you have had in the past. Energy workers can help you clear these from your field if they are negatively affecting you. The more you are able to identify what might still be around, the more empowered you are to get free of it. If you have had a partner who was sexually wounded, it is possible you are carrying some of their wounding. This would be important to clear, as would any direct wounding you have suffered from that or any other connection.

You may also want to do the following healing ritual. This is a very powerful energy cleanse that you can do on your own:

Visualize pure white light coming in through your crown chakra and then slowly see it swirl throughout your body. Let it swirl through every part, every cell, every chakra, clearing all unwanted energy. Then focus this swirling light intently in the genital area, asking that all old wounding or dysfunction be cleansed out.

As we transform the old unhealthy sexual beliefs and clear out the old wounds, we become free to fully connect in sacred sexual union with another.

Emotional Healing

If you are carrying anger, distrust, sadness, guilt and/or shame of any kind from past relationships, this tends to get reflected in your current partnerships. This does not mean these relationships will be ruined or damaged, it simply means you must watch your emotions and your partner's emotions to notice when old issues are coming to the fore. The more healed our hearts before entering into the relationship, the easier the lessons will be to learn. The more wounded we are when we enter a relationship, the more challenged we are likely to be by whatever arises.

The most significant emotional factor needed for successful relationships is each person's ability to see and take responsibility for their projections and to understand how their partner's attributes and issues mirror their own. Projections are feelings, attributes or judgments we are experiencing inside, which we put onto others in order to defend against recognizing them in ourselves. When one or both partners are unable to recognize their projections, the relationship cannot progress in a healthy way and old emotional issues will have little or no room to be resolved.

As an example, if I have an unconscious belief that I am unlovable, I may find myself feeling that my partner does not love me. Or I may act in "unlovable" ways that make it impossible for my partner to show me love. While my partner may actually be acting in an unloving way to me, it is my inner belief that is driving 50% of this dynamic. An effective way of owning our projections is to see everything in the outer world as mirroring something about us; thus, if I feel my partner is being inconsiderate or unloving, I look inside myself to see if I am being inconsiderate or unloving either to my partner, to others in my life or to myself. It may be that both my partner and I are acting like this, but when I can own my projection and do my inner work, the issue can be resolved for me. Conversely, if I will not own my projection, the issue becomes impossible to resolve.

If you have or have had a partner that refuses to own their projections, thus invalidating your perceptions and holding you always to blame, it does not matter how self-aware you are or how hard you may work, there is no way this relationship can be healthy. You can become emotionally healthy, but you cannot make your partner do the same. Still when one person in a relationship makes an immovable commitment to growth, the other person sometimes opens to growing at least enough to keep the relationship from disintegrating. Whether or not this turns out to be true in your relationship, making that commitment to growth will create a positive outcome for you.

As an example, if you have a partner who is rarely home, and when confronted says something defensive such as "I will not be trapped," than I would suggest looking within for a part of you that fears "getting trapped." Work intensively with this fear in yourself while ignoring your partner's absence for a while. Once you have worked with your issues, several things may happen. You might identify that you have a need for more personal space, and so while your inner child might have felt abandoned by your partner's absence, your adult might actually need the time alone. You might have found a belief that if you are in partnership your personal space and sense of autonomy has to be limited, and that this was a necessary sacrifice for a "good" relationship. If this has been the case, then without any change on your partner's part, you may begin to enjoy your time alone more. Another possibility is that as you withdraw your focus from your partner's behavior, they may begin to be home more often. This may occur because your partner has felt safe in the relationship as long as you got upset when they were gone. Once you stop being upset and begin to enjoy your own space, your partner, assuming he or she really wants to be in relationship with you, is likely to notice the change and become scared you might leave. Or they may feel relieved that every time they wish to go off somewhere that they do not have to feel guilty about hurting you. That will free them up to get closer to you again, and want to stay home more. If, however, the deeper issue for your partner is a desire to be out of the relationship, or a deep fear of closeness, it is not likely they will change their behavior, and as you get healthier, you will want to end the connection. As you own your own ability to enjoy time by yourself, you will be less entangled energetically and therefore more likely to simply end the relationship, freeing yourself to find a more compatible partner.

Keep in mind no matter what happens in a partnership, what is important is our ability to understand that all attributes which elicit an emotional response in us are reflecting parts of ourselves. This understanding will propel us to a new level of personal power and health. From here we can create evolved loving partnerships.

If you are currently in a partnership, I suggest you do the following: Make a list of the qualities of your partner that bother you the most, as well as a list of what you most appreciate and admire about them. Then begin to look inward to understand what the mirrors are for you.

If you are not currently in a partnership, think back to times when you were. Notice both the positive and negative patterns. Think about why the relationship(s) ended, and then look within for your part in things.

Once you have identified the issues and/or the beliefs the relationship mirrored, you will be able to work on transforming your inner qualities that are dysfunctional, and to own their positive qualities as attributes in yourself.

Interpreting mirrors correctly can take a great deal of mental flexibility. Sometimes the projected issue is easy to see: feeling unlovable, needing more freedom, etc. Sometimes it is much more complicated. The following are designed to help.

Examples of Common Mirrors in Relationships

1. A partner who always blames

Your possible inner reflections & beliefs:

I always feel guilty about everything.
I deserve to be blamed.
If I really love someone, I will take the blame for them.
Someone is always blaming me/victimizing me.

I am afraid I am not powerful enough OR I am afraid I am too powerful. If I always take someone else's blame, I do not have to use or test my power.
I use my partner to keep me in a state of powerlessness.
I am the stronger one so I should pretend I am weaker so as not to threaten my partner, because no one will love me if I am stronger than they are. (Can substitute better than, nicer than, etc.)
My mother (or father) always took the blame. I should be like mom or dad to defend their behavior. (But I really blame them for this.)

2. A partner who is emotionally distant

Your possible inner reflections and beliefs:

I am too scared to get close. I cannot trust people not to hurt me.
People always hurt each other when they get close.
I cannot keep my sense of self if I get too close.
I would feel trapped if my relationship were really intimate.
People always leave me or abandon me, so I will not allow myself to be close.
If I let someone really get to know me, they will not love/like me.
My father/mother was distant so I do not deserve to be close to someone
My father/mother was distant so I feel safer/more comfortable with such a familiar dynamic.

3. A partner who is overly dependent, clinging.

Your possible inner reflections and beliefs:

If my partner clings to me because they are so insecure, I can avoid noticing that I am equally insecure.
People let me down, abandon me emotionally and physically. If someone is needy enough, I can count on them not to leave.
I need someone to take care of me, but cannot be direct about this.
Since I only got attention from my parent(s) when I took care of them, I feel loved only when someone needs me.
My needs are not important. I do not count. I am unworthy.
I am afraid to be myself. If I have to take care of my partner, I have no time for myself.
Since my partner is such a child, I can pretend to be a grown-up.

4. A partner who is controlling

Your possible inner reflections and beliefs:

I cannot trust myself to make the right life decisions.
I get scared if things feel out of control.
I am scared to take any initiative.
I am scared of being wrong/ making a mistake/ failing.
I am scared to take responsibility for myself.
I am not good enough/smart enough/deserving enough/competent enough to take charge of my life.
I will not be loved if I assert myself.
My needs do not count. I do not deserve to ever have my way.
Other people always know better than I do.

5. A partner who is critical

Your possible inner reflections and beliefs:

Self-Judgments:
   I am not good enough
   I do not do things well enough.
   I cannot measure up.
Perfectionist beliefs:
   If I do not do things perfectly, I am not doing enough.
   If I am not perfect, I am not good enough.
   If I am not hard on myself (or if someone is not hard on me), I will not improve.

6. A partner who is angry

Your possible inner reflections and beliefs:

I am angry but I think that feeling is unacceptable for me, so I will not let myself realize I am angry.
I am angry but I get scared of my anger.
I direct anger toward myself for not measuring up to my unrealistic expectations

7. A partner who is an alcoholic or a drug abuser

Your possible inner reflections and beliefs:

I feel empty so I fill myself by focusing on my addicted partner.
I fill my life by being addicted to relationships.
I numb my pain by being addicted to relationships.
Life is full of suffering.
My needs are not important.

Use this list as a rule of thumb for any quality of this nature that you see in your partner. If your partner is cynical, look for your inner-cynic. If your partner leans toward negative thinking, look for that tendency with you. Conversely, if we admire our partners because they are successful in the outer world, look within for the part of you who needs to get out into the world. If they are leaders, find your inner leader. If they are intuitive, find your own intuitive nature.

As we work on issues inside us which our partners reflect, we grow and change. In a highly functional relationship both partners continually grow from the reflections they provide each other. My husband and I often laughingly remark how we have switched roles in various areas over the years, but this phenomenon has really occurred because we have owned the characteristics the other was reflecting for us. This has allowed us to express pieces of ourselves we may never otherwise have found, as well as to identify areas of ourselves which we needed to heal or transform.

Another phenomenon occurs when one partner has worked on healing the dysfunctional issues the other is reflecting and then finds the relationship no longer tolerable. For instance, if early on they needed someone to be distant and they have worked on healing their own emotional wound around a distant parent, they will then be ready for sharing intimacy, and a distant partner becomes unacceptable. If the other partner refuses to do their own healing work, the relationship will end.

Projections and Reflections of the Inner Male and Inner Female

Carl Jung was the first of the modern psychologists to give us the concept of the inner male and the inner female by presenting the archetypes of the anima and animus. Jung understood that many of the projections which occur in relationships has to do with the unhealed or undeveloped inner male (the animus), or female (the anima.) Because of gender imbalance and inequality in our society, it is rare to find people who do not have some of these issues. Both men and women tend to repress their inner opposite, but for different reasons.

Men in our culture are often taught to hate and/or scorn their inner female. This message gets programmed in many ways. Men who have tyrannical, authoritarian fathers are shamed into repressing and feeling contempt for their inner females. Weak mothers, especially mothers who do not stop their partner from abusing their children, are likely to have sons who have intense and usually unexpressed rage at mom, which then gets focused on females in general and their own inner female in particular. Social institutions, whether religious, educational or recreational, often shame or embarrass males who are trying to express or honor their inner feminine. These males develop a belief that in order to be a "real" man, they must pretend that part of them does not exist. The more insecure a man feels, the more likely he is to repress and oppress his inner female.

When men are not allowing themselves to express this yin or female energy, they seek a partner to balance them. A heterosexual man may then be hateful and abusive to the woman in his life, reflecting his feelings about the female part of himself. Or he may artificially honor this woman on the surface because of guilt about his mother, but through passive/aggressive or other subtle forms of behavior, undermine her well-being. Homosexual men are equally likely to respond to their partner's feminine in whatever way they respond to their own inner female.

Women operating from the patriarchal paradigm of "femininity," repressed their yang or male energy. This has shifted considerably since the advent of the women's movement in the 1960's, but we still have vestiges of it. When women refuse to own their strength and competency in the world, they tend to seek partners who will do it for them. Traditionally, this was the only route most women had available to them. Modern women have fought for and successfully created the right to express their inner males; however there are still women who repress their inner male in some areas of their lives. When women repress their male energy, they disconnect from feeling whole and fully empowered. Their power goes underground, surfacing unconsciously in manipulation, controlling behavior, martyrdom and other forms of self-denial, and resentment.

Because the archetype of the powerful feminine was suppressed during patriarchy, many women do not know how to access this for themselves. They have had no models and therefore have not known how to access this very wonderful energy and may begin to repress all their feminine energy because they believe it to be weaker and therefore feel more vulnerable than when they are expressing their inner male.

A woman who saw her mother tyrannized by a domineering male partner and/or was herself tyrannized by a man, may have decided the only way to be safe in the world was to scorn her own female. She may then primarily express herself through a dominating inner male energy in order to feel powerful. Typically, this woman would approach relationships by building a metaphoric fortress around her emotions. She is likely to be successful in the work world since our culture has rewarded this type of personality, but her relationships will not be healthy. If she is heterosexual, she is likely to either choose a man who is repressing his own masculine and will be passive and placating, or a strong male she views as her equal where they create a relationship that feels like a war zone. The passive man will provide her with a feeling of emotional safety but will never be fulfilling. The latter may seem passionate, but it will have no emotional depth and intimacy. Neither type is likely to allow much growth. Lesbians who are repressing their feminine are likely to create the same type of emotional dynamic in their partnerships.

There are also men who repress their own male nature. A man who is repressing his male is likely to have seen his mother hurt by his father's, or another significant male's angry and/or domineering energy. If he had a warm relationship with his mother, he would then try to be her "hero." For some men this means taking on the male warrior/protective energy, which if unhealed, is the rescuer. For others it means expressing only a passive or nurturing female nature because of guilt feelings developed in childhood. These guilt feelings may stem from being unable to protect mom from abuse, being furious with mom for not being able to get herself out of the situation and then feeling guilty about the anger, picking up on mom's negativity toward male energy, or even feeling that he could never measure up as a "man" in his father's eyes so why bother.

Any time we repress an aspect of ourselves, it creates anger and resentment. For the male who "rescues," the anger will be at his partner for not being successfully "rescued." If this is a man who has repressed his masculine expression, he will likely convey his anger in one of the following dysfunctional ways:

1. *Passively expressing this resentment by acting inept, irresponsible or helpless thereby eliciting his partner's rage (resentment) and then acting victimized.*
2. *Being passive as above, but acting as if his partner is invisible when she/he starts expressing their rage.*
3. *Withdrawing all his energy from the relationship. Energetically, this is a refusal to give any energy to the partner; instead he will suck his partner's energy. This creates extreme entanglement made more destructive by the amount of resentment each person in the relationship will hold.*

Whenever one or the other partner is repressing and/or oppressing the inner male or female, any love partnership will be energetically entangled. We must achieve androgyny, a healthy balance of yin and yang, female and male, if we are to get disentangled and create evolved relationships. Becoming androgynous does not mean men act like women and women act like men. It means that women will express a strong and loving feminine nature while simultaneously having full access to their yang energy for material manifestation, protection, boundary-setting and leadership. Men, conversely, will express a strong male energy simultaneously having access to the intuitive, flowing, nurturing side of themselves. From this, a wonderfully healthy partnership can form. This is equally true for same-sex couples. If you are feeling you are not in balance, look to past or present partners to show you the mirror of what qualities you need to own and transform.

As we work out our emotional issues and balance our male and female, the tangles in our energy field unknot themselves. The true energy of love which has been blocked can now begin to flow in a loving partnership. Joy and well-being begin to emerge. Two people with this energy configuration are empowered, and therefore no longer invested in projecting their fears, anger, and unmet childhood emotional needs onto each other. Sexuality can now become an ecstatic exchange of love and soul essence. Together the partners, in their sexual connection, invite cosmic light and love to surround them. The family created from these partnerships is warm, loving, protective and fair, and creates a healthy environment for children and animals to thrive.

PARENT/CHILD RELATIONSHIPS

Your children are not your children.
They are the sons and daughters of Life's longing for itself.
They come through you but not from you.
And though they are with you, yet they belong not to you.
You may give them your love but not your thoughts.
For they have their own thoughts.
You may house their bodies but not their souls.
For their souls dwell in the house of tomorrow...
					Kahlil Gibran

Our children come to us so we can love, nourish and keep them alive until they are old enough to move into the world on their own. We do not magnetize these souls in order to imprint our own beliefs, desires, or ego needs onto them. They are not little pieces of us. They are their own entity, their own microscopic piece of the Divine. Ideally, we magnetize a child as a way to bring more loving souls into the world so that the world may be filled with more light. We are not here to mold our children, but rather to provide a safe container where they can develop; and when we become too small to contain them, we need to lovingly wish them safe passage and send them our love and blessings on their journey. To understand that as parents, we are simply the vehicle is a rare gift indeed. It is also one we dearly need to cultivate.

I imagine in the ideal parent/child relationship, there are cords of light which bond the two. These cords emanate from both parents to the child, but the cords are infinitely flexible, vibrating at a high frequency, and serve only to send love and encouragement. There are no tangles, no knots. On an emotional level, this means no guilt, no shame, no expectations, just a pure flow of heart energy. When the parents are in loving relationship to each other, this will amplify the love, encouragement and light these cords conduct.

The cords from parent to child are a conduit for parental love. I suspect this conduit does not travel in the other direction. This is not to imply that children do not or should not equally love their parents. It means that it is the parent's obligation, the parent's spiritual contract, to provide for the child, not the other way around. The child's obligation is to provide for their own progeny, whether those progeny are children or other creative manifestations of the Divine. Children who have been raised in this type of energetic field send love back to their parents out of natural gratitude and appreciation, not out of a sense of obligation or duty.

From the Beginning

From the moment of conception an energetic conduit starts to form between parent and child. It is quite thin and permeable in the early stages of gestation with the soul of the child not fully connected with the developing body, but by birth the connection is well in place. How a child is born, how they are welcomed into the world by both parents is important.

Birthing practices have come a long way in the last 40 years, but people still need to use caution and creativity in order to make sure that a birth is designed in a way that honors the incoming Spirit. Caesarian sections, except in rare cases, are for the convenience of the doctor or connected to the mother's fear, and potentially interfere with the energy flow of the infant. In my opinion, drugs for the mother or the baby can create issues in the energy field, and so ideally should not be taken. Despite my Jewish up-bringing, I think circumcision is a rather horrible, primitive rite. When I became pregnant and imagined interfering with my offspring in that way, I found the idea appalling. I could not justify tampering with a baby's genitalia. What right was it of mine to modify the body like that? Think about what that does to the Spirit. Circumcision must surely be experienced as deep trauma in the energy body. It would break my heart to do that to my son. What I find most disturbing is that so few prospective parents question standard medical procedure or cultural tradition, even when with a little independent thought, some empathy and intuition, it might become clear that these practices are potentially, albeit subtly, harmful. However, the larger issue is that we are culturally trained to not be conscious of what our children are actually experiencing. If we were, we could not do large numbers of things we do to them, and circumcision is one.

Typical births need no medical intervention. I birthed my children at home. I became educated about the process so that I could do this safely, and for all three births called in a team of friends who also became educated about birthing, and who had different areas of expertise. For my first two children, I had midwives attending me, but when my son was born there were no more available midwives, having been harassed by the Ob/Gyn community in our area, so my husband and I called upon a friend who was an EMT.

Our deepest focus beyond safety, was on the soul of the child entering the world. The environment was prepared with this in mind. While, by law babies in our state are required to be treated with eye drops in case either parent has syphilis, I found there was an alternative drop which was legal and did not sting the baby's eyes. By going through natural childbirth in the comfort of my home with only caring, spiritually attuned people in attendance, my children came into a calm warm world surrounded by the energy of love. This is quite a contrast to the traditional hospital delivery room. And unlike many hospital births, my children were not whisked away for unnecessary bathing and medical prodding and probing. While my first birth was challenging, my second and third births were remarkably easy and I felt wonderful and joyful immediately after all three. Imagine how the energy fields of parents and children are honored in this method of birthing. The conduit is free to form in its natural state. The energy of the mother and father immediately envelop the child, protecting their field from harm and discordance. For those uncomfortable with home birth, a hospital birthing room can be used to create a similar environment if the parents are assertive and educated about the process.

As children grow, the conduit which is already flexible and permeable simply expands. Thus the child is free to explore their world while connected to the protective energy of the parents but not restricted by it. Little children need structure. They need protection. They need guidance. When young children "misbehave," they are simply trying out new behavior, testing their limits or in some cases, acting out their parents' unresolved issues. If a child's misbehavior is simply a matter of not knowing what is expected or playing with the limits to see how far they can push, it is a rare toddler who does not respond to a parent getting down to make eye contact, holding the child firmly while saying "no, it is not okay to..." I think it is important even for a very young child to add a reason. As an example "it is not okay to hit because hitting hurts and it is not okay to hurt others." Also be aware, that foods with processed sugars, chemicals and additives, as well as lack of sleep can cause children to "misbehave," as can food allergies. So pay attention to these things as well.

There is never a need or reason to hit a child in order to get them to behave. Nor is there ever a good reason to shame a child. In my opinion, it is cruel to physically or emotionally hurt a child. Slapping, hitting, paddling, humiliating and screaming at children create holes or tears in their auras. Some children are more sensitive to this than others, but I think all children are negatively affected. A quick swat on the butt of a young child is not likely to do energetic harm, but this too, is an unnecessary way of using discipline. As we honor ourselves and understand why we want to retain or reclaim the integrity of our energy field, we will begin to shun those so-called "acceptable" child-rearing practices.

If a child is misbehaving because of the unresolved issues of their parents, things become more complex. In order for this to get resolved, parents must take an honest look at themselves, their own experience of being parented, and their relationship and current situation. If parents are willing to confront what is going on with them, and are willing to work at resolving it, their children will respond positively and the behavior will shift. This is a wonderful gift we get from our children who by their very being, direct us toward our own growth and healing. I had to face and clear up many things about myself, which I might never have had the opportunity to see if I had not been raising my children. When parents change and heal, the energy field of the entire family clears and shifts. However, if the parents are too scared or feel too inadequate to face what is really going on, it is likely their child's behavior will become worse and the whole family will suffer.

As children enter adolescence their need for their parenting changes dramatically. Adolescence is ideally a time to activate one's inner power, to explore, to experiment. We need to embrace our teens and their high-spiritedness, and work for cultural changes that support this important developmental stage. A society which knows how to honor the spirit of its teenagers and young adults provides a socially flexible container in the same way good parents provide the familial one. This allows adolescents to gradually transition into adulthood and enjoy the freedom of this transition before taking on adult responsibilities. If parents are in right relationship to their budding teenage children, which means they have that strong flexible conduit in place without the co-dependent knots, their children can safely venture outside their old boundaries knowing they have the security of their families to support them when they need it. This can unleash fresh and wondrous energy into the world.

Sadly, our culture has created a counterproductive system for teens. Families, too insecure to question the status quo, typically do their best to push their teens to conform to restrictive, fear-based societal rules and norms which ultimately serve to undermine their ability to come into healthy adulthood. If a teen is lucky enough to feel free to experiment and explore while being supported and protected by their family, they are likely to have to struggle with the energetic entanglements of a public school system operating out of a belief that teens must be controlled/reigned in. Rather than empower and mentor adolescents to become fully themselves, schools are more likely to bind teens up in silly rules, dishonor their initiative and creativity and if they do not rebel, drone and bore them into a mental and spiritual stupor.

Good parenting of teens involves not just having a proper energetic relationship to them at home, but validating their distress at the ways they and/or their peers are being treated at school. They may also need information on how to protect their auric field as the emotional chaos of high school (and sometimes middle school,) can overwhelm a sensitive teen. Providing these things gives teens a way to begin to feel in charge of their own journey toward adulthood. If these teens have come from loving families, their heart chakra will be open, and with the proper guidance and encouragement in adolescence, their solar plexus energy becomes highly activated and can propel them into their life purpose. Parents need to release judgment and expectations that can limit their child's flow of energy, in order to allow this journey to continue unobstructed.

Once your child has entered adulthood, a whole new phase of relationship can begin. It is an evolutionary imperative that our children grow beyond us. Adult children become our teachers of the future, teachers of the evolving world. We, on the other hand, have the accumulated wisdom of living through various personal and social cycles. We have the perspective which comes with this living and can share our wisdom with our children as they begin to take over leadership positions which we have previously filled. By this time, the energetic conduit needs to be totally voluntary between parent and child, based only on love. The parental contract has been fulfilled. Now there is affection, love and appreciation for each other which grows from a healthy family garden. All interactions come from this source and not from obligation, guilt or repentance.

Guiding the Older Child

Being a mother has been one of the most miraculous and challenging experiences of this lifetime for me. As my children have grown older, what they need from me changes dramatically and this demands that I stay flexible and creative in how I relate to them. An interesting parental issue arose some years ago that I think is instructive to share. My oldest daughter was getting close to completing her junior year in college. She suddenly became enthralled with the idea of taking a year off from college, heading out West and working. She figured she would establish residency and ultimately finish her degree in another state. She first presented this to me by thanking me exuberantly for how we have raised her to follow her path, and said she knew I would totally understand and support her plan. To her surprise and irritation, I was not enormously thrilled about the idea.

While, she has always been an independent spirit, she was not always clear on her readiness to venture forth into the world. This is where parental guidance comes in. We had always provided her with a lot of freedom and leeway, but did so within a safe structure that was tailored to her personality. For example, when she was a senior in high school she did not have a curfew on weekends, but we gave her a 9:30 curfew on school nights. She needed the early curfew during the week to keep her focused and grounded, but she was savvy enough to take good care of herself in "weekend mode," and a curfew then would have created unnecessary constriction that she would likely have found a way to rebel against.

When she presented me with the idea of stopping her education for a while, I encouraged her to just finish up her degree and then to take as much time as she needed to travel and explore. Her college experience had been excellent. While she had faced some interpersonal challenges, she met them successfully. Her academic performance was outstanding – a change from her nonchalant attitude in high school. And while she was attending a large state university, she had magnetized interesting, like-minded people and some wonderful learning opportunities. The most dramatic being the creative-writing seminar she had enrolled in. It was a class of only 15 people, and she immediately connected with her professor. This man had recently published a novel which shot to the best seller list and received enormous critical acclaim, while my daughter was in his seminar. People were calling in from all over the country to get into this creative writing program, and she was set to take another seminar from him in the fall. This was a synchronicity to me that suggested she needed to stay where she was and complete her degree. Knowing my daughter well, I also knew that whatever my view, she was clearly going to make her own decision.

We had planned a family visit to see her before this latest development occurred. It turned out our visit was scheduled to occur a few weeks after the time my daughter began to contemplate taking a year off school. This gave my husband and me great opportunity to think out what might really be going on, to surmise what she might most need from us, and to create a strategy which would serve as strong guidance, but ultimately assure her of our blessings no matter what she decided.

I put together a list of "PROS" and "CONS" – except I could not think of any pros. I left that part blank. If she could come up with reasonable "pros" it might change our view of things. We also created some financial penalty for her taking time off. We told her she could use whatever was left in her college fund whenever she returned to school, but that it only had enough in it to cover tuition, and we would not at that point be responsible for her room & board. This way, we still made it possible for her to finish school when she chose, but she would have to be more responsible for her living expenses.

If she felt the Universe was compelling her to go, then she would have to do it on her own. This would not have been all that difficult for her. She had been a waitress at a restaurant that was part of a large national chain and could "passport" to another of their locations anywhere in the world, thus guaranteeing her a base income and flexible hours. So we did not make this impossible, only something that would challenge her enough to see if leaving college at that point really was important for her. We also let her know that even if she did not have our permission, she would always have our love and blessings.

By the end of our visit, she had decided to finish up her degree. However, if she had chosen not to, we would have needed to let her go. In order to keep the energy flowing properly between us, we would have had to surrender any control. We gave her our guidance. We presented a small challenge that she could have overcome if this had truly been her path. And we knew that we should never block her way or assume that her decision should be about what would make us happy. This was not about us, this was about her. No matter how foolish her choice might appear to us, if she had decided to leave school then, I have no doubt she would have learned from it and ultimately made it work in her interest. It might have been a harder road, or simply what she needed at the time. By not taking this personally and at the same time still giving her parental guidance, we honored her right to make her own decisions and thus left the parent/child conduit working in a healthy manner.

Ironically, a few years later our younger daughter decided to leave college for a while and accepted the potential challenges we presented to her. This clearly was part of her path and led her on an important part of her journey. Each child is an individual, and as parents, our obligation is to do our best to help them sort what really is the call of their Spirit versus what might be an interesting or engaging whim. We were also careful to create options that allowed both girls to take ultimate responsibility for their choices and thus, for their life.

Any time we try to control another's behavior, we energetically attempt to take power away by imposing our own fears, desires and beliefs onto them. Sadly and ironically, parents have been conditioned to believe that in situations like this they should attempt to control their children's decisions. Children are extremely susceptible to suffering energetic harm when we do this to them. Because they have depended on us for their survival and feel bonded to us in numerous ways, it is difficult for a child, even a young adult child, to defend or protect themselves from being drained energetically when their parents behave in a controlling manner. The younger the child, the more vulnerable they are to giving up their own sense of self in order to comply with the family rules.

Teenagers, who enter adolescence with some sense of self, face a deep wounding as well as a difficult dilemma if their parents try to control rather than guide them. Again, there is a great irony here: parents often act controlling because they are scared some harm will come to their children and therefore believe that by imposing controls they are protecting them. Instead, of course, they may end up doing the harm.

Another reason parents become controlling is to keep their children from being different or developing different beliefs than they have themselves. These parents are seeing their children as extensions of themselves and often imagine that they are really helping their children by treating them in this way. This is another way parents unconsciously take energy away from their children and thus disempower them. In these situations, parents are not honoring the conduit as a channel for their love and encouragement, but rather are knotting up this channel, drawing their children to them more tightly. If a child or adolescent complies, they give up parts of themselves; if they rebel, they are likely to incur their parent's wrath, panic or both. This parent then may fight harder to entangle their child in order to keep them attached, and a potentially dangerous cycle develops.

When parents are taking rather than giving energy to their child, the only way children have to save their sense of self is to break away. Teenagers can do this through rebellion. Unfortunately, rebellion motivated by this need often creates more challenges because often other authority figures are called in to "control" them. This can cause more harm to their field including any damage done by medicating them into compliance. The strongest teens break free even if it means leaving home at a fairly young age, but this leaves them vulnerable to other forms of physical, psychological and energetic danger. Others will wait it out, and when they are old enough to be on their own will begin the breaking away process. Sadly, many more will simply adapt and try to go through life without having activated these inner vital parts.

Younger children who have controlling parents will typically be either the "perfect" child or act out. This acting out may come from the deepest part of their soul which is trying to save them. Tragically, once again, our society will often intervene, offering drugs as a solution and thus literally lulling them into submission. These drugs may also disconnect some children from their feelings which, in turn, disconnect them from their own energy source.

The opposite of this type of parental control is neglect. This often happens with older teens when parents get worn out from trying to control them and then throw up their hands with statements like "Go do what you want, you probably will anyway." This leaves no feeling of love or guidance for the child who, in turn, may subtly try to become entangled with the parent in order to feel reconnected to them. This does not mean a teen will not go ahead and act on whatever they "wanted" to do, but it does mean that the energetic configuration which develops from this negative interaction is likely to keep whatever they choose to do from working out well.

If we had said to our daughter at the time she wanted to take a break from college, "Sure, go ahead and do whatever you want," we would no longer be providing her with the container she still needed. She was just 20, and not yet across the bridge to adulthood. Even though she had a good connection to her Self and thus had internal resources which could have led her to making a good decision, she might have experienced a sense of being abandoned by us.

There are no hard and fast rules for how much of a container an older teen or young adult might need. This varies with each child. When my younger daughter was seventeen and was a few months shy of leaving for college, she stated clearly that she felt able to decide when she needs information or help from us, and asked that we not volunteer it. She also made it clear that it was important we not worry about her because she said "it sucked her energy." Prior to this pronouncement, I had never considered that parental worry could do this. She, of course, was accurate. Worrying about one's children is not helpful and can be harmful to a child. This is because worry sends an unconscious message that you do not trust this child to be okay. Children unconsciously pick this up and it makes their path more difficult. This erodes their sense of self-confidence and will drain their third chakra energy. While we then respected our daughter's wishes, we still stayed alert to how and when she might need guidance and to ways that guidance could be shared with her without our overreacting or draining her energy.

It is a delicately balanced dance to accomplish this. Certainly it is not necessary or possible to do perfectly, but if, as parents, we pay attention to how our words and/or actions might affect our children energetically, and if we listen to their feedback, then it becomes a dance we can master.

This is a central challenge for parents of teenagers and young adults: we need to listen; to give enough freedom; to be sensitive to their deeper needs and to anything which could negatively impact their energy. We also need to stay separate from the dictates of mass culture including inappropriate pressure from school, from other parents etc. in order to provide the container for optimum growth.

Before moving on to this next section, I want to stress the impossibility of parenting perfectly, as well as to assure you that you might have raised perfectly wonderful children without having followed similar guidelines to the ones I've just presented. Often I find that parents of grown children go through a great deal of sadness and guilt when they learn new ways of parenting which they didn't have access to when raising their children. So, remember to go easy on yourself.

Reclaiming Ourselves and Reconnecting Our Auras

No matter what you have experienced through your development as a human in this lifetime, there is nothing that can keep you from becoming whole if you are committed to it. The following suggestions are some ways to activate or to continue this deeper process of healing.

Re-Birthing

Take a moment and think of what you have been told about your own birth. Large numbers of you would not only have been born in a hospital, but would have been birthed from mothers who were drugged. Your father, if he was there at all, would have been out in the waiting room. You would have come into a delivery room that was cold with bright harsh lights, and as soon as you came out, you would be swatted on the butt because physicians carried a belief that healthy babies could not breathe on their own. That done, you would have drops that stung placed in your eyes, and been carted off to be bathed and prodded. If you were a boy born in the U.S. and not of Jewish or Muslim descent, you would likely have been circumcised immediately without anesthesia. Think about this. You came out to this world pure, open and loving, and you were immediately traumatized. Imagine how this disrupted your energy field. Imagine how this type of birth disrupted your mother's aura and disconnected your father from the birthing process.

Imagine now that you could change your birth. Close your eyes and take some deep centering breaths.

Visualize your parents excitingly awaiting your arrival, free from their own wounding and from any problems in their relationship,. Imagine that you were conceived from their ecstatic connection and drawn into this incarnation on that energy. Hold the idea that each time they think of you during their pregnancy, they immediately get a deep sense of their love for each other. Notice what this does for the energy between them. Notice what this does for you.

Create a new picture of your birth: A picture where your parents are feeling competent, empowered and in charge of the birthing process. Get a sense of how excited they feel as your mother goes into labor. Picture the environment you would have most liked to be born into. Remember, you survived your birth so you can choose to envision being born on top of a mountain as an example, without worrying about your safety.

Now, let yourself be born... let your father, in his most loving state, be the one to catch you as you slide out of your mother. See his smile as he realizes the miracle he is holding. Perhaps you will notice there is a glow around all three of you. (If your relationship with your parents has been too painful and/or abusive for this to work for you, change the picture. Make up a new father and/or mother to be there for you. Or envision your biological parents coming to the realization that despite their love for you, they are not equipped to raise you, so they bless you and give you to a loving couple who will be able to fully be there for you.)

Breathe into how wonderful this feels to be born in love and beauty and peace. Feel the warm glow of all three of your hearts joining in a golden beam of light. Notice how good it feels to be birthed in a way that does no damage to your Spirit or the Spirits of your parents. Let your father place you at your mother's breast and feel her ecstasy at birthing this wondrous being who has now come to join her on the earth. Feel the love emanate from her to you, and let yourself surrender to this love. This is how the healthy conduit forms and your life on the planet begins. If you had siblings at birth, see them join you and your parents in the radiance of this familial love.

If you can feel as well as see the above imagery, it will start to re-weave any energetic holes created by dehumanizing birthing practices. It will be even stronger if you feel Divine love surrounding and protecting you. If you birthed your own children in a way you now feel was not best spiritually, re-envision their births and send the newborn part of them this love, warmth and radiance. You may want to pass this imagery along when those close to you become pregnant. Thus we can welcome more and more of our children into this world in a loving and peaceful way.

Because hospitals now have birthing rooms, if prospective parents will be firm with their doctors ahead of time, there is a strong likelihood of creating a hospital birth where all are honored. When parents are mature and fully educated about the birthing process, my preference is to promote home births where the birthing environment can be controlled to be optimally beneficial to the Spirit of both the parents and the newborn child.

Activating More Healing

Once you have visualized your birth to honor your true spiritual nature, you might want to think about your parents' general attitude toward you and any other children in the family. Also think about their methods of discipline. If you were treated abusively through experiencing or observing violence, sexual assault and/or molestation, harsh discipline, verbal criticism or cruelty, or through being expected to be someone you were not, be aware that your energy field has been negatively affected. The healthy conduit which should have formed between you and your parents was distorted or in more extreme cases, shattered. If you have done effective inner child work and deep emotional healing, you have minimized the effects on your energy field. And if you have done additional work with a good energy healer to repair your aura, it is likely that you have successfully changed any negative energetic configuration which existed between you and your parents as well as you and your children. If you have not yet done this work, I strongly recommend you seek outside help to do this. It is difficult to heal these negative configurations on our own.

Now think back to your adolescence. How would this time have been different if you had been fully encouraged to be yourself, to think for yourself and to speak your truth all the while feeling safe, loved and honored by your parents? Imagine a protective glow around you while you venture forth to stand up to peers, teachers and any others who try to impede your genuine expression. Imagine that you voice your perceptions and have them honored, in and out of your family.

Visualize a school where the teachers are there to aid your evolution, where the social norms have shifted from those of competition to those of cooperation so that friends are always caring and encouraging of each other. Imagine this environment promoting individual talents and lauding all forms of innovative ideas and expression. Nothing would be considered "too weird" but rather viewed and appreciated as creativity. The adults and older teens in the environment are there to help you channel these creative flashes into poems, stories or plays, new movement, new music, new technology, new ways of relating, new ways of perceiving. School is a learning community, not an "educational institution." Let yourself breathe into this imagery. See that young adolescent that you were, flourishing in this new experience.

Let yourself conjure up a picture of what you look like at twelve or thirteen. If you feel you are unattractive at this age, use your imagination to change your appearance. We are all beautiful, but all too often this beauty goes unrecognized, especially if our self-esteem is low. Because early adolescence is an enormously self-conscious time, many of us carry shaming beliefs about how we looked. Usually, looking at a photograph from that time can help. If you were actually unattractive at that age, it is because your true self had already started to hide. Look into the picture to find the real Self of this young girl or boy – see their Divine spark and then use your power of visualization to alter the outer self – a flattering haircut, flattering and/or "cool" clothing, straighter posture, straighter teeth; all this can do wonders. See your parents looking at you with pride, honoring the young man or woman they can see about to burst forth, while being clear about respecting your personal boundaries. Breathe into this. See that young teen surrounded by parental love, encouragement and trust. Let yourself re-travel that journey in a way that empowers your Spirit rather than deflates it.

Think back to what might have caused you to hide your Divine self at this time. Was it the insensitivity or authoritarian belief system of your parents? If so, change this. Was it school and/or your peers? Again, create the new school with new healthy peer norms. Do your best to step outside of conventional experience to create a learning environment where you are empowered to choose your own courses with teachers as guides rather than authority figures. See also that the teachers have created a sense of community where there is respect and caring for all students and differences are not just tolerated, but appreciated for adding depth and brilliance to the tapestry. In a self-directed learning environment, in a community that honors all and therefore is not steeped in competition, the classic social back-biting of those early teen years, shifts as well.

This is the developmental phase where we can activate our capacity to utilize our power. Perhaps this is why society has been so quick to repress and suppress teenage energy. If our parents were not able to help us come forward with this power, our connection to our Spirit withers in some way and must be reclaimed. Parents that understand how to create the appropriate energetic container are able to give their young teenagers tools to withstand difficult peer interactions, early "broken-hearts", and dishonoring or violating teachers.

If this young teen you see in the photograph did not have those inner tools, imagine you can now provide these for your teenage self. Empower this part. Help him or her be and express their authentic essence. See this happening in your mind's eye. It is almost as if you can breathe life back into your adolescent self through your intent, through your ability to love, validate and honor this part of you.

By looking at yourself at this age and sending love, encouragement and wisdom, you can help this little teen part of you stand up straighter, speak louder and more authentically, and withstand any peer derision. Simply by sending this energy of love, encouragement and wisdom, this part of you will come out of hiding and begin to connect with their (your) Spirit. See yourself telling this teenage part that they have a spiritual path, a path that was in place before they were even conceived. Imagine how the world would change for our young inner teens when we tell them there are higher beings surrounding them who all wish to help them on their path. Let yourself feel this – breathe it deeply into the center of your being.

Now do this with the older teen inside you. The older teen is generally not as vulnerable to peer or parental pressure and carries even more focused power than the younger teen. This part is also naturally sexual. It is a time of life when life force energy surges through us. This part is also acutely aware of all the contradictions and hypocrisy in the adult world. Use the school imagery above to see this part of yourself steeped in creative and stimulating mental pursuits. All of life is approached passionately by this older teen energy, and high-spiritedness and fun-lovingness infuse every interaction. When you feel fully in touch with this part, affirm him or her, letting them know how much you appreciate them. As with the younger teen, breathe this part into the center of your being.

Work with this imagery twice each day for two to three weeks. You only have to spend a minute in the morning and a minute at night envisioning and breathing in this new feeling of empowerment. When you feel deeply connected, see this teenager integrating into your adult self so that wherever you go, whatever activities you engage in, this vibrant youthful aspect participates with you. As you work with these teenage parts you will see new levels of confidence develop which will become more operative in your present life. You will also be having more fun and generally finding yourself in higher spirits.

As you reclaim this part of your Spirit and feel this energy connected to all aspects of your life, you will find your ability to create a positive reality for yourself deeply enhanced. If you have had a difficult relationship with the parents who raised you in this lifetime you will feel empowered to change this. They will no longer have any power to usurp any part of your Spirit; therefore you have nothing to lose when you treat them with compassion.

Remember compassion should never include sacrificing your emotional or spiritual well-being. It is in no one's interest for you to get re-victimized. While, in some cases, it is possible for those of you with abusive parents to be kind and cordial, it is better to stay away than to re-engage in the old dysfunction. Your risk is greater with these parents if the abuse has not been brought out into the open. If the secrets are still in place, subtle energetic levels still operate which could endanger the work you have done. So be careful.

However, if there are no longer secrets and if you have done your healing work and severed the energetic cords, you will be able to see that even the most awful circumstances provided you with the choice to develop the inner resources which have allowed you to get to this point in your life. It is okay to be grateful for your ability to survive these circumstances and for the strength and depth you developed because of this. Understand too, there were loving, gentle ways for you to develop these resources, but developing them in the context of an abusive childhood can be utilized to your benefit now. Having survived abuse, you are in a better position to help stop abuse on the planet than those who have no experience with it. As you absorb this awareness it allows the soul parts which have fragmented in response to the pain, to reconnect in a new way.

If you have a difficult relationship with your own children, realize the more deeply you are connected to your own Spirit, the more deeply you can encourage them on their path. Children still need us in various ways, no matter what stage of life they are in. As adults, we can continue our development without our parents, but it is a great gift when we have parents who can still help us along. It is thus an awesome emotional gift we can give our children when we model a path of growth and then encourage, honor and applaud them for their own. If you have not yet been able to provide this for your children, realize the more you empower your own Spirit, the easier it is to move into "right relationship" to them.

Let yourself visualize each of your children. Notice their soul shining through them. If they are at a defiant or currently at a difficult stage, it is okay to think back to an earlier picture – go wherever you need to in order to see their Essence. Remember that sweet innocence they were born with. Let yourself connect to their inner Light. Once you get a clear image of this, superimpose this onto the inner picture you hold of them now. Hold this image a few times a day for a few weeks. Every time you see this child, see their light. If you will do this with consistency, you are likely to experience startling results.

To recap from the Gibran poem at the beginning of this section, it is the parents' obligation to send loving energy and encouragement to the child, not the other way around. This has been deeply misunderstood in our culture. Parents often believe, consciously or otherwise, that their children owe them something. Children often are aware of this from a very young age. They begin to believe it is their job to make their parents look good and feel adequate. They feel an obligation to make their parents happy and often to make up for what was missing in their parents' childhoods. Shifting these beliefs and reclaiming the power of our inner light allows us to cut free from the old destructive configuration. This is the karmic resolution our soul seeks.

When we collectively come to the realization that love can exist only in freedom, and from pure heart energy – then as a culture we will create new healthy models of parenting. Until then, we must continue this quest as individuals. The more of us who break free from parental and societal tangles, the more of us there are who keep a loving conduit between ourselves and our children. This greatly affects future generations as we add loving energy to the web of life and amplify the energy needed for global transformation.

Karmic Connections

As a rule, family members come into the world with karmic ties to one another. These patterns may be dramatic and intense. Some are based on deep love. Others are based on deep challenges; lessons our soul has chosen to learn in this lifetime. Some, of course, are based on both. Karmic ties are energetic configurations that are incomplete. This translates into contracts that need to be fulfilled. Issues that are unresolved create a magnetic field to draw life situations that provide opportunity for completion.

No matter what the karma at birth, there is always the potential to work it through for optimum soul development. As an example, if a child is born to a parent who has abused them in another lifetime, to optimally finish the contract, the parent has to not repeat the pattern. For the child, he or she needs to break free of the negative beliefs about the self which were formed from the abuse and not yet worked through. The highest resolution of this contract would be for the parent to treat this child with gentleness, love and understanding; this in turn, would make it easier for the child to break through old guilt and shame. However, if the parent has not grown enough in their own spiritual and emotional development, there is a strong likelihood they will repeat some form of abusive behavior, which will have the same emotional and energetic effect on the child. Even if the parent is not willing to do their share of growth, the child, once grown, has the option to move through the old pain, transform and thus complete their karma. This means that this particular soul would not need to come back again to work this out, and the parent will have to find another way to complete their own karma. We always have the option of working through our part of the karma even when the other souls involved choose not to.

Other common types of karmic issues that come through in parent/child relationships are those of self-worth, personal power and competition. I have noticed that parents who have difficulty taking responsibility for their own negative behavior and thus tend to blame others, often have children who feel inwardly to blame for things they had no part in. While this is easily explained by psychological theories of conditioning, I think there is something deeper going on here, driven by the karmic energetic configurations of parent and child.

People who blame others tend to experience deep, unconscious levels of shame. When we carry this shame, we feel that we are defective in some way; and we may compensate for these feelings by pretending to ourselves that whatever we do is beyond reproach. Any criticism threatens to break through that defense and release the shame into consciousness which will create great psychic discomfort. Unless this person is committed to soul growth, their inability to deal with this discomfort may lessen any motivation for breaking through this pattern, even though that is the optimal purpose of this configuration.

This type of parent may well magnetize a child who has an energetic configuration that has formed around guilt. This means that the soul of the child carries a belief that they have failed in some significant way, or done something wrong. This child then would often feel a sense of having erred in some way or not having done enough. What a perfect match. The parent can blame in order to cover their inner shame, and the child will take the blame to validate their own inner feeling of guilt. Conversely, parents who struggle with guilt may draw in children who are dealing with shame and therefore project fault onto their "guilt-ridden" parents. The energetic resolution occurs when the parent owns their shame or guilt and works it through, thus helping to free the child from theirs. Or when the child reaches adulthood and chooses to get free.

There are numerous potential configurations. Some are easy; for instance a child who needs deep encouragement to be themselves might magnetize parents who are skilled at this. Children who are holding fears from other lifetimes might be drawn to stable, comforting parents in this one. Many types of configurations, both easy and challenging, can exist simultaneously. Be aware that parent/child relationships facilitate both parties' growth no matter what their nature. We have the choice to resolve them optimally together or simply to resolve them by ourselves, separately. This is where free-will comes in. We always have the option as adults, to view all the karmic lessons presented to us from a perspective of higher awareness and with an attitude of gratitude for the opportunity to grow. This choice is necessary to bring them to their resolution.

SIBLING RELATIONSHIPS

Inherent in sibling relationships is the potential for remarkably deep and abiding love. Whether because of genetics, shared early environment, and/or previous soul connections, we usually are able to have a very special connection with our brothers and sisters. In a healthy loving family, all children are honored for their own uniqueness. They are each seen as a special gift to the family unit. The parents do their utmost to provide for each child's needs, foster individuality and encourage them to develop their own talents, which minimizes the likelihood of any deep sibling rivalry.

When we look at this type of family from an energy point of view, the configuration that is formed would look something like the following. The parents would be in the center of a circle that was formed by the children. When the children are young, they face into the circle, and loving, protective light flows from the combined hearts of the parents to the heart of each child. The children are sending and receiving loving beams of light to and from each of their siblings as well. As children reach adolescence, they turn to face the outside of the circle in order to enter the world. This is a gradual process of each child developing their own resources to face the world at their own pace. As this change in the circle occurs, the parents are still beaming their love and protection, but each child has full freedom to venture out on his or her path. Because we are holographic, and thus each of us contains the whole, the energy configuration of the family unit stays with this growing child as he or she ventures out and gives them a strong sense of security on their journey.

Let yourself imagine this from both your family of origin and from the family you may be creating or have created. Close your eyes, breathe deeply and sense this. Feel love emanating from your parents' hearts and love emanating from the hearts of your siblings being beamed to you. Then beam love from your heart to them. If your parents were too unloving for you to feel this, make up a new family, but you may still want to include your siblings in the circle. If you were an only child or had only one sibling, you will have to envision a different geometric configuration. An only child might be standing in front of the parents, facing inward as a young child, and then outward. Two siblings might stand slightly apart at an angle in front of the parents. If there is only one parent, just adapt this as needed. Feel the glow of the love that is emanating from everyone and realize that as you do this, you amplify it, since you contain the whole of that love. Then switch the scene, and put yourself in the parent role if you have your own children.

If you and/or your siblings have children, see the family circles all linked to each other. Put your family of origin's circle in the center, and see the new partners and children in these outer circles adding their heart energies and ultimately creating new circles. It begins to look like a molecular structure, with all the circles connected, amplifying the love and continuing to create totally new configurations. If you include several generations you will begin to see infinite numbers of configurations. When all are connected in love, our planet will be wonderfully transformed.

Sibling Issues

While I think it is unrealistic in our culture for there to be no sibling rivalry, in healthy families this does not run deep. Part of the reason for sibling rivalry in our society is the collective belief that holds competition in such esteem. Birth order plays an important role as well. Older children are typically given more power in the family, but also less nurturing. Resources tend to expand as the parents grow older, so youngest siblings generally have more economic ease in their lives. Parents are also maturing and are likely to be more relaxed and therefore, less controlling. Oldest children may have had the advantage of parents being more active and playful, while the youngest children may get more stability and quality emotional time. Older children will typically resent the younger ones for having more material things and attention, and younger children will often envy the older children for their aura of authority. Middle children have their own role to play, as do oldest daughter vs. oldest son, and youngest daughter vs. youngest son. Again, even in a functional family, some of these issues are likely to be operative, but their impact on the energetic connections will be negligible and disappear over time.

Hostility and/or abuse between siblings is typically a result of parental dysfunction. Sibling abuse can be caused by a parent aligning with one child against the other(s), or by an older child acting out their own abuse on the younger ones. I have worked with many people who came to therapy alienated from their siblings, and later when they were able to remove themselves from their dysfunctional family role, became awed by the amount of love and sense of connection they developed with their brothers and sisters.

When children are being abused by their parents, I have seen two polar responses in the sibling group. In some families, siblings respond to the abuse by bonding tightly together, protecting and nurturing each other the best they can. Conversely, in other abusive families, the dynamics are such that the siblings are alienated from each other. Sometimes, both configurations exist at once. In one very abusive family, twin sisters were able to bond and energetically protect each other, while their brother, who was deeply disturbed, would act abusively toward them. They were able to reach adulthood with their hearts and Spirits much more intact because of what they were able to provide each other.

In another abusive family, all five siblings would bond together. They would go outside when the parents were getting drunk, and have meetings about how to help each other manage and survive the family situation. Imagine the energy field that would surround these children as they were doing this. While it would have contained much pain, their support and love for each other would also be energetically amplified.

On the other hand, many abusive families go about systematically separating the children from each other. One way this happens is by one or both parents scapegoating a particular child and rewarding the others for doing the same. This can be an intentional or an unconscious process. It is devastating either way. By using their children to carry out their unhealthy agenda, parents create disruptions in the aura of all their children, and the disruptions are increased by keeping each sibling isolated from each other, leaving them all the more vulnerable to the negativity of the parents.

Less dramatic ways the energy bond between siblings is interfered with includes one child being selected as a parent's favorite, thus giving that child preferential treatment and usually more responsibility for the parent's emotional well-being. Ironically, while the other child or children feel more rejected, the "selected" child is more invaded and entangled.

Another way to interfere with the sibling bond is for each parent to align one of the children getting them to side with them against their spouse. Siblings are then emotionally and energetically separated by the "us and them" mentality which exists within the family.

A damaged sibling bond can be reconnected if the family chooses some healthy and successful intervention or when the children grow up and go through their own healing process. Each adult child will have to release enough of their parents' dysfunctional energy from their own field in order to be free to relate to their siblings authentically.

If you were set up in your family to be alienated from your siblings and have not yet reconnected in adulthood, take some time to analyze the dynamic that was present in your childhood home. You might even make a chart of the family alliances and how that affected your relationships with one or more of your siblings. If there are siblings you still do not get along with, notice if you are putting characteristics onto them from their early family role, or whether you really believe that they are unable to separate from the negative family role and be themselves. Do your best to give them the benefit of the doubt. You may want to write out all your gripes about them and see which ones, if any, are still operative. The next time you are with them, imagine them as they could be if they were not influenced by the family negativity. Then see what happens. Sometimes remembering them as very young children can help you break free of your negative feelings. It is very rare that children in families do not share some warm and fun times together no matter how dysfunctional the family. Again, it has been my experience to see many siblings who believed they did not like each other and had nothing in common, awed by the deep love and support they found in each other once the healing took place. Be aware however, if you are the emotional pioneer in your family, that is, if you are the only one of the sibling group who has faced their pain and sought to heal, your other siblings may withdraw more from you as they are still afraid to face the real issues in the family.

FRIENDSHIPS

Remember, all relationships in our life are reflections of parts of us. Sometimes they are wonderful creative parts, sometimes they are wounded dysfunctional parts, but always they are important mirrors. The more conscious we become, the more we are able to attract people who will help us learn our deepest lessons, resolve our most challenging karma and support our growth and life's purpose.

In our modern society, friendships have taken on a stronger role than ever before. Many of us are geographically separated from the families we grew up in. With the rate of divorce and the large number of adults choosing to stay single and/or childless, we need friendships to fill in the spaces traditionally filled by family members.

Because of our cultural conditioning, friendships between women tend to be deeper, more emotional and therefore more potentially growth-producing than friendships between men. For the same reason, women tend to create more drama and more difficult situations with each other. This leaves women ripe for inner transformation from these relationships should we choose to use these challenges as opportunities for growth. Certainly this is not unavailable to men. Men who break through the cultural injunction and get close to their friends may also find these friendships can propel spiritual and emotional growth.

Friendships, like all other important relationships, tend to either facilitate soul growth or help us stay stuck. Who we magnetize into our circle is determined by our conscious or unconscious intention. If you think about your closest friends throughout your life, you may begin to notice the synchronicities that brought you together. By interpreting these synchronicities, we can begin to see why we drew certain friends into our lives at different times.

You might want to make a time-line of your closest friends, starting as far back as you can remember. Even pre-school and kindergarten friends can be significant. Under each friend, write in the year the friendship began, as well as the year that it ended (if this is relevant.) Make note of what circumstance brought you together, and if you are no longer friends, what circumstances ended the relationship. Then spend some time thinking about the deeper meaning of that friendship. This would include what you learned about yourself and the world from this particular friend. Notice specifically what these friendships mirrored about you. Were any special qualities in you nurtured or developed through these relationships? Were there painful situations that taught you important lessons? Notice if you are the type of person to keep your friendships vital and to let them go if it is the time to do so.

Those of us who have chosen a path of conscious growth in this lifetime generally have had to leave behind friendships that did not support our growth. Realize if you stay in any relationship that does not promote or at least support your growth, the energy connection will tend to pull you down. If people leave a friendship, it does not mean that they stop loving each other, it only means that staying in each other's fields is no longer serving a positive function. If you find yourself with friends where there are unhealthy cords between you, cords that in any way restrict your growth or well-being, it is important to sever those cords. This may allow the friendship to transform into something healthy or conversely to whither and ultimately end.

If you are trying to disentangle from the unhealthy aspects of a friendship and your friend does not want this to happen, an interesting process generally ensues. As you cut and thus disentangle the old cords, you will likely feel some initial freedom. Then you may find this friend creating a crisis or other type of drama as a means of drawing you back in. This process is typically unconscious for the person who is hoping to keep the status quo. A typical scenario might go like this:

You and Kathleen have been best friends for 10 years. Much of your friendship has involved sharing problems you are having in various romantic and familial relationships. As you have grown and healed, you have begun to find you do not need the type of input and support that Kathleen has given you, because you have learned to trust you own awareness and perceptions. You might also find that you feel frustrated trying to provide ongoing support to her, as she never seems to make any real changes in her life. Of late, your friendship tends to consist solely of you being the person she comes to when she is in pain. She may also have the expectation that you must always be there to help her. While you want to be loving and compassionate, you might begin to notice how drained and/or irritated you feel when you are with her. This is an important signal that something must change. You might want to say something like: "We never have much fun anymore. Let's go to a movie or out to hear music" (whatever the two of you typically like to do that has been enjoyable in the past.) You might also add that you would like the relationship to be more than just a discussion of personal problems. Probably Kathleen will agree. But what you will generally notice is that even if you begin to do activities which used to be fun, if she has not made some inner changes, you will not feel that you are having a good time. This may be because she finds a way to talk about her problems anyway, or it may simply be the vibrational field the two of you create when you are together is dense and therefore feels heavy.

At this point, it would be good to notice where the unhealthy cords exist between the two of you which tend to create a negative field. Then go ahead and release the cords – doing that in the same way I have suggested with other relationships: imagining you can pull the cord out from your own field, kiss the end you have disconnected and send it back to Kathleen with love. You will begin to get that sense of freedom I mentioned above.

If Kathleen is really set on not growing, it is also likely that within a few days she will call you with some "irresistible" problem, where she wants your insight and/or help. Or maybe she will just be so depressed that she will imply or actually threaten to "end it all." The amount of escalation of the drama will match her level of dysfunction as well as her desire to hang on to the old. It will also come as a test of your commitment to be true to your Spirit. If you can respond in a loving but detached way, refusing to go into your old role, you can keep the cords from re-attaching.

Another extreme scenario may go like this:

Kathleen calls saying her boyfriend just beat her up and she is scared and desperate. Her expectation of you, based on your previous behavior, is that you will run right over and rescue her, bring her to your house, take care of her kids, whatever the situation seemed to call for. This time, in order to transform the friendship, you will have to respond differently. A positive response to this could be "Oh, Kathleen, I am so sorry. I know that must be awful for you. Let me give you the number of the domestic violence shelter. I know you can change your life with that help." Then you must get off the phone. Use the same thing if there is a threat of suicide (look up the number for the suicide prevention hotline). If the call is less of an external emergency, but comes in the middle of the night, it is really appropriate and necessary to say that you will not deal with it now, but will check in with her in the morning. When you check in, keep it short. Say empowering things about her ability to resolve whatever has come up and then end the conversation. If you let yourself get sucked back into the old behavior, the old cord will re-attach and you will have to start all over again.

As you read the above example, notice if you currently have dysfunctional friendships in your life. If so, ask yourself what these friendships have provided you in the past. Did you feel valuable and important because your friend always needed you? Did you feel safe knowing if you always helped her, she/he would be there to help you? Are you still stuck in the classic co-dependent pattern of believing you can only be a good person if you are sacrificing yourself for another? Once you identify what has truly attracted you to and kept you in this type of relationship, then you must ask yourself if you are really ready to get free. This needs to be done with as much honesty as you can muster.

Just because we know something is unhealthy for us does not necessarily mean we are ready to change it. Yes, of course, your Spirit is urging you to, but maybe there needs to be more ego-healing before you are ready. If you realize you do not yet have the current motivation to change the situation, this is okay. Just stay as conscious as possible each time you interact with this person. Notice how you feel beforehand, how you feel during your interactions, and what feeling you are left with. Journal all your fears and concerns about setting new boundaries with this person. If you wish, you can create a conscious intention to become ready soon and then just observe how this happens. You will likely be amazed at how your conscious intention will set things in motion and the change will happen somewhat effortlessly. Your job is simply to get out of your own way and notice that any obstacles that arise are signals for deeper awareness and/or healing.

Often, we recreate unresolved family relationships in our friendships just as we do in romantic partnerships. As you analyze the dynamic of emotional connection with your closest friends, see if this is operative. Energetically this occurs when we have unresolved emotional issues. These issues create a magnetic energy configuration in our aura which draws people to us that resonate with this pattern. Whenever our friendships are not healthy, this is a sign that the old configuration is still there and needs to be transformed.

If you have many experiences where you have felt betrayed by friends, look for the pattern of betrayal which existed in your family and is now lodged in your belief system. This old belief is creating the energetic configuration that draws this pattern to you. When you heal the original pattern, the betrayals will disappear. Betrayals where friends turn out to be emotionally untrustworthy may also mirror a hidden part of yourself that you cannot count on. According to Carolyn Myss in her book **Sacred Contracts**, we all carry the archetype of the saboteur who will seek to undermine us as we near our desired goal. Until we develop a positive relationship with and a new "job description" for this saboteur, it is hard to break out of self-defeating patterns like drawing people to us who will not treat us fairly. When we recognize and own the "mirror," we become empowered to identify and transform this inner betrayer and will no longer draw friends or experiences of this nature.

There are other possible mirrors when you experience the feeling of betrayal from friends. It is possible that you are finding trustworthy people who become engaged in a mutual drama where they act in an uncharacteristic way, either actually betraying you or doing something that you interpret as a betrayal. The mirror here might be reflecting a disowned and dis-empowered part of yourself who believes that people are unpredictable and hurtful, and that ultimately you will be victimized by them. Again, when you identify and heal the parts that hold these beliefs, you rearrange the energetic patterns and begin to magnetize friends who will consistently have your best interest at heart.

Our friendships can and often do mirror positive qualities and beliefs as well. Friendships can encourage and inspire us to express new ideas, unrecognized talents and other serendipitous parts of ourselves. When I look back on my early childhood friends, I see important soul connections. One friend especially comes to mind. Besides sharing her somewhat wild imagination and irrepressible creativity and wit with me from kindergarten on, she introduced me to great literature and philosophy while we were in high school, and Yoga on one of the few times we saw each other after college. While I have not seen her now for over 35 years, if there is a time when we do reconnect, it will no doubt be as significant as always. It is obvious to me that this connection was a very old one. From the time we were very young, a part of our soul recognized each other and this instantly drew us together.

As children and teenagers, our friends can be our salvation from deeply dysfunctional and painful family situations. Many clients tell me of childhood friends and their families who provided solace and modeled sanity for them. These friends and families were magnetized for this purpose. They provided these clients hope as well as a sense of balance which would become more significant as they reached adulthood, chose to heal old wounds and actualize their soul potential.

WORK RELATIONSHIPS

Spirit is deeply at play in our workplace though people are rarely conscious of this. Spirit's work here is often indirect, yet provides us with remarkable challenges for growth and healing.

Workplaces in our society are riddled with people's unresolved emotional issues. Because of the large number of people in our culture who never emotionally finish adolescence, workplaces often are full of "acting out" teenagers in adult bodies, many of whom are in positions of influence and authority. Clearly in this environment, ego issues abound and it often feels as if our Spirit gets left at the door.

The typical workplace is structured in a way that invites people to recreate the dysfunction from their family of origin. Because it is rare to find a workplace that encourages individual responsibility where people can manage their own time, stay accountable as their position dictates and work in the way that is most efficient for them, the boss or supervisor, through their position of authority takes on the role of the parent. In turn, co-workers may take on the role of siblings. In this dynamic, people tend to replicate the dysfunctional roles they were given in their family: the Hero, Clown, Scapegoat or Lost Child; roles they unconsciously adopted to feed their parents' dysfunctional needs.

It is likely that our workplace has drawn souls we have connections with from other lifetimes. Adding that to the replicated family dynamic, work becomes a wonderful opportunity for soul development if we are willing to meet the personal and interpersonal challenges. In order to do this, we have to extract ourselves from the sickness in the system. As we do, we begin to resolve many of our personal and interpersonal issues. It will then become clear if our job matches our soul's higher purpose or if it is now time to move on to something new.

Because people generally associate their jobs with survival needs, work tends to have a strong base chakra vibration. Since the base chakra is also associated with tribal consciousness and tribal connection as well, it is consistent for family issues to arise in this environment. As we evolve to the point where we understand and perform work as Divine service, the energetic vibration will incorporate more heart chakra and crown chakra energy. This will cause a dramatic shift in "workplace dynamics."

If you have experienced difficult interpersonal challenges in your workplace relationships, ask yourself if you took this job because you believed it was aligned with your soul purpose and thus could help you develop and utilize your unique gifts, or did you take this job because you needed a paycheck? If you were drawn to this job primarily for base chakra reasons, chances are you have found yourself embroiled in situations and interpersonal issues which reflect what was still unresolved for you from your own family. The risks you need to take to resolve them will help you develop the inner security to move from the lower to the higher chakras in your relationship to work.

A Deeper Look at Childhood Roles in the Workplace

If you were the Hero in your family, the child that took care of your parent(s) and made the family look good by gaining positive recognition out in the world, you may well find yourself covering for your supervisor's incompetence, taking on more than your fair share of tasks and/or mediating the conflicts of co-workers in an attempt to keep everyone happy and functioning. Family Heroes in the workplace often find themselves having great influence and responsibility, but no genuine authority. Therefore they are not able to change unfair and/or unhealthy policies and practices. As a result, they often feel overwhelmed, believing it is their responsibility to make sure all work endeavors are successful even if this means unfair and unacknowledged personal sacrifice.

In order to extract yourself from this drama, you need to be prepared to set boundaries that are unlikely to be welcomed by your boss or co-workers. The energetic configuration here is similar to all other co-dependent relationships and so noticing where the cords might be tangled will help. Take some time to ponder and/or journal on what your job really is. If you and your employer had a written contract, what would you expect from each other? You might want to write up a contract that clarifies fair expectations for your job. We are paid money, which provides us with food, shelter etc. for services we perform which ultimately keep our world running. There needs to be a fair exchange. What essentially is being asked is for you to "earn your keep?" When you perform your end of a fair contract, the energy should be flowing freely. When you get enmeshed in unconscious unhealthy dynamics, you will feel the entanglements.

To be ready to extract yourself means you need to value yourself for who you are, not for what you do or how well you care-take others. These are third chakra issues of empowerment and self-esteem. Part of the way we strengthen our third chakra energy is to act with integrity. That means we have to fulfill our part of the contract. As we support our self-esteem in these ways, we become able to activate our personal power to get free of the old family roles.

Be prepared for inner resistance as you begin the process of staying true to yourself rather than to the expectations of people in your workplace. You may be giving up a level of status given to you by the person in charge and perhaps also by your co-workers. But that status only feeds your ego, not your Spirit. As you free your self-esteem from needing others to recognize and give you approval, you will be amazed at how free you become. There's a wonderful saying on one of Wayne Dyers *Inner Wisdom Cards*: "Other people's opinions of me are none of my business." Try walking through your workplace and your life holding that awareness. Once free, miracles can begin to happen. I have often seen people suddenly offered a new, exciting job or be transferred unexpectedly to a much healthier work environment.

If you find or have found yourself being victimized in the workplace, it is likely you have recreated a family dynamic of being the Scapegoat. You may be scapegoated for "whistle-blowing" or in other ways telling the truth about the office dysfunction; or you may be scapegoated on a personal level by being the brunt of others' jokes, derision and/or hostility. Again these are third chakra challenges. The first scenario asks that you learn to hold your sense of well-being, knowing you have spoken from your heart and honored your integrity. Often children are scapegoated in families because in telling the truth they are challenging the denial system that the parents hold so dear. It is rare that a child can continue to hold on to their sense of self when they are bombarded with negativity from the rest of their family. When this is recreated in adulthood, this provides another opportunity for healing this wound.

We have to heal our third chakra issues to resolve the scapegoat scenario as well. When we are derided or insulted by others, we are seeing a mirror of how we inwardly dishonor ourselves. Think about when you were treated disrespectfully by others. This can extend beyond family members to school and peer groups. Notice what stage of development you were in, because this is the part of your inner child that will need your attention. Also notice if your ego has some attachment to being in this role? Perhaps some of your identity has formed around this dynamic, and you feel "safer" knowing that people will ultimately mistreat you, rather than getting taken by surprise in case they do. Or maybe this gives you more fuel for your outrage since life always treats you unfairly. To uncover the deeper reason may demand that you seek outside guidance through therapy or another therapeutic modality. The transformation of this pattern will change your life.

If you find you are generally liked but not taken seriously in your workplace, this probably indicates you have been in the Clown or Mascot role in your family. Typically this role is occupied by the youngest child who acts cute and entertaining as a way to lighten up the tension in the family. While this child is valued in the family because they are fun to be around, they typically underachieve because they feel their value comes in entertaining others and not in developing a sense of competence. For workplace "Clowns," the mirror is asking you to take yourself and your gifts seriously and once again to detach from the opinion of others.

Lost Children, the fourth family role, tend to feel as invisible in their work settings as they did in their families. They are likely to do good work, not seek recognition and not make any waves. The inner belief is to support those in authority by never inconveniencing them or drawing attention to themselves. This typically leads to feelings of isolation and disconnection from one's core. In this role, one goes about their "duties" so to speak, but their inner self is not participating in the process. If you recognize yourself here, use it as a signal that you need to do more emotional healing. Again, this is a third chakra issue. Your lesson is to know that you count and are of value just by being who you are.

As we listen and follow the stirring of our Spirit out into the world, we will find we are released from these lower chakra issues. If this is a difficult task for you, then look more deeply at your resistance which is likely to be made up of old beliefs about yourself and the nature of the world.

SOUL GROUPS

James Redfield speaks a great deal about soul groups in his book ***The Tenth Insight***. Groups of souls both in this dimension and others were drawn together for a higher purpose. The humans in the group needed to work out their individual soul issues with each other in order to actualize this higher purpose. Through their work, they reconfigured their energy fields and thus were able to carry out their mission. When we take this concept and generalize it to our daily lives, our view of friends and community takes on a whole new meaning and perspective.

In our modern world, people are usually involved with several different groups simultaneously. When we begin to look at these groups as souls coming together for a deeper purpose, we are able to see things heretofore hidden, and we can open to a level of growth not previously identified.

There are typically two distinct types of groups we participate in: groups we consciously choose, such as a close circle of friends, life-partner, like-minded colleagues, people who share similar interests, etc.; and groups we find ourselves in, such as our families, work groups, parents of our children's friends, people in our religious or spiritual communities, teammates, neighbors, service groups, etc. Any group like these where the relationships have longevity is likely to be some type of soul group.

It is also a frequent experience that one of your soul groups will begin to intersect with another of your soul groups with no conscious effort on your part. You will find that people in one group have connections with people in some of the other groups. I visualize this as a group of circles, many of which are concentric and connected to each other in varying degrees, some that barely overlap and others that significantly overlap.

Take a moment and think about the groups you are in. You might want to draw them on a chart noticing which groups overlap and which do not. Notice that the energy is intensified in the groups which have a lot of overlap. These will be most directly connected to your soul's mission. Ponder their deeper purpose in your life and even in the life of our planet. Think about the overall characteristics of these overlapping groups and what they mirror in you. Look at the most positive characteristics and imagine each soul in these groups owning these characteristics and creating an intention to amplify this out into the world. Creative groups would send out creativity to all; socially conscious groups would send out justice; groups formed around spiritual awareness or development would send out compassion and consciousness to all.

Realize then, that these groups which can serve so many different functions in our lives, at their deepest and most purposeful can shift the world.

****

To sum up this chapter, remember that all relationships in our lives serve as mirrors of our inner development. These mirrors allow us a deeper understanding of ourselves and others. The more intimate our relationships, the more likely they are to uncover aspects of ourselves which we may have blocked from consciousness. Group situations such as workplaces, can also serve to be profoundly informative about our development.

We can choose to learn from all the relationships in our lives, and it is up to us to make the most of this feedback. As we own our projections, interpret all mirroring presented to us, heal our disconnected parts, transform our old belief system, honor ourselves and others and lovingly refuse to participate in unhealthy connections, we clear our energetic field. As we clear our field, we intensify our ability to send pure love out into the world. The more love we project, the more we attract. Soon we find ourselves surrounded by loving people who are connected to their essence and to the energy of universal love and illumination. From this, we continuously strengthen the power of our Spirit. All sense of victimization has fallen away.

Romantic connections become based on the principles of equal and loving partnership. The old model of separation with its power and control issues dissolves. Parent/child relationships honor the miracle of procreation, gestation and the spiritual essence of all incoming souls. Children are free to be themselves and to be loved for who they really are. Parents connect with their spiritual guidance and thus are able to be in the flow of life. They are able to carry out their parental role feeling empowered, loving and blessed, rather than scared, guilt-ridden and isolated. Sibling bonds are healed, allowing the most positive aspects of ancestry and genetic coding to amplify, while the old dysfunction falls away. Friendships are magnetized to encourage, inspire and support the development of all involved. Workplace connections are formed from our hearts and our spiritual vision, not from our base chakra or unresolved childhood issues.

As we align, we begin to recognize our soul groups and participate in pre-birth contracts more consciously. As these contracts become clear, we feel both empowered and committed to carrying them out for the highest good of all involved. Loving and enlightened energies become amplified as we commit to this process.

From this alignment, all relationships in our lives are magnetized to us from the stirring of our Spirit with the intention of infusing all life with love and illumination, rather than from old karmic issues and unresolved emotional pain. The families we create will easily provide the love, security and guidance to continue this into future generations. Our communities will reflect this health and well-being, and we will see our social institutions magically and magnificently transformed. We will explore evolved families and communities in the next two chapters.

8: FAMILIES FOR THE NEW PARADIGM

To create a society filled with conscious, loving, spiritually evolved people, we must look at transforming the powerful institution of the family. In its evolved version, families consistently honor the Spirit of all their members while providing them with unconditional love, nurturance and support, as well as physical and emotional safety. Each family unit is headed by empowered adults who are connected to their essence and who know they can co-create positive reality for themselves, their children and their world. Relationships are equal partnerships based on honesty, love and mutual respect. Not only can families like this sustain us through these times of change, but more importantly they will allow us to build the kind of social and emotional foundation we need to propagate and maintain a just and healthy world.

For decades our families have been in a state of flux. While this instability has given rise to a multitude of previously hidden and therefore unexplored social problems, it has also allowed us to finally see and begin to heal what has not been working. In addition, it allows us to create new versions of family. We are in the early stages of this with the rise of blended families, single-parent households, same sex couples, and families with children headed by gays and lesbians. I think we will find families continuing to transition over the next several years with the final configurations not fully predictable.

It is interesting that there has been such controversy and fear over the idea that marriage could extend beyond consisting of one man and one woman. While some of this is propelled by homophobia and the political agenda of the religious right wing, I think the deeper motivation is driven by the inaccurate belief that if we keep the outward form of the traditional family, it will create safety and stability. As we evolve, we come to realize the fallacy of this. We understand true safety and stability come from creating healthy inner dynamics in a family unit which has nothing to do with gender or sexual orientation. Simultaneously, we also recognize the wisdom of creating strong, stable family units; they simply will not look or act like their traditional counterparts.

The overwhelming changes we have seen in the nuclear family began in the late 60's. We started to question the value of the traditional family and simultaneously to challenge the institution of marriage. Some saw marriage as a societal ruse to keep women oppressed. Monogamy was often viewed as a silly moralistic tradition that stifled people and interfered with their spontaneity and creative expression. We started to believe that happy fulfilled parents meant happy fulfilled children, but what we believed we needed for happiness and fulfillment did not always jive with the needs of our children. What we forgot was that children need a sense of stability to thrive.

The upside of these changes was a new insistence on gender equality which, in turn, provided models for a marriage based on genuine partnership, a prerequisite for emotionally healthy families in two-parent heterosexual households. The downside, as we know now, is that many children were wounded in this shift.

Children born from the mid 60's to the mid 70's became the first casualties of a sky-rocketing divorce rate; of fathers who were questioning their own roles and no longer felt the obligation to provide for their children; of mothers who, in seeking to fulfill themselves, dragged their children along on their adventures or quests for meaning. Huge numbers of adults were experimenting with drugs and overusing alcohol, often ignoring or harming their children in the process. Children were often exposed by both their divorced parents to a series of lovers, live-in or otherwise. Economic instability plagued these new family configurations because divorce laws had not caught up to the growing and enormous need for child-support enforcement. Women were pouring into the workforce, being paid substantially less than their male counterparts, and facing inadequate childcare which also had not caught up with the increased demand. Many young children were left to fend for themselves after school. It was not a pretty picture.

This reconfiguration of the family has continued, but we are maturing some as a culture and learning ways to provide children with stability despite these changes. Many people who came of age in the 1960's and 1970's waited until they reached their 30's and 40's to have children. This newer generation of children has had a better chance of stability whether their parents stayed together or not. We have become more adept in adjusting to change. We have learned (or relearned) that children need a stable environment with a strong sense of connection whether through extended family or a strong network of family friends and community.

Some of us have created new models of marriage that promote individual growth and fulfillment while providing a secure and loving environment for our children and ourselves. Since there is now far more cultural permission to live authentically, many people have felt free to stay single (with or without children), to be in same-sex relationships, and to have live-in partnerships. While we are still working out the glitches, still experiencing the fall-out of this social transformation, this wider array of choices is part of our spiritual evolution.

Despite the problems we have today with children who are acting out violently, there is also progress afoot. Part of the reason today's children are seen as so extreme is because they refuse to put up with the dishonoring and abuse that older generations assumed was fairly normal. Rather than listening to these children and finding ways to treat them more respectfully, our societal response has been to prescribe drugs and devise more oppressive rules. Even the term "zero tolerance", a widespread policy that began in high schools in the mid-90's, speaks of the problem because it implies that the only thing that matters is whether or not a rule is broken, as opposed to the motivation causing a child to break a rule. Looking at what is motivating these children can both help design rules that are more reasonable and help troubled children to keep rules that are truly important.

On the other hand, children who are raised in loving families, families who have made empowered choices and have a sense of social justice and spiritual connection, are showing levels of remarkable development. These are the children whose parents have honored their Spirits, and these are the children who will be a significant force in the evolutionary shift. This chapter will look deeply at the types of families which produce these empowered children.

THE EVOLUTION OF THE FAMILY THROUGH THE RECLAIMING OF FEMININE POWER

Many of the positive changes in our families over the past 40 years are the result of our reclaiming the archetype of the powerful mature feminine. This archetype is fully available to both men and women, although at our present stage of development it is more easily accessible to women. As I have already pointed out, female power is about intuition and connection; it is an inner power that holds its ground while nurturing ourselves and others into wholeness. It is about control over the self rather than control of those outside the self. It is connected to the rhythms of our bodies and our planet. While female power in itself does not create outer change, (we need to utilize powerful mature male energy for this) a culture that dishonors or diminishes the powerful feminine archetype cannot produce emotionally or spiritually healthy people.

The most obvious beginning of this reclamation has been seen in our birthing practices. It is certainly in the gestating and birthing of our babies that we make direct contact with the essence of feminine power. The Lamaze method of educated natural childbirth which began to gain popularity in the 1960's started this new wave that put women back in touch with their birthing power.

Prior to Lamaze, modern women were cut off from fully experiencing this amazing and powerful event because they were drugged during labor. Typically they were uninformed about the birthing process which created fear and therefore more pain, and kept them from feeling any sense of control. This prevented them from connecting with their own internal power. In addition, birthing mothers were separated from their partners and others they loved, and found themselves in a cold and uncomfortable delivery room where, more often than not, they were instructed to go against their primal instincts. For example, the practice of giving birth to a baby while on one's back is not a natural way to give birth and makes birthing significantly more difficult and painful. Yet traditionally women were not allowed to move into a more comfortable and natural position.

Natural educated childbirth also reestablished the importance of breast feeding. In previous decades women had been discouraged from nursing their babies. Bottle-feeding was touted as the modern thing to do, and often doctors told women that their breast milk was not suitable to feed their infants. Women did not know that the colostrum, which the breasts produce for the first 48 hours after childbirth, is a clear liquid, and thus they believed the doctors when told that their "milk" was too thin. Ironically this colostrum is full of vital nutrients and immunities. Because women were not educated about this and were culturally encouraged to bottle-feed, they gave up the remarkably powerful experience of providing all the necessary sustenance to keep their babies alive and healthy for the first six months of their lives. They also gave up the emotional closeness and well-being that can come for both mother and child during nursing. Both birthing and then parenting of infants had become frighteningly devoid of Spirit. With the re-emergence of feminine power in the birthing process, Spirit could begin to be part of the birth and early life of the baby.

Lamaze also made a significant difference in the role of the father. Men were welcomed as part of the birthing process and were now able to be directly included in this powerful experience. We know now that infants create deep bonds with people who are with them in the first 24 hours after their birth. With natural childbirth, mothers and fathers could be with their newborns. The absurd concept of isolating newborns in a nursery began to fall by the wayside as parents insisted on keeping the baby with them. When we interfere with the birthing process and separate newborns from their parents, we set up obstacles to creating conscious family. As this process has shifted, fathers have been able to bond with their babies in new ways, giving rise to very different family configurations and parenting styles. It has become normal for fathers to participate in caring for infants, changing diapers, rocking their babies to sleep, etc. When one has such an intimate connection to his or her infant, being an active parent throughout the rest of their child's upbringing follows naturally.

As women began moving into the workforce in record numbers, co-parenting became essential for a healthy household. Even fathers who were unwilling to take responsibility for household chores were more likely than their own fathers to provide care for their children. To do this in a loving way demanded that these men tap into their feminine qualities of sensitivity and nurturing. It also meant that men no longer needed to be emotional outsiders in their family. In the traditional patriarchal family, men had the economic and social power, while women often had the emotional power. Typically, mom and the children would be emotionally connected and dad would be isolated from this circle of warmth. Because this type of family structure could not give rise to an emotionally healthy family, the emotional bonding between mothers and their offspring often became unhealthy. As fathers take a more active role in the birthing and care of their children, the emotional configuration of the family can now change.

With women bringing home paychecks, men were freed from having to be the primary or in many cases, sole breadwinners. Sociologists know that cultural norms develop around our survival needs. Before and during the industrial era, physical strength was important in many of society's jobs. With the advent of post-industrialism, as we move from a manufacturing to a service-oriented society, the skills needed to sustain employment and therefore livelihood, have changed as well. To provide good service to people means we need to be emotionally aware and available, and have good communication skills. We need to use the feminine part of the self to master this, and men as well as women need to develop these skills to be adept in our new service economy.

For children to be raised in a conscious family, they must have parents who are whole, who have developed both the male and female strengths in the self, as well as who have owned their shadow parts. Men need to embrace their feminine side without sacrificing a well-developed masculine side. Women need to activate their male side, standing up for themselves and their children, while staying emotionally connected and nurturing. Ideally there will be more than one parent because the job of parenting is incredibly demanding. For single parents a strong loving supportive community can help fill this gap.

A healthy, spiritually evolved world can be created only by whole individuals. As the structure of family becomes an organically unfolding process fully committed to honoring the Spirit of each soul, new paradigm families embrace evolved concepts of birthing and child-rearing. Without the reclaiming of female power, this would be impossible.

THE DYNAMICS OF CONSCIOUS FAMILY

Close your eyes for a moment and imagine how it would feel to be born into an emotionally healthy, spiritually evolved family in which each parent feels happy and fulfilled as well as nurtured and enhanced by the marital relationship. In this family, parents understand that they are empowered to create the lives they desire. They are committed to honoring the Earth and all its life forms. They believe that each person born on the planet can make a loving and unique contribution and that all may live in simple abundance.

Breathe deeply and imagine that this family is giving birth to you. This birth is taking place in a family home where the energy field holds love, respect and nurturance. Notice that your mother is inwardly prepared and in charge of your passage through her into the world. She is able to flow with her contractions and mentally instruct her cervix to open as you push your way out of the womb and into this new life. Imagine your father is there to catch you as each of your parents' hearts overflows with gratitude for your arrival.

See the room filled with people your parents have chosen to welcome you: siblings, other relatives and dear friends. All are attuned to the sacredness of this event and have only love and good wishes for you. As you slide out of your mother's body, you feel the love emanating from your father's hands as he holds you and gently lifts you to your mother's breast. Once you are nursing, tasting the sweet liquid which will provide your body with the best possible nourishment, your father gently cuts the umbilical cord; thus, you are transitioned in the gentlest way from one world to another.

Feel yourself as this infant in a state of total peacefulness as you are immersed in the protective and loving energy field of your new home. Drink in the loving looks from your new parents and the others who are there to honor your entry to the Earth plane. Perhaps the room is also filled with the ethereal music your parents chose for this occasion and the fragrance of fresh flowers. Notice how whole and loved you feel as this infant. Let this feeling permeate through every cell in your body. Feel how this type of birth can create a natural faith and optimism as well as an immediate awareness that your purpose for incarnating could be carried out with ease. If this loving and protective field were maintained throughout your childhood, your Spirit would remain empowered and there would be no obstacles to manifesting your full potential.

Because few if any of us are born into such circumstances, our process is much more challenging. Nonetheless, *imagining* how we might have had a different journey in this lifetime if our passage had been joyful, peaceful and conscious begins to bring this image into our future.

In spiritually evolved families, conception is often conscious, not only planned but an event experienced by both parents in the midst of their love-making. Imagine how this begins to nurture the soul as well as the developing body of the fetus. Imagine if it were a universally accepted idea that all conceptions came from parents calling in a particular soul to incarnate to them and that soul agreeing; or from a soul's desire to incarnate with the parents and the parents consciously agreeing. At our level of human development, most of these agreements are unconscious, but as we take the evolutionary leap, our ability to remain conscious through all conceptions and births will be second nature.

Communication is open and flowing in evolved families. People consistently speak from their heart. Everyone is free to express his or her deepest feelings knowing that their feelings are important to the rest of their family members. All ideas and points of view are welcomed. Creativity and creative expression are held in high esteem.

The adults in the family are ultimately and equally responsible for decision-making, but the opinions of the children are solicited and considered. Children know that their voice counts. The adults understand how to base family decisions on a win-win model, so that any disagreement between them is worked out in such a way that each feels good about the outcome. This model is also used with the children when the decisions involved affect them directly. The more conscious and heart-centered the family, the more the parents are able to honor the gifts of each child and provide safety and encouragement so all the children may blossom according to the dictates of their Spirit.

Be aware though that at this stage in our evolution, even children who choose to be born into conscious families and feel their Spirits empowered, will be influenced by the beliefs of our culture. The norms and experiences they will be exposed to, can separate them to some degree from their Spirit. This is why parents must commit to staying conscious about and separate from the limited and often destructive cultural beliefs of our society in order to nurture, support and protect their children. Many parents are too scared or mystified by popular myths to validate their children's perceptions of what is wrong or crazy in the culture; in conscious families, this is not the case. Children are helped to understand that the culture creates these negative conditions out of fear, and they are given tools to operate within the culture as effectively as possible without internalizing its negativity and dysfunctional belief system.

Conscious families in the current transition need to assess whether or not to segregate their children from the larger culture. Much of this assessment needs to be based on the temperament of the child. As an example, a young child who is getting energetically worn down in public school needs an alternative. This can mean being home-schooled or going to a Montessori, Waldorf or similar type of school. Sometimes even a small church-run school can work if it has a loving energy and is open-minded. Conscious children are able to sort out any religious "indoctrination" when they have the backing of their families.

As children grow older, they have more resilience to deal with difficult cultural experiences. Because my two youngest children went to a Montessori school through sixth grade, they were well prepared for taking on the challenges of the culture when they transitioned to public school. My son was able to breeze through middle school and high school pretty much unscathed by the energy there. However, my youngest daughter, who was in high school some years before my son, hated it. She was involved in numerous activities, had many friends and was popular and seen as very successful, but the high school administration (which had been replaced by the time my son went there), sought to control its students by creating a hostile authoritarian environment which my daughter found intolerable. Because we were able to validate her perceptions, as did many of her teachers and some of the guidance staff, she was able to maintain her connection to her Spirit despite or maybe because of her overt response to the environment. She ultimately decided to graduate in three rather than four years, something that a wonderful guidance dean was able to work out for her, yet her pronouncement of, "I would never send a child of mine to that school," still rings in my ears. In retrospect, I feel strongly that it was perfectly fine for her to be there. While her Spirit was challenged, she also was given a hands-on education of what was not working in our society. It was not pleasant, but it was an important experience and no doubt will fuel her passion for carrying out her life purpose. Had she not had the support she needed from teachers and her guidance counselor, or had she gotten depressed, we would have sought another avenue for her.

Conscious families are tuned into their children's emotional and spiritual energy and feel empowered to carry out whatever needs to happen for their child's well-being. We had very little money when we put our youngest daughter in a fairly expensive Montessori school, but because we knew that she needed to be there, we always trusted we would have enough. Remember that conscious families always operate out of empowered beliefs so they do not put up roadblocks to doing what they know needs to be done for their family's well-being.

As we evolve, I believe it will become easier to protect our children's Spirits. In conscious families, we know these children have come to our planet and into our family for a purpose. We know they each have a special contribution to make to our world. That contribution may not be anything we are equipped to understand. Our world is shifting so rapidly that our job as parents may solely entail creating a loving and empowering process rather than focusing on developing any specific talents. Certainly, providing an enriched environment filled with books, music, puzzles and art supplies is necessary, as well of course as making sure our children spend plenty of time outside in the natural world, but essentially we need to follow our child's lead rather than taking that leadership into our own hands. This is very important because it is the only way to insure we are not projecting our desires onto our children. By focusing on the process and following their lead, we are allowing them to flower into full bloom through watering, fertilizing, adjusting the temperature and beaming them with light.

Again, you might want to take a moment and fantasize about what it might be like to go through childhood having your perceptions validated and being thoroughly encouraged to follow your inner leanings. Notice how it would feel to be provided with whatever resources, material and nonmaterial, you may need to do this. Create a dialogue with your Spirit asking how it would have responded to this type of environment. You can write this out. If you use the non-dominant hand to be your Spirit, your supra-conscious mind will likely speak to you directly. If you do not wish to write this out, do a meditation where you can carry on this conversation with your Spirit; when you come out of the meditative state, journal on your experience.

Understanding and Honoring the "Threshold Period"

Part of conscious child-rearing involves a deep awareness of developmental stages. Conscious parents know that toddlers must explore their world, and so they naturally adapt their environment to be baby-safe and baby-friendly. They understand the importance of children developing a sense of competence when they reach elementary school age, so they provide their kids with the tools they need to feel good about themselves in this stage. Adolescence is the time to develop a sense of identity separate from one's parents, and healthy families honor and guide their children through this individuation process.

As a society, we have carried a belief that adolescence ends around when teens reach eighteen. This is not accurate. Developmentally we do not reach adulthood until around thirty. We are just beginning to understand the last stage of adolescence and identify what is needed to cross this final bridge into adulthood.

In looking back at my own life, I see what an important developmental time the ages from 18-30 were for me. Ideally this should be a time of exploration where we become empowered to activate our life's sacred purpose. And from my personal experience, this certainly was the case. However, I needed to leave home and take some interesting and unconventional risks at the time to make this happen.

When both my daughters had entered this age group, I came upon a magazine article on teenagers which spoke of the "thresholding stage." This article identified 18 as the beginning of this stage, noting it was marked by the need to have a great deal of space from the parents, while at the same time needing to feel the parents are there for guidance. That struck me immediately because it was what I was observing in my own children. It also struck me that if we understood this more clearly, we would release our young adult children from the burden of having to define what they want to do in their lives and would allow them to more comfortably postpone "real jobs," relevant schooling and family responsibilities.

Astrologically, we all pass through our first Saturn return between the ages of 28 and 30. While astrologers have long understood that this is the age when people step fully into adulthood, our culture has shown a great deal of ignorance of this. Because of my awareness of this cycle and my own threshold experience, I had raised my children with the idea that college-aged kids rarely knew what they really wanted to do in their lives and that undergraduate school was simply to get an education, not a profession. Thus, as my oldest daughter graduated with a Bachelor's degree in English, it was perfectly fine with me that her next step would be to move to Northern California and work in a natural foods store.

It was more of a challenge for me to feel excited about my younger daughter stopping college after her first year. She had been at a school in Colorado, and she knew she would not return home to Illinois. Her goal was to travel, but since she had no money or car, she started her new life in a tiny mountain town where she knew many people, a half-hour away from where she had attended college. Because she wanted to save money for a car, she did not want to pay rent. She decided she could camp out when she was not staying with friends, and still work. I joked about my daughter being "homeless in Paradise," but it was only partially a joke. She was homeless. Cell phones were not yet popular, and while we had given her a phone card to call us, we could not reach her by phone. I had to deepen my faith and to trust what I knew of her, not what I was conditioned by our culture to believe. And what I knew was this: she was a very healthy, charming, lovely and loving young woman who was also strong, independent and resourceful. I knew she would be successful, and I was not disappointed. Within a few months she took a job as a nanny, where she had a nice place to live, even provided with organic food and was able to save enough money to buy herself a car for her travels.

As I pondered the process of both of my daughters and what they were going through, I began to formulate a fuller theory about this threshold stage of development. I realized they are going through a rite of passage. It is our lack of awareness of the need for this rite that has left so many young adults at loose ends. In addition to families emotionally supporting this passage, it would be wonderful if we had some curriculum for high school students that loosely outlined a process to meet the developmental tasks between eighteen and thirty. This process needs to allow and encourage diverse forms of self-expression and travel as well as social and community participation. European culture, by the way, does a much better job of fostering this. If our young people could be guided to identify intuitively, what they need for their own rite (or series of rites), we would see a deep and positive shift in our society. Instead we try to put these young adults into narrow boxes.

While I was writing about this, an editorial appeared in the teen section of our local newspaper. A high school student wrote about a discussion she had with her mother in response to her mother telling her she should get married just out of college. I am going to quote this young woman directly because she eloquently supports my point:

"My mom said that it would be great if I got married straight out of college. I told her I would marry in my late 30's just to irk her. It's fun to irk my mom, within reason." (Note: I have included this because it shows so clearly the psyche of the older teen when seeking a sense of their own power in relation to their parents.) *"Marriage at a young age may leave people with the impression of opportunities missed... They may begin to resent the restrictions and limitations (real or imagined) their marriages put on them... They may also wonder if they are able to stand on their own two feet. After going from the protection of parents to the protection of marriage, they may not have an idea of their resourcefulness... People who marry at a young age also may not have a good sense of themselves."* She then pointed out that when teens' views differ from their parents, it may take them a while to sort out what is rebellion and what is really coming from inside of them. She went on to say, *"People may lose themselves in how the world perceives them. They may come to identify themselves as someone's spouse... not as an entire person on their own."* Written by Yanny Siu, as printed in the *State Journal Register*, Springfield, IL., 9/11/01

The salient points made by Yanny Siu, who as a high school junior was 16 or 17, outline the developmental tasks of our modern thresholders:

- *Breaking free from their parents' views so they can clarify their own.*
- *Learning that they can depend on themselves for survival and well-being.*
- *Getting free from societal perceptions and conditioning.*
- *Developing an unwavering sense of identity that will not allow them to lose themselves in an external role.*

It is pertinent that this obviously bright and healthy young person could see so clearly what she needed, whereas her mother, who, I have no doubt was a loving and effective parent, was unaware of the deeper task at hand. Like so many parents, her mother was making the assumption that one becomes ready to step into full adulthood (marriage) upon graduating from college. This is a telling example of the changes our society must make as we develop spiritually, and the changes we will make when we focus on empowering the Spirits of our children and readying them to raise conscious families of their own.

When older teens are encouraged to follow their own heart and spiritual path, they can make any number of "right" choices. For some teens, college and a higher educational experience in general provide the gradual independence they need. Their lives are still structured for a while, and some "adult" responsibilities held at bay. If they are being intellectually and philosophically stimulated, great growth can occur. Those who thrive in undergraduate school may then choose to take some time after graduation to explore other aspects of the world and other aspect of themselves. This can be through self-supported travel or the Peace Corps, or simply finding an interesting place to live and a way to be self-supporting, free from the pressure to get on a "career track." For others, it will be a much more individuated journey, with each person feeling free to choose ways to explore themselves and their world while learning self-sufficiency. Encouraged in this manner, our young people would be far healthier and happier and in turn, would activate a new way of being in our world.

Because many parents these days are scared, they believe they must control their children in order to insure their well-being. Whether the teens' response is compliance or rebellion, they are not being equipped with what they need to cross the slow bridge into healthy adulthood. We need to be more conscious about this threshold period, helping parents learn to encourage, trust and support a deep and individualized exploration. The more emotionally healthy and conscious a family, the more children will have strong internal resources and a vibrant connection to intuitive guidance. These are children we can trust, and we must allow them to follow their journey whether it makes immediate sense to us or not.

Conscious families understand that life purpose and choice of a life partner often develop and blossom after crossing the threshold into adulthood. We need to give thresholders plenty of time to plant their seeds and to learn to tend their own garden. Sometimes an empowered thresholder will choose to get married and/or have a child before completing this process because this may be part of their path. So while generally I would encourage doing this later rather than sooner, we have to trust and empower each individual to find their own way. For those who have not been raised in conscious families, teachers and other influential adults ideally should be helping them to hear their inner voice, to listen to their intuition and to honor the stirrings of their Spirit.

Letting Go

Another important aspect of creating conscious family is learning when and how to let go of your children. It is this "letting go" process that ultimately empowers them to move forward in their own development. I have observed how this works with my own children. In addition to our consciously protecting and honoring their individual Spirits, the independence we encouraged as they became adolescents helped empower them to carve out their own way. This freedom allowed all three of my children to make their own decisions and learn to balance work and play, so that by the time they went off to college, they were used to setting their own limits. Because we trusted them, they saw themselves as trustworthy and therefore continued to act in a trustworthy way. Our trust allowed them to make decisions from their core selves, rather than from a place of repression or rebellion.

To trust our children does not mean that we should expect them to be perfect or to always make good decisions. It means that we trust them to be okay, to think out their decisions and to take responsibility for them. When teens feel this type of trust, they are more likely to be honest with their parents.

As parents, my husband and I decided to stress what we believed to be most important. We might prefer that our teens not drink alcohol, but we needed them to not drive while impaired or with someone who was, even if that meant staying at a friend's house until 5 in the morning until they sobered up. We might hope that they would not smoke pot, but we really needed them not to smoke cigarettes, and to not try crack, ecstasy, heroin or methamphetamine. We might have hoped our teens would not be sexually active, but what we really needed is that they not engage in exploitive sex and that they protect themselves from disease and pregnancy.

If we had seen any self-destructive behavior attached to our own children's experimentation, we would have intervened, and they would have ultimately appreciated this. As parents, we have to have a strong intuitive connection with our children so that we are able to differentiate between our letting them experiment and find their own way versus our going into denial and thus neglecting them when they really need us to set limits. We also have to trust our children and ourselves to allow them the freedom that was so important in the early stages of this "letting go" process.

Ideally our job as parents through this important stage is to let our children go out, explore, fall on their face if this should happen, all the while providing support, encouragement, unconditional love and the belief that they will succeed in their goals. It is also our job to help them develop their ability to deal with the consequences of any choices that turn out differently than they hoped. Sometimes this may mean giving them direct help, a loan for example or a temporary place to live, but more often it is simply letting them know we see them as resourceful people who are able to turn things around for themselves and learn whatever lessons are being presented to them. We offer ourselves as an ongoing resource for guidance, letting our children come to us for what guidance that they need.

Think back to your own experience in this threshold phase of life. Take some time and ponder or journal on what life was like for you in high school and then again what it was like when you first left your parents' home. In high school, did you have the freedom you needed so that when you entered this threshold period of your life, you were in touch with your inner resourcefulness? If not, what might have worked better? Did you feel support and encouragement from your parents? Did you find yourself limited by getting into the role of parent, college or graduate student, spouse, etc. before you were ready? If you gave yourself the freedom to pursue your own journey at that age and your parents were not supportive, did you end up feeling guilty for experimenting and following your dreams?

Ponder the following:

- *What worked well for you at that time in your life?*
- *What was painful for you?*
- *What decisions are you proud of?*
- *Are there decisions you regret?*
- *How did you make your decisions?*
- *How were your parents helpful?*
- *How did they make your passage more difficult?*
- *What beliefs were you carrying from our society which held you back?*
- *What societal beliefs did you rebel against?*
- *If you rebelled, how did that rebellion work out for you and what did you learn from it?*
- *Do you fear that your children will make the same "mistakes" you did?*

If you are currently or soon will be raising teenagers, it is important that you have processed your own experiences at that age so that you can release past issues and therefore be free to effectively be present for your children. I strongly encourage you to step beyond our cultural norms and keep an open dialogue with your teens so you can guide and thus help them on their path. Give your child as much freedom as they can responsibly handle. Say empowering words to them, letting them know you trust them and are there for them, but that you will assess what they need and structure rules accordingly. If you pay attention to both their strengths and weaknesses, you will know the right amount of freedom to allow them.

Should you find yourself feeling fearful about breaking free of cultural norms that do not resonate for you or for your teen, do some deeper work on your own issues. Perhaps consult a therapist to resolve these. Read books on healthy teens that reflect your value system. My book, *Journey to Wholeness*, devotes two chapters to the inner teenager and is full of exercises to help you resolve your issues about this period in your life.

You might want to ask yourself what you do to facilitate your children's independence. Are you able to empower them by giving them the freedom to explore, to experiment, to test out their own boundaries and beliefs and, at the same time, do you give them age-appropriate guidelines? Do you have a sense of what these are? If not, seek out solutions. In addition to books on this subject, talk to anyone you know who seems to allow their children to make their own way without abandoning them, and use these people as a resource.

Here is a list of some of the qualities to look for to assess the well-being of your older teens and their readiness to move into the world.

- *What types of problem-solving skills have they developed?*
- *Do they have a belief system, philosophy, or a general way of looking at the world which is basically positive and loving?*
- *Do they have the ability to maintain their self-esteem even in the wake of failure or mistakes?*
- *Are they able to see the lessons that different experiences, including so-called "failures," can provide them?*
- *Are they adventurous without being reckless?*
- *Do they trust themselves?*
- *Are they able to speak up, at least to you, when they feel that they or others are being treated unfairly?*
- *Are they able to accept the consequences for their behavior?*

Remember, too, that as parents we have good information for our children, but we need to be careful not to give them information based on our own fears or conditioned responses. We need to learn to give information in an objective, non-judgmental way for it to be optimally received. Information is different than advice. If we are giving advice, we are implying that it needs to be followed in order for our children to make the right decision. If we share information, we are giving them the tools to make a more informed decision. In addition to sharing information, we need to communicate from our internal belief that we believe they will be successful in their pursuits. If you have doubts about this, do your own work first, looking at all the beliefs and fears you carry which create a feeling that if you do not control the people you love, some harm may come to them or to you.

Incorporating Our Children's Partners and Spouses

Trusting that our children are being led by their Spirits in choosing their partners and spouses is a way to hold the spiritual energy field of the family as it expands. Children that have been raised in a Spirit-directed household will naturally be drawn to relationships based on deep soul connections. Because of this, it is unlikely that there will be disharmony in the energy field of the family as new people enter. However, there are no guarantees. If there is disharmony, this is clearly an indication that the family is being called upon to grow.

From my observations, creating healthy extended family takes work on the part of the parents. Seeing the Divine in each additional member is the way to begin. It takes commitment to support our adult children and not get entangled in their lives. We have to be committed both to honoring and living our own life, while welcoming new family members and continuing to provide emotional support, encouragement and any requested guidance.

I would encourage parents, if at all feasible, to set up yearly or bi-yearly family vacations for grown children and their families. These should be short enough to ensure that everyone involved is also able to have vacation time away from you if they choose. Those with limited funds can set up family camping trips for a long weekend. The ideal is to provide each of the children with separate accommodations so they can be with their own family unit while spending a lot of collective time with their parents and siblings and siblings' families. How successful this is obviously depends on how much a family truly enjoys time together, how much they have in common and how much fun they have with each other. It is important not to force these getaways but rather to offer. If this is done correctly, it creates a wonderful extended family experience that allows young cousins who may live at a distance from each other, to bond deeply. It gives siblings and their partners an opportunity to know each other's children well, and it clearly keeps the extended family operating as an energetic team, keeping the family energy field strong. This healthy field will create protection and harmony for all family members as they return to their own day-to-day lives.

Family vacations, such as these, also allow grandchildren to experience their grandparents, aunts and uncles in a neutral and relaxed setting. These gatherings provide easy opportunity to share family stories, history and wisdom, and allow a larger group of conscious people who are bound by genetics and/or love to collectively empower each other, which creates an incredible resonance for the Spirits of the next generation of children. It also creates a field of encouragement for adult children to deal with any family or other problems they may be having and to feel a supportive group cheering them on in their life purpose.

Another outgrowth of this experience is that it sets the stage for a supportive network to form quickly and easily if aging parents, or anyone else in the family, experience a debilitating illness or other type of tragedy. The spirit of co-operation, appreciation and love surrounds the group and so all challenges are eased.

If we are to survive on planet Earth, we must make the commitment to create conscious families. Remember, they do not have to be biological families. You might wish to assess the consciousness of the families you have created to see where they are strong and where they are weak. Be careful to go easy on yourself. Many of you will have raised or partially raised your family long before you became more consciously aware, or you may have had a spouse or ex-spouse who would not support your awareness. Trust that this was in accordance with Divine plan and gave all members of your family their necessary tasks to become who they are meant to be. Start from the present. Think and pray for the wisdom to help infuse your family with more consciousness.

One last point: healthy, conscious families do not come together motivated by unhealthy first chakra issues. There is no call for family loyalty here. There is no sense of having to do things out of obligation. Rather, this family comes together from their hearts, so that shared beliefs have been reached individually and shared activities are participated in because of a desire to spend time with loved ones. There is great tolerance for diversity and no belief that all must be like-minded.

Family Ritual

Different families have different ways of establishing family norms and family traditions. In our family, we began to create family rituals from the start. My husband and I designed our wedding around our spiritual views. We created an altar in our living room and had a friend conduct the ceremony we wrote together. The woman who officiated at our marriage knew that in esoteric traditions, entering into marriage was in itself seen as a type of spiritual initiation, so we were blessed to be able to have this awareness passed on to us at our marriage ceremony.

All of my children were born at home, and all of their births were consciously honored as spiritual events. A week after my oldest child was born, her birth team reassembled to do an initiation ritual for her as a way to fully welcome her to the planet.

We created our first daily family ritual when my oldest daughter was three. I had just returned home from a spiritual conference which inspired me to address my daughter's "hyper" behavior at the dinner table. We decided to begin each dinner with an attunement. We started off simply: doing an "ohm" chant and then naming all the foods on the table. This created a way for her to be mindful and thus settle down naturally. As this evolved and the children grew older, we left out the naming of the food and created an attunement that included a gratitude prayer, a prayer for the well-being of the planet, and positive intention for health and abundance.

We still begin our family dinners by holding hands and saying this (the "ohm" got lost somewhere along the way). Though my step-daughter and my oldest daughter both asked if we could skip the attunement when they first started having boys over for dinner, they were good-natured when we refused. Because we do not take ourselves too seriously we reacted with amusement when, before we did our attunement, they would explain to their friends that we were just weird, or they laughed a bit or made faces during the attunement. While the issue has not come up again for several years, I suspect they rather enjoy showing their friends what we are really about.

We also began to create rituals for significant family events. Before we moved to a new home, we would light a candle and go through the home we were leaving, thanking it for all it had given us and naming special memories we had for each room. As we started life in a new house, we did a ritual in which we created intention for what we wanted the change to bring to us. We did a ritual as we closed up my mother's apartment after her death. Each New Year's Day we pick tarot cards for the coming year and talk about what they might mean for our development. When each of my children left for college or left to begin another phase of their life, we gathered for a ritual send-off where each of us would give them a special symbolic gift to take with them that holds our wishes for them, and they would pick tarot cards about their new venture. While my son was not open to picking cards as he set off to college, he was open to having a goodbye ritual which we made clear to him was completely optional. We have also done family rituals to heal the Earth and pray for world peace, creating the specifics as we go.

I urge you to consider creating rituals for your family. Be creative and keep them short and meaningful, adapting them to the ages of the children involved. I would also suggest not insisting on serious behavior. Serious intent and serious behavior are not the same thing, and children unconsciously know how to discern this.

It may be difficult for you to implement these things if you have a spouse, partner or children who are not immediately open to this, but I would encourage you to stress its importance, and work to adapt it in such a way that family members can at least attend, if not participate, with some degree of comfort. Younger children will naturally follow your lead.

Realize that the purpose of ritual is to consciously address and celebrate as a family the sacredness of our day-to-day lives and our ability to be co-creators of our reality. Rituals help us stay mindful and grow more conscious. There are numerous ways you can implement this. Let your heart, Spirit and imagination lead the way.

ENVISIONING THE FAMILY OF THE FUTURE

As we evolve as a species, our families will also evolve. We need to create strong, healthy, spiritually based families for our well-being. This becomes even more obvious in a time of great change and upheaval. As the traditional household of mother/father and children becomes rarer, who constitutes a family is far less important in our evolution than the material, emotional and spiritual sustenance our families can provide for its members and the growth and well-being our families can promote.

Much of the psychotherapy and other healing methods of the last 30 years have given us ways to release our soul's karma; in others words, to shift dysfunctional, self-defeating soul patterns. As these soul-patterns shift, so does our electro-magnetic field. As the electro-magnetic field around each of us shifts, the field of the earth will ultimately be filled with the vibration of love and spiritual enlightenment. More and more souls will come to Earth with no need to work out individual karma, but with the sole (soul) purpose of helping the present transformation. Perhaps many are here already.

As a healed soul conjoins a healthy new body, a new species is born. Rather than Generation X, we will have Generation Light Beings. In the meantime, those of us already on the planet who are working through our karma are simultaneously activating our Light bodies. As this process becomes more widespread and conscious, our genetic structure will begin to shift as well. What this means for the family is yet to be seen, but it will likely expand us beyond the structure of couples or single parents choosing to have and raise children together, to groups of conscious adults being there for each child.

It is interesting that the idea of legalizing marriage for gays and lesbians is such a controversial issue. A healthy society wants to promote stable relationships. Not only should we give gays and lesbians the legal right to marry, we should encourage it. The negative response and fear to this points to how dysfunctional our present society is.

If opening the idea of marriage to extend beyond a man and woman also opens the idea of more than two people marrying, and if all these people are emotionally and spiritually healthy, where is the harm? Clearly, for this to work, we need people who are Spirit-directed and very emotionally mature. But when one considers the abuse and dysfunction which occurs in so many traditional marriages, who is to say this would not be an improvement. When we think about evolution, we need to open our minds to numerous possibilities. Certainly, the more like-minded loving adults involved in supporting and raising children, the easier raising a family can become. I am certainly not talking about the practice of polygamy as we know it where one man has several wives. Traditionally in that situation, there is an enormous power imbalance between spouses. If families do in fact evolve to include people having more than one spouse, they would be made up of empowered adults who love each other choosing to create a household and thus a conscious nuclear family together.

Adults in conscious families know how to be intimate without being invasive. They have well-developed communication skills and the ability to work through any conflict to the highest good of all involved. And they understand that it is the people we allow to get closest to us who can be our greatest teachers, showing us where we still need more development. Evolved families form from a desire to join together to create a particular frequency which enhances each member of the family unit as well as the members of the community – a frequency built on love, on heart energy which will enhance the world. Those who have come here to raise conscious children will be drawn together to provide exactly what each new soul needs for their optimal development.

Two books come to mind as I think about a new concept of family: Starhawk's ***The Fifth Sacred Thing*** and James Redfield's ***The Secret of Shambhala.*** In Starhawk's futuristic novel, an intentional community has formed in what was formerly Northern California. It is sometime in the 2050's and because of the scarcity of water and the political shifts early in this century much of the United States is living under a totalitarian government that keeps its control because it owns the water rights. This intentional Northern California community has managed to stay independent from the larger repressive political system. It grows its own food, collects its own water, builds its own houses, provides its own healing. People gather together in family groups based on affinity. There might be six or more adults of various generations in each household, all caring for the children who live there. The community itself is an extended family and all members help with child-rearing. There is not much partnering for life; rather, people might have several love relationships with community members. Family extends to current lovers, past lovers, blood relations and their lovers, and dear friends. Jealousy and possessiveness do not exist because everyone in the community feels loved, secure and valued. Sexual love is expressed freely but never exploitively. Spirituality is interwoven into all aspects of their lives.

Cooperation and commitment to the sacredness of the Earth and its elements are not only the essence of this community, but also at the core of what is needed to survive. Once someone is a member of your family, they always remain so, no matter how the relationship changes. Children born of one coupling are always considered family by both parents long after they have ceased to be lovers and all of the parents' successive lovers and their offspring become part of the family as well.

We are beginning to create some of this now. A friend of ours immediately reached out to the new wife of her ex-husband, stating unequivocally that their children would be siblings so they needed to realize they were family. While this new wife was a bit hesitant at first, with time she not only softened but ultimately bonded deeply with this woman and her child. When her husband died, our friend and her son went to live with this woman and her two young children in order to help them through the mourning process. They began to share responsibility for each other's children and would joke about being each other's wives. This is the model of family that Starhawk presents us in her novel. It seems to be a wonderful model for our future. While a more traditional-looking family model will still be in place for some, these new family configurations will more and more be able to provide the same stability and security as the traditional family.

What we most need from family is to know that there are other human beings who love us unconditionally, cherish us, enjoy us; and be there to support and encourage us through life's challenges and celebrate our life's victories. We need, as well, to form cooperative economic groups, thus minimizing stress. For example, imagine a house of four or five adults, some of whom are lovers, some of whom are not, but all of whom love each other dearly and are committed to sharing resources with each other and raising children together. Imagine that each adult is fully empowered, willing to do his or her share, is emotionally and spiritually healthy with good communications skills and a compassionate heart. Each of these adults is committed to being Spirit- rather than ego-directed as well as committed to self-awareness and fairness. Each has the ability to see any conflict that arises as an opportunity for more growth. With self-awareness comes the ability to know and accept one's shortcomings and thus to be able to identify one's part in any conflict. This provides the needed resource to resolve the conflict. People at this evolutionary level could carry out these new images of family without creating the old family dysfunction and they would provide an enormously loving and secure field in which to raise conscious children.

As more and more of us have released our old emotional and karmic baggage and become committed to being Spirit-Directed, we realize that we are not far away from being evolved enough to handle the above scenario. Numerous adults have healed emotionally, honed their interpersonal skills and are now committed to soul growth. Our ability to communicate honestly has been through a quantum leap and we recognize how we have thirsted for authenticity. There are huge numbers of us committed to healing the Earth and to living in harmony with her and her creations. We truly can do this. We need, however, to start projecting these images into our culture so that we can begin to provide people with a more concrete vision, which in turn will strengthen and amplify the field of our intention.

In **_The Secret of Shambhala,_** there are wonderful images of evolved human beings, their culture, and their families. In the society Redfield presents, humans lead their lives from their intuitive guidance and appear to operate in full consciousness (although they are still developing, so what might look like full consciousness to us may be simply a point along the way). While couples may work long distances apart from each other, they have the ability to send thoughts and intentions to each other telepathically to insure that family members will stay deeply connected with one another no matter the physical distance.

Conception is always conscious in this culture, with sex having evolved to an ecstatic energetic connection that does not seem to involve genitalia. Here in Shambhala, they are no longer talking about the merging of the physical sperm and egg, but rather calling the Spirit in through the resonance created by the parents' "energy merge". This Spirit then begins a physical manifestation initiated through the conscious intention of both parents. All conceptions come from an intuitive message sent from the soul who wishes to incarnate. The parents are able then to ponder why this soul might want to come to them and how the qualities they intuit of this soul would help the development of their family. (P. 163)

The choosing of a mate is conscious as well, with people being led to each other through synchronicities. All members of the society consciously know they have a spiritual mission to fulfill, so are not drawn to each other from an unhealthy place and there is no dependency on family members to meet each other's unmet needs. The psychological dysfunction rampant at our present level of evolution appears to have vanished.

Another essential point in the Redfield book is that this new society fully understands that each generation is to go beyond its parents. Thus a strong focus in child-rearing is to insure that the collective wisdom which has already been accumulated is passed on as early as possible to create a foundation for youngsters to move beyond what is already known. Ancestors record their own life lessons, going back seven generations, as a means of helping the youngest group in the community by providing them with the existing collective wisdom.

I urge all of you to envision healthy, conscious, evolved families. Meditate on this. Draw pictures. Make movies. Create songs and stories that tell of the coming possibilities and then begin to watch it unfold.

9: SPIRITUAL COMMUNITY

We are by nature social creatures. We long for a sense of belonging and support. If we look at this from our own energy system, we realize that it is the feeling of group connection, the tribal consciousness of the first chakra, which is at the foundation of successful living on the planet. As large numbers of people wake up spiritually, we will be shifting the nature of this tribal consciousness. At present the general consciousness of the planet has become harmful to our well-being, insisting that people conform to norms that are emotionally, mentally and spiritually dysfunctional. The change which is now occurring has given each of us the awareness that we can create our own tribal norms and that we can create them out of compassion and enlightened consciousness. We are now ready to experience community in a way which has rarely been available to humans on this planet.

People who have meditated in a group setting often talk about what a wonderful experience it is because the group energy helps them go deeper. Experiences such as these teach us what is meant by the concept that we are all connected. Our sensitivity to energy expands greatly in such a setting and it is frequently the case that identical or related images will occur simultaneously in the meditations of several participants in the group. All participants are affected by the positive energy generated in the environment and thus all of them experience a greater sense of well-being. Imagine, then, how this would become amplified with a conscious group of loving and healthy people creating cooperative networks as well as cooperative living communities all over the globe.

When describing the lifetime I spoke of in Chapter 6, I mostly detailed the negative parts of that experience: being imprisoned, executed, and fearful for the well-being of my children. What I did not speak much of, because it was not relevant to the chapter, were the memories I retrieved about the village where I had grown up during that lifetime. When I tuned into that community, the feeling I experienced was simply remarkable. This was an enlightened community based on love, support and Divine purpose. The sense of well-being I had there was more profound than I have ever experienced in this lifetime (and I have a good life!). From the moment of my birth, probably from the moment of my conception, I was enfolded in the most awe-inspiring love. The entire community was energetically aligned with Divine love and Divine guidance. No one suffered. All had what they needed. Food was abundant. The climate was gentle and the natural beauty, pristine. We all knew we had come to Earth to fulfill a higher vision. There was no competition. There was no ill wished for anyone, on any level. The entire village supported the higher mission of each individual. All members felt it their responsibility to welcome and nurture each soul born into their community. They felt deep gratitude for this opportunity. While this was not the time on Earth that this type of community could become a universal experience, I believe there have been prototypes of these societies scattered throughout the ages. We are now coming to a time where we have the potential for all to live like this. How many of us will actually create this option remains unclear.

When I facilitated weekly spiritual development groups, I realized that the norms developed in these groups strongly support spiritual community. These included loving intention, deep honesty about our strengths and weaknesses, speaking from the heart, tolerance and non-judgment. All participants understood that we are all interconnected, all One. Therefore we were all conscious that the love and positive energy we put out into the group and into the world affected the whole, and vice versa. This created an even stronger commitment to send out more love and joy. Another value that these groups supported was the honoring and empowering of the Self. We understood that each of us brought a special energy, a unique Spirit, to our group and it is our honor as well as our responsibility to support and encourage its full development. There was so much gratitude expressed in these groups; gratitude for all of life, gratitude for all our lessons and gratitude to be a part of a group of people who shared this. One of the many things I have learned is the great value people place on being able to share from this level. This tells me two things: first, that our society has been shamefully bereft of these opportunities; and second, that there is a great collective hunger which longs to be satisfied through genuine spiritual community.

While many people attend church, prayer and bible study groups for this reason, the groups I facilitated differed from any traditional religious path because we held tightly to the belief that there are many ways to the Divine and many ways to Enlightenment. We did not judge another's behavior. We did not ask people to conform. We did not advocate any lifestyle rules. We did hold a high criterion for acting honorably, coming from the heart and living in as much harmony as possible with the Earth. Since we knew there are many similar groups of this nature around the world, we kept in mind that we are building a frequency with many souls who are presently on the planet to usher in this evolutionary shift. We were a small part of a much larger movement which is bringing forth a global spiritual community.

My vision of what is to come is similar to the vision James Redfield gives us in ***The Secret of Shambhala.*** As I mentioned earlier, the humans in Shambhala have already evolved beyond us. Like the village of my past, they are all committed to spiritual growth, cooperation and connection. They are able to control climate and manifest whatever they need for their material comfort through thought forms amplified by earth-friendly technology. There is no hunger. There is no ill will. There is no disease. This group of humans is invisible to us in the outer world because they are vibrating at a higher frequency. Speeding up our frequency is what we need to do as well. This is the way we literally become Light. We are not made of clay. We are made of molecules that can vibrate at any number of frequencies. The more joy and love we are able to hold in our hearts and the less fear, guilt, anger and shame, the faster we vibrate and the more we radiate.

Look into your heart for the moment and see the longing there: the longing to be filled with light; the longing to be part of a greater whole; the longing for commonality with people who are committed to their Spirits, who are committed to bringing harmony, peace and well-being for all living things on our planet, including the planet herself.

Exercise: Conscious Community

Notice if you can create and hold an image of a loving group of people who live in conscious community. Start with the physical environment. Does it feel right to picture yourself by the ocean? In the mountains? In the desert? In the heartland? Notice the physical environment that resonates most strongly for you. Breathe in this imagery and notice its fragrances. Can you smell the salt or brine of the sea? Or the sweet mountain air? Or the dry warmth of the desert, or the wild flowers of the prairie? Maybe you find yourself in the cities surrounded by large numbers of people. See the people all around you emitting love and healing energy.

Breathe into this for a while.

Think about what forms of shelter you might want in your community. Do you see glass or wood or stone, or perhaps a material we are not yet familiar with? How would you want these shelters to be placed in relation to each other? What kind of groupings of people do you see living in these shelter units? Are there traditional or extended family groups? Do people live alone? Are households multi-generational? Do people group together in households because they are involved in the same tasks? Or perhaps people come together as soul groups: groups who have been together in the Spirit world and have collectively chosen to come to Earth.

Notice what it is like to live among people who are relaxed and happy, who have a life without stress. Imagine everyone taking time to start their day in prayer or meditation then taking time for a leisurely, healthy breakfast either alone thus allowing for quiet and contemplation, or with family members, co-workers or friends.

Realize that in this community, everyone sets their goals by allowing an inner intention to unfold. Perhaps tasks performed each day simply arrive in that person's consciousness during their morning prayers or morning practice. Or perhaps in your community, you would prefer groups of planners who outline what needs to be done together and then allow each individual to focus their talents in order to make their contribution. Let your imagination design your community for you.

Imagine you are in a body that feels strong and vibrant. Notice if you can feel your chakras spinning, or in other ways attune to your energy body. Imagine your heart feels both full and light. This fullness fills you with joy and gratitude, and the lightness brings you ease and flow.

See yourself dress for your day in simple, comfortable, Earth-friendly clothing. Then notice yourself preparing to begin your work. Take a few minutes and let the contribution you make in this community come to you intuitively. Do you go out into the community? Do people come to you? Is your purpose in homemaking or child rearing? Do you work alone or as a team, or both? Notice how you feel while performing your work. Notice how it feels to meet others in the community, knowing without a shadow of doubt that they deeply care about your wellbeing and the wellbeing of your children and your animals; that they deeply value and support your work.

Allow these images to come to you spontaneously and feel how living this kind of life would be for you. You might actually be able to feel your cells quickening, vibrating faster, simply through this visualization. If so, enjoy this sensation.

Take some centering breaths again and think about your community's schools, its libraries and cultural and recreational places. Imagine the community health care facilities. Is there a building or a site for a governing body? What about a responsibility team, a new paradigm police and justice system that does not capture people and punish them, but rather helps individuals stay accountable to their own sense of honor and to their community contract. Are there spiritual meeting places? Notice how all these branches of your society are organized. It may be that some of you are here to help transform these societal institutions. If you feel this is so, let yourself go in-depth in one or more of these areas, and journal on the ideas that arise in you.

In order to transform our planet, in order to save our planet, we desperately need to create images of harmonious, spiritually-connected, earth-friendly life-styles. I urge all of you who are able to visualize this, to speak of it, to stay internally focused on it, to write of it, to draw it. If you make movies, put it in your films. If you write books, let these images spread through your writings. If you work with children, provide these images for the children. Talk about them to your loved ones. Share them with your friends. The more we do this, the greater opportunity we create for this to happen.

The Collective Resonance

Be aware that we are creating collective energy frequencies all the time. Unfortunately, many of them are fear-based and hold the energy of powerlessness which, besides disconnecting us emotionally and spiritually from our essence, impacts our immune system and leaves us vulnerable to disease. If we collectively participate in this resonance of fear, we will not create a new world that supports and enhances the Spirit; rather, we will be vulnerable to creating a world that is even more repressive. The more repressed, the more powerless people feel. As you can see, this can begin to spiral downward and these energy spirals are then filled with fear and the rage it invokes.

The energetic aftermath of September 11th is an interesting example. As tragic as the events of that day were, the immediate resonance created appeared to be one of unity and love. The media kept showing us ordinary people who behaved in extraordinarily loving, courageous and evolved ways. Our hearts were saddened but full at the same time.

Then the political rhetoric began to infuse the collective with rage and revenge and fear images, with the media broadcasting these negative frequencies out to the masses. Once we began our military action, the resonance began to shift even more. More and more fear-based thoughts were poured into the collective, thoughts filled with fear for our well-being; and ego fears our country would be humiliated if we did not "flex our muscles." We were bombarded with horror stories of what these terrorists could do to us, and these were used as justification for prolonged and, in many cases, totally unprovoked aggression under the name of security and freedom.

We all need to take responsibility for the creation of the collective resonance. We need to stay conscious. We need to stay connected to Spirit. If there are enough of us committed to this, we have the ability to not only stay out of the fear-based energy currently crossing the planet, but to amplify the energy of love, faith and well-being which helps us spiral upward into enlightened consciousness.

The following exercise will give you a sense of what I mean by the collective resonance, and help you stay detached from the negative frequencies currently being broadcasted. You might want to get into a very comfortable chair, light a candle and breathe yourself into a deeply relaxed state.

Imagine a room filled with loving, highly conscious people. There is uplifting music being played and everyone in the room is focusing on their heart chakra feeling it fill with Divine love. They then beam this love to everyone else in the room. See yourself looking in on that circle. Notice how everyone looks, the expression on everyone's faces.

Now become part of the group. See yourself in this group closing your eyes and breathing deeply until you feel totally calm and aligned. Then begin to focus on your heart. Rub your hands together and place them over your heart feeling the warmth melt any blockages and feel your heart open wider and wider. You will begin to experience a sense of overflowing love. See and feel yourself beaming this love to all of the others in this room and allow yourself to receive their love, drawing it into your heart. Notice that the entire room is pulsating with this love. You may see intricate patterns of energy connections between everyone in the room. You might even experience delectable fragrances and notice how the music harmonizes with all of the other energy rhythms to create this ecstatic experience. Your sense of personal boundary may shift so that you begin to feel yourself dissolving into this collective love. In a trusting environment, where there is no desire consciously or unconsciously to invade or manipulate anyone's energy, it is completely safe to allow your boundaries to dissolve into the collective resonance, and allow the ecstasy of that experience to envelop you.

Imagine now that someone in the group gets up and opens a door, and one by one, you all walk out to a beautiful courtyard. Each person removes their shoes and standing barefoot on the earth, joins together in a circle and holds hands. Feel the bottom of your feet on the lush warm grass. Then allow the sensitivity in your feet to grow until you are able to feel the energy of the Earth enter your soles, let it expand through your feet then up through your entire body, filling it with the deep resonance of Mother Earth. Realize that everyone in the group with you is experiencing this simultaneously. Again, bring your awareness to your heart and beam love to all, receiving their love simultaneously and feeling the Earth's melody pulsating through every cell of your being.

See now that there are circles forming like this everywhere on the planet: on the beaches, in the deserts, up in the mountains, on farm land, in the jungle. Circles of people everywhere, all connected with the Earth's resonance and all beaming love from their hearts. See the beams of love traveling in every conceivable pattern around the globe. Breathe this. Feel this. Smell this. Some of you will hear the music created by this vibratory patterning. This is part of the Collective Resonance. The more we allow ourselves to invoke this on our planet, the more we create our new world.

We did an interesting experiment in one of my spiritual groups. Each group meeting started with a check-in where members state briefly how they are feeling. One woman came to group drained and angry and therefore was an ideal candidate for the following experiment. I asked her if she would be willing to sit in my waiting room during our opening meditation because I wanted to use the meditation to build a loving field which would help shift her energy. She was happy to oblige. Before she left, I used dowsing rods to measure her energy field. It extended about 6-8 feet beyond her body. She then left the room, and I led the group in a meditation that included all of our members meeting in a wooded grove. I named each group member aloud to help anchor and intensify our collective energy. As we all met in this grove, we formed a circle around the woman who was sitting in the other room. Then we pulled in Divine energy through our crown chakras and beamed her love from our hearts. When I intuited in the meditation that she had received the energy, I had each person visualize her joining the circle in the grove and we then swirled loving Divine energy around ourselves as a group and ultimately out to the world. After the meditation, we had our member come back from the outer room and measured her energy field with the dowsing rods again. Now her field extended so far I had to walk into the other room to get the measurement. She extended about 25 feet. She reported that she felt great and at one point suddenly had goose bumps while out in the waiting room. As each person shared their experience of the meditation, it was clear that we were all affected and all were feeling wonderful from this resonance.

While the above was a conscious experiment, we are always building and affecting the collective energy field. All of us have experienced walking into a room full of people and getting a sense of the energy in that room, knowing if it feels good or uncomfortable; heavy or light. We are all able to sense the existing energy field, the existing resonance. Often we ignore it, or it is so subtle that we do not bother to "read" it. Yet what the above shows, is that the energy we bring in can significantly impact a group if we hold conscious intention. And while it is easier if there are several people committed to this, even one of us can affect the collective field.

You might want to try experimenting for yourself. If you know you are going into a negative environment, create a force field of light around yourself for protection before you enter. Do this by centering your breath and envisioning this light beaming from your heart and solar plexus. It does not matter if you can see the field as long as you can feel it. Allow it to extend evenly around your body at least a few feet. If you walk into a room that feels heavy and you were not prepared ahead of time, do this once you enter. Then go to the crown chakra, consciously pull in Divine light and Divine love, and then beam it out to everyone in the room through your heart chakra. Wait and notice the effect. If you are able to beam this light to everyone in the room, the energy will create a shift, no matter how small, and may unconsciously motivate others to put out more positive energy. If this is an environment you enter frequently such as a home or workplace, do this consistently for a while and notice the results.

Taking Charge of Our Vibrational Field

There are various frequencies operating on the Earth simultaneously. The higher frequencies are closer to the frequency of light. The more quickly our cells vibrate, the higher our frequency. The term "enlightened" suggests that as we become more conscious, our cells vibrate more quickly and we become filled with the essence of light which brings us closer to the Divine. When we are ego- driven, our energy is denser; slower. Because there are so many of us committed to living from Spirit rather than ego, there is now huge potential for large numbers of us to become "enlightened" which will shift the collective energy field of the planet. The more conscious we can be of our own positive, loving and thus higher frequency energy, the more we send this out into the larger resonance with intention and the closer we all get to making the evolutionary leap. A loving compassionate heart appears to generate the highest frequency of all, so the more love we can feel, the more quickly this shift can occur.

Paradoxically, large numbers of people are also holding the denser energy field of fear, and our media constantly bombards us with this dense energy. We need to continuously re-attune ourselves to the resonance of Spirit or we become vulnerable to participating in the fear resonance. How we affect the collective energy field happens both consciously and unconsciously. When we are unconscious of our own fear or negativity, we are not able to neutralize this dense resonance and we run the risk of becoming too weighted down to send out that higher frequency. The more we are able to observe ourselves, the more empowered we are to stay conscious and therefore to positively affect the whole.

The more emotionally healthy we become, the more high frequency loving energy we are able to emit. This happens whether we do it consciously or not. However, the more mindful we become of the quality of our own energy, the more we can amplify and direct this energy as we disperse it. Conversely, the more scared or hostile we become, the stronger our negative energy. Because negative energy has a slower, denser frequency, it is like slogging through a swamp. We literally get bogged down, and like swamp land, the energy becomes stagnant and unpleasant.

All of us contain this positive and negative energy. Since we are complex beings, even the most enlightened person can have a pocket of darkness here and there, and the cruelest person, can still have pockets of light. The more we develop spiritually, the greater our commitment needs to be to notice our pockets of darkness and neutralize them. This is the ongoing challenge for all of us, and when we realize how our energy impacts the larger whole, it becomes even more compelling.

Those of us committed to growth, to leading a spiritually evolved life and making this world a more loving and evolved place may find it extremely painful to see parts of ourselves that are not aligned with the highest good. My most direct experience of this comes with my work. I would like to imagine that my ego never gets involved with those who come to seek my help. But the deeper I go into self-realization, the more I have to notice that there have been times when I have put judgment onto someone I have worked with. This judgment of them had nothing to do with them or with their issues, but rather with my ego feeling I was not being given the credence or credit it believed I deserved. My ego would like to fight with my Spirit, rationalizing and minimizing my inner reactions, so I need to stay highly conscious.

Because I am extremely kinesthetic, I have learned to recognize any constriction in my energy field, especially if something is misaligned emotionally. My normal state is to feel open and loving with everyone I work with. I know any sense of constriction is a signal that the flow of my love is being blocked and that I have to be pro-active in examining my motives and neutralizing this energy. As soon as I realize this, I put strong prayer and intent to get out of judgment and back in a loving flow with this person.

Since I have activated a high level of personal power, and because I have a position which wields some authority, I have to be even more diligent to recognize and neutralize my dark energy because this power means I could do greater harm than average, despite my conscious intention. If I refused to face this part of myself, this negative energy would seep outward and have a more destructive effect. Be aware that neutralization occurs as we integrate all these parts in ourselves, loving them just because they are part of the human experience, but giving them no power.

Any powerful leader or teacher who has not tuned into and committed to neutralize their potential for darkness can create great harm. They may start with a loving heart and an enlightened awareness, but if they are not continually diligent, they have the ability to negatively impact the collective resonance in a considerably larger way than most individuals. While we cannot control others, we can become clear about recognizing our own resonance and thus our own dark pockets. The more we are able to recognize this in ourselves, the more we will recognize this in others. As more of us learn to do this, not only will we not be misled by that type of leader or teacher, but also we will help hold the larger field in a way that can minimize their destructive influence.

The less able we are to recognize our flaws, the harder it is to see the flaws in others accurately because we are likely to be projecting our disowned flaws onto someone else. As an example, if I have an arrogant part of myself that I am not able or willing to see, I am at high risk for my vision to be distorted. I will either not see arrogance in others and perhaps give them more influence than they deserve, or more likely, I will project the quality of arrogance onto others, whether it is there or not, and judge them harshly. This will both create disharmony in my field and make it difficult for me to see this person in an objective way. If, on the other hand, I can notice the arrogance in myself, forgive myself for this, and stay conscious to not operate out of that arrogance, I will be shrinking the dark spots in my own field. And I will become more skilled at observing this quality in others accurately when it is relevant to my personal or the collective well-being. As I go through this process, I can also see that arrogance is a shadow side of authority and I can integrate these qualities and use them for positive ends. So as we integrate our shadow parts, we refine our own resonance, and are far better able to understand what impact we are having on the collective.

Suggestions to Observe and Transform your Individual Resonance.

To keep the concept of the collective resonance in your mind as you go through your day-to-day life, you might want to practice the following:

Start each day with an intention to stay conscious of your energy. Look at your mood to help you notice the frequency of energy you emit at any given moment. If you are feeling expansive, notice the love and joy that permeates your energy field. Then begin to beam this loving, joyful energy out to the world. You can start seeing it radiate through your house and then your community, town, state, country and finally around the globe.

If you find your energy is heavy or dense, make a commitment to work on your emotions and/or beliefs in order to shift this. Sometimes just breathing in Divine light and/or Divine love will automatically transform your energy. Sometimes we just need to allow ourselves to be heavy for a while, but when that is the case, I suggest you ask that the heaviness stay contained so that it will not impact the people around you. Simply staying conscious of the heaviness can shift the frequency enough to facilitate this.

Once you have a sense of your own energy, focus on the collective resonance in your household. There are several ways to do this. One is by sitting quietly and intuiting what type of frequency each member of your family is sending out that day. Some of you will be able to see this visually, others will get strong feelings. Still others of you may find a more auditory cue, imagining their energy as music – smooth, flowing, harmonious, jagged, discordant, fierce, etc.

Let your imagination relax so the images can flow easily into your consciousness. Then imagine sending each household member loving and soothing energy.

If you have difficulty doing this with anyone in your household, take it as a sign that you have some emotional issue to work out with them, and make a commitment for this to happen. You may be holding anger or negative thought forms which will impact on their field as well as your own. Once you are able to send love freely to each member, notice what happens in your mind as you do. Notice too, how their field is affected?

Young children typically will soak in loving energy with ease. Beaming them love should immediately soften their field. Teenagers, especially teens who have been deeply hurt, may have resistance at first. If you receive only a withdrawn or hostile response as you do this, go deeper into your intuition and ask what needs to happen for this teen to trust you. It may be that you have overlooked something painful that has happened to them. It may be they are so caught up in a negative relationship with someone significant in their lives that it has affected and temporarily hardened their own field, or it may be that you have had a tendency to create enmeshment with this child, and they know no other way to be self-protective. Do your best to be open enough to allow the truth to come to you intuitively. This can then lead you to what might need to happen in order for their energy to shift.

If you find your adult partner is resisting your positive loving energy, there is a likelihood of one of the following: 1.) they are so angry at you or hurt by you that they are afraid to let your loving energy affect them; 2.) they are so wounded from events in their own lives that they are afraid to open to anyone and have not learned other strategies to protect themselves; or 3.) they do not know how to keep their sense of Self and allow your energy in.

Be as honest with yourself as possible here. If their responses are due to anything in your relationship, do your best to state your part in the situation directly to them, make a commitment to work on it, then give it some time and see if their energy will shift. If not, it might be best to end the relationship. If it is not a relationship problem, but rather something they have brought into the relationship, create an intention to stay non-reactive to their wounded patterns, and keep beaming them positive energy. If ultimately there are no changes, again you may choose to separate yourself from their energy.

If you find little or no resistance in your home and you consciously and consistently beam love out, you will notice how everything begins to improve. Quite likely you will see less squabbling and more kindness. Your household will start to feel better and better, and perhaps goals that seemed far off will begin to be met with ease.

Bring these techniques into your work life and social life as well. Notice who can easily absorb your loving energy and who may resist it. Remember that noticing is emotionally neutral; there is no judgment or anger when we are simply noticing. Send loving energy out consistently and then pay attention to the transformation which takes place. If there is a strong culture of negativity in your work or social life, you may not see any dramatic change immediately, so look for incremental change. If the resistance is negligible or non-existent, the shift may be miraculous.

Check in with yourself at intervals throughout the day. Perhaps as you sit down for a meal, or as you get into your car. Stop and take a moment to scan your energy, adjusting it if need be, and then to send out love.

When I am conscious of feeling expansive, I beam this out to anyone I see. For instance when I am driving in my car, I will beam this love to everyone I notice on the street. While simply feeling expansive impacts the collective, to direct this beam to individuals that you see amplifies this. Imagine if all of us did this on a daily basis. This is the level of collective consciousness that truly will transform the planet. We all, ultimately, have a responsibility to be energy activists. As my husband likes to playfully say, "We owe it to each other to have a nice day."

If you notice yourself feeling a little uncomfortable with your expansive, loving energy, check in to see if you experience guilt about feeling joy. This is an all too common phenomenon in our culture. We are often schooled to believe that our joy somehow is unfair to those suffering in the world, as if there is a limited quantity of joy to go around. Joy is limitless and available to all. When we understand the collective resonance, we realize the more we can feel joy, the more we raise the vibration of the collective energy field, which brings even more joy to our world.

Creating Community

There are many ways to define community. It may be our circle of friends, or our neighborhood or town. It may be a group of people who share the same religious or ethnic background. It may be our workplace or work connections, or other groups of individuals with whom we share something in common. The more conscious we become, the more we are likely to create a community that supports our evolution.

The types of communities which will give rise to the most rapid and positive change will consciously incorporate many common principles. These include:

- **The conscious awareness that we are all connected, all One**
- **Cooperative rather than competitive systems**
- **Authentic communication – speaking from the heart**
- **Environmental stewardship**
- **Creativity**
- **Freedom from conventional norms**
- **Ethical behavior based on mutual respect**
- **Caring for all humanity and all living things**
- **A deep understanding of energy and how it works in our world**

The more communities we create of this sort, the more loving and enlightened the energy field of our planet. One of the basic tenets of this type of community needs to be to have faith in one's ability to align with the loving forces of the Universe and therefore to Co-create what we each need. This keeps us free from the fear paradigm which has been so pervasive in our culture.

Assess your life in terms of your community by pondering the following questions:

Do you have like-minded friends? Are you able to feel totally yourself when you are with them and to consistently speak your truth? If not, ask yourself what keeps you from this. Do you believe there are no other people in your area who share your views? Have you tried to talk about your views in a non-judging way? Have you gone to lectures or yoga centers or natural food stores where there is a likelihood of meeting people who will have your same view of the world? Are there healing centers in your community that offer ways for people to come together and share their process as well as their light with each other? Notice if you hold some fear or self-defeating belief that may keep you from meeting others who share your values.

If you do have like-minded friends, are you consciously aware of building an energy field together which raises your collective frequency? You might want to think of additional ways of structuring this. For instance, begin a weekly or monthly group that focuses on the collective frequency and how each individual can expand their own consciousness and the evolutionary force on the planet.

Another way to support the collective evolution in a more conscious manner is to bring suggestions to groups you belong to that are working for causes consistent with the values of the new paradigm. These suggestions can include beginning each meeting with a short meditation where people release distractions and stress with the out-breath, and draw in powerful feelings and images of love, harmony and creativity with the in-breath. People can also focus on speeding up their vibrational field and feeling others around them doing the same. The goals of the meeting and the larger goals of the group can also be put into a positive intention statement in this opening meditation.

In addition to the above suggestion, those of you who attend a lot of meetings might want to incorporate closing your meetings in a new way. Take time to give loving feedback to praise people for their positive input thus reinforcing this type of participation and energetically raising the group's frequency. Incorporate suggestions about how to improve the effectiveness of the meetings in the feed-back session. Before formally closing the meeting, take a moment to feel gratitude and to focus on positive images of your future work together. Sending light as a group to any who are in need is also a wonderful way to end. Let your creativity lead you while you stay conscious of how you can enhance the energy field of the groups you participate in.

We Are the World

We really are the world. We are part of the great collective force of existence. We are the creators. The quality of our energy is totally in our hands. When we beam our loving Spirit-directed energy into the world, we transform our families, our communities and ultimately, our planet. Let us walk together with empowered Spirits. Let us walk together with open hearts. Let us walk together in Divine love and consciousness, and to quote a Steven Stills song, "Let the Peace Begin."

About the Author:

Judith Corvin-Blackburn is an author, teacher and transpersonal psychotherapist who presents workshops around the country. Her work blends lessons from her personal journey, studies and training in many transpersonal, shamanic & humanistic techniques, and her highly developed intuition and strong connection to Higher Guidance. She is author of 2 books: *EMPOWERING THE SPIRIT: A Process to Activate your Soul Potential* and *JOURNEY TO WHOLENESS: A Guide to Inner Healing*. Leading people to activate their highest potential and create planetary change has been her passion for over 35 years. She lives with her husband in the beautiful mountains of Western North Carolina.

She offers online classes on *Empowering the Spirit* through her website at www.empoweringthespirit.com.

Learn more at www.empoweringthespirit.com You may contact the author at healingconcepts@hotmail.com

Printed in Great Britain
by Amazon